ST. BONIFACE, FULDA.

BONIFACE OF CREDITON
AND HIS COMPANIONS

BASED ON LECTURES DELIVERED IN THE
CATHEDRAL CHURCH OF BRISTOL IN 1906

BY THE

RIGHT REV. G. F. BROWNE

D.D. (CAMB. AND OXF.), D.C.L. (DURHAM), F.S.A.

BISHOP OF BRISTOL

FORMERLY DISNEY PROFESSOR OF ART AND ARCHAEOLOGY
IN THE UNIVERSITY OF CAMBRIDGE

WITH SEVENTEEN ILLUSTRATIONS

LONDON
SOCIETY FOR PROMOTING CHRISTIAN KNOWLEDGE
NORTHUMBERLAND AVENUE, W.C.
48 QUEEN VICTORIA STREET, E.C.
BRIGHTON: 129 NORTH STREET.
1910

PREFACE

This little book had its origin in a course of lectures on Boniface delivered in the Cathedral Church of Bristol in 1906. In the autumn of 1909 the writer carried out an old proposal to visit the scenes of Boniface's work and residence, and to follow up so far as might be the traces of the English men and women who joined him in Germany when his pioneer work had been attended with a large measure of success. This Preface is written at the time when King Edward is lying dead; and the writer is not without hope that an active realization by Germans of the debt owed to England by Germany, and by Englishmen of the labour and lives given to Germany by their predecessors eleven and a half centuries ago, may do something to further the efforts of the late king in the direction of a more peaceful understanding between the two empires, sprung as they are from a common stock, and tied from their early beginnings in Christian bonds.

A diocesan bishop in these busy days really cannot find spaces of time adequate for the marshalling of complicated material. Things have to be done from hand to mouth as it were. The writer can only hope that any who may glance at this little book may be less acutely conscious of its defects than he himself is. On one point he wishes to repeat a caution given in his little book on *Alcuin of York*. The varied spellings of names are not misprints or blunders, though any reader may well think that they are when Grypho, Gripho, and Gripo, appear for one and the same man, and Cynihard appears in almost as many spellings as there are letters in the name.

The writer desires to thank earnestly, for help given, the Librarian at Fulda; the Director of the University of Würzburg; Dr. G. F. Warner, Mr. C. H. Read, and Mr. O. M. Dalton, all of the British Museum; and Professor H. J. White of King's College, London. They are none of them responsible for any errors that may have found their way into the text.

Thanks are due also to the editor of the *Treasury* for the use of the blocks of illustrations of articles by the writer, which appeared in that magazine in February and March of this year.

The numbering of the Bonifatian Epistles is that adopted by Wattenbach and Dümmler, *Mon. Germ. Hist., Epistolarum*, tom. iii, Berlin, 1892.

G. F. BRISTOL.

May 9, 1910

CONTENTS

CHAPTER I

CHAPTER II

CHAPTER III

CHAPTER IV

CHAPTER XI

CHAPTER XII

CHAPTER XIII

CHAPTER XIV

CHAPTER XV

CHAPTER XVI

LIST OF ILLUSTRATIONS

γ

BONIFACE AND HIS COMPANIONS

CHAPTER I

The main dates of Boniface's life.—Willibald's Life of Boniface.—Othlon's Life of Boniface.—Collection of letters, &c.—Early life.—Boniface in Frisia.—His return to England.—His final departure.—Earlier English missionaries.—Alfred the Great and Frisia.—Earlier English ardour for missionary work.—The state of religious life at home.

THE main dates of the life of Boniface may be stated as follows :—

He was born at Crediton in 679 or 680, and was ordained priest at the age of thirty. In 716 he went out to join the Northumbrian Willibrord in his missionary work in Friesland. After a short return to England he finally left our shores in 718. He went direct to Rome, and in 719 received a commission from Pope Gregory II to preach the gospel east of the Rhine. Before executing that commission he worked with Willibrord in his archdiocese of Utrecht for three years. He then worked among the Hessians, with so much success that he was summoned to Rome and was consecrated bishop on November 30, 722 or 723. He returned to work in Hessia and Thuringia, the latter corresponding roughly to the modern Saxony. In 732 he received the pallium and became an archbishop without a see. In 738 he again visited Rome, and on his way back he spent some time in Bavaria and founded the sees of Salzburg, Passau, Regensburg, and Freising. In 741, on the death of Charles Martel, whose sons and successors Carloman and Pepin greatly favoured him, he estab-

B

lished four bishoprics for Hessia and Thuringia, namely, Würzburg, Eichstätt, Büraburg, and Erfurt. From 742 to 744 he held at the request of Carloman and Pepin mixed councils of clerical and lay persons to regulate the affairs of the Church. During the same period he founded monasteries at Utrecht, Fritzlar, Fulda, Amöneburg, and Ohrdruf, sending to England for monks and nuns to take charge of them. In 744 he proposed to occupy the see of Cologne, and to make it the head of a metropolitical province. It chanced, however, that the see of Mainz came vacant, and the ecclesiastics and lay folk so pressed him that he became archbishop there, with Cologne, Spires, Worms, Tongres, and Utrecht, as suffragan sees. In 747 Carloman retired to the abbey of Monte Cassino. Pepin became sole governor of Austrasia and Neustria, and in 752 was crowned king at Soissons. In 754 Boniface resigned his archbishopric and consecrated Lul of Malmesbury as his successor in the see. He then pushed up into the north parts of Frisia, and at Dokkum on the river Bordau he was martyred with his whole party of more than fifty persons on the eve of Whitsunday, 755, at the age of seventy-five.

That list enables us to see the chronological position of Boniface in relation to other prominent English persons. He was ordained priest in the year of the death of Aldhelm, Abbat of Malmesbury and first Bishop of Sherborne. He received the pallium about the time of the death of Bede and the birth of Alcuin. When he died in 755, Alcuin was a youthful assistant to the Archbishop of York in his capacity as Head Master of the School of York, an office which Alcuin himself eventually held. The English Boniface was in close relations with Pepin when he became King of the Franks, but not nearly so close as the relations in which Alcuin was with Pepin's son Karl when he became the Emperor Charlemagne.

We possess a very interesting Life of Boniface, written by one who was evidently very well informed. The name of the biographer was Willibald. This was the name of a nephew or other near relation of Boniface, who was a very famous traveller, and after visiting in great detail the scriptural places in the Holy Land returned to Europe to help Boniface in his missionary labours, and was by him consecrated first Bishop of Eichstätt. The biographer Willibald used to be quite naturally supposed to be the same person as the Bishop of Eichstätt; but in more critical times, abundant reasons for rejecting the identity have been discovered, and the sound view certainly is that Boniface's biographer was not the bishop his relative, but a trusted presbyter of the same name.

Willibald's Life of Boniface must be regarded as quite trustworthy. He addresses it to Lul, a Malmesbury student, who succeeded Boniface as Archbishop of Mainz in 755, and to Megingaud, Bishop of Würzburg, and he states that it was written at their command. He describes how careful he had been to learn, from those who had seen and known the work of Boniface, everything that he had to write of the beginning, middle, and end of his life. Details of his life were known to many in Tuscany, Gaul, Germany, and Britain; he had obtained them from all quarters. Lul and Megingaud had themselves told him much. From internal evidence, Willibald's Life of Boniface was written during the reign of Pepin le bref, the father of Charlemagne.

A writer three centuries later put on record the tradition that Willibald wrote the history on wax tablets and submitted it in that form to Lul and Megingaud, and when it had passed their scrutiny, it was written on parchment. The whole description reminds us of Bede's account of the inquiries which he made to ensure accuracy, and of the submission to King Ceolfrid of the original draft of his Ecclesiastical History, before the book was written out in its complete present form. Considering the very high regard in which Bede's life and labours were held by Boniface, we must regard it as very probable that Willibald did all that lay in his power to proceed on the lines so well laid down by that great father of true history.

It is a valuable testimony to the truth and adequacy of Willibald's Life of Boniface, that the monk Othlon, who was engaged to write a Life of the Saint some three hundred years later, took Willibald's Life bodily and added almost nothing to it beyond invaluable detail and documents more invaluable still. He was a monk of Regensburg, or Ratisbon, and he compiled the biography for the monks of Fulda, Boniface's own special foundation. He has, it is true, something to tell which is very interesting to us of the Church of England. We know from statements in the letters of the time of Boniface and Lul that Boniface sent to England for religious men and women to come out and help him to deal with the pagans. Othlon made it his business to state, from the records at his disposal, the names of the principal persons who responded to the call of Boniface. In this way we know the names of six of the men and six of the women, with something of their relationships; and we know the several places to which Boniface sent the men and the women to work.

Othlon's preamble to his biography is interesting in its connexion with his special purpose, and is instructive in general respects.

"I have endeavoured to obey your request, my brethren of Fulda, so far as the poorness of my skill has permitted. You have asked me to set forth in clearer language the Life of our holy father Boniface, which the holy Willebald wrote in old times in a style distinguished and elegant, but in some places so obscure to a feeble intelligence that it is difficult to say what the meaning is."

In the Appendix will be found a typical example of Othlon's idea of the way to make Willibald intelligible to a feeble intellect, and also a palmary example of the additions which he fortunately introduced.

Abbat Egbert of Fulda, Othlon proceeded to remind those who had set this task, had made collections illustrative of the work of the founder of the monastery. He was abbat from 1038 to 1058 and was now dead; he appears as Eppo in the lists. Egbert had applied to Pope Leo IX for permission to get such information as was contained in the papal archives, and had sent a copyist to Rome to transcribe the materials which existed there. By this and other means, a considerable amount of information which Willibald had not possessed, or at least had not used, was at the disposal of any one who desired to write on the subject in Othlon's time. We may regard him as writing at the end of the eleventh century, not far off the year 1100.

In two special respects Othlon found that the Life which he was to simplify was deficient. That it

should be so on one of these points was only natural.
Many remarkable letters or details from letters were
not mentioned by Willibald. Considering the difficulty of transmitting news, and the impossibility of
Willibald's doing what in these days is almost a matter
of course, that is, sending out a request that any one
who has any letters of some person lately deceased
will lend them to the biographer, it is only likely
that after Willibald's time many letters written by
Boniface, and many pieces of information which he
had sent by letter, would find their way to Fulda. The
other point has real value; it is illuminating. "I have
found," Othlon says, "that very many remarkable
accounts of miracles, which I have read in other
books, are not contained in the Life by Willibald. It
may be," he continues, "that the writer passed over
the wonderful works of Boniface in ignorance." It is
more likely that we have here a useful warning about
the growth of miraculous stories.

So far as the letters were concerned, Othlon remarked very justly that the letters which in his time
were in the library of Fulda, letters from Boniface
and letters to Boniface, were the great foundation on
which the knowledge of his marvellous successes was
built. "There is to be seen with what respect he was
received in the beginning by the Roman Pontiff, and
how the Pontiff sent him to preach to all the peoples
of Germany, and with what great labour he brought
that same Germany to the faith of Christ, and how
he rescued Germany not only from pagans and heretics
but also from false Christians and depraved priests,
as it were from the ravening of wolves." Taking the
whole position into review, Othlon determined to learn
all that he could from these and all other sources, and

to insert each piece of information in a fitting place in the Life by Willibald. See Appendix A.

The parents of Boniface were people of good position, probably connected with the royal family of Wessex. He was sent in early boyhood to a monastery at Exeter[1], to be brought up under Wolfard the Abbat. It is clear that he was one of the English colony in Devonshire, not one of the native Britons of Damnonia. We must bear in mind that the Damnonian Britons were still under their own British king, and still maintained their own British ecclesiastical rites and ceremonies. Aldhelm's famous letter to their king, Geraint, was not written till after Boniface had left Crediton his birthplace, and Exeter his first school. At Exeter he showed from the first a great desire for the religious life. After a time he sought a monastery in which he could obtain more advanced teaching, and he found what he wanted at Nutscelle, or Nuiscelle, near Winchester, a monastery of which no trace was left after the ravages of the Danes. Some writers place it at Nutsall, some at Nursling, and some at Netley. He bore still, and for long after this, his proper name of Winfrid, or Winfried.

At this West Saxon monastery he lived for many years. At the age of thirty he was ordained priest. His reputation for learning and business stood so high that, on the recommendation of the Abbats of Wessex, he was appointed by King Ina to proceed as their representative to Kent, and there lay certain matters before Archbishop Brihtwald. The occasion was certainly a serious one. A sudden difficulty had arisen in Wessex, and hasty action appears to have been

[1] Adescancastra (castrum ad Iscam).

taken by some of the more rash of the ecclesiastics.
By advice of the king, Ina, a synodal council was
held by the chiefs of the churches. More prudent
counsels prevailed. It was determined that an explanation must be sent to the archbishop, in order
that he might not ascribe to them the fault of having
acted without consulting him. Winbert, Winfrid's
own abbat, and Wintra, Abbat of Tisbury [1] in Wilts,
and Beorwald, the Abbat of Glastonbury [2], are specially
named by Willibald as among the many who selected
Winfrid for this delicate mission. He quite fulfilled
their expectations, returning in a short time and
delivering to the king, in the presence of the chief
ecclesiastics, a reply from the archbishop which they
found satisfactory. It had evidently been a matter
of much anxiety, for the story ends with a statement
that Winfrid brought to all a great rejoicing. What
the occasion of the difficulty was we do not know.

It was manifest that a large career was opening
for Winfrid in England. But in one sense that
career was not large enough for his desires. He had
determined that he must seek in other lands an opportunity for devoting himself to the conversion of pagans
to the true faith. All of the kingdoms of the Heptarchy were by this time professedly Christian, though
it is true that the conversion of the South Saxons, our
Sussex, was not effected till after his birth. Brihtwald, the archbishop, had thirteen bishops present at
one of his councils, in the year probably of Winfrid's
visit to him. Things were too well advanced at home
to satisfy his larger aims. He resolved to go to the
nearest pagans, the inhabitants of the territory called

---

[1] Disselburg.   [2] Glestingaburg.

Frisia—roughly speaking, Holland.   He took with
him two or three of the brethren, for the sake of
bodily and spiritual help, set out amid the tears of
his monastic friends, and came safe to a place where
there was a market of things for sale, called London [1].
It is curious to note how the idea of a concourse of
people come to buy and sell clung to London in the
earliest times.   Willibald describes it as a "forum
rerum venalium"; Bede as "multorum emporium
populorum terra marique venientium"; [2] Tacitus, six
hundred years before, as "copia negotiatorum et com-
meatuum maxime celebre". [3]

From London Winfrid sailed for Frisia, and arrived safely at Dorstat, a town on the river Lek,
represented now by Duuerstede in the modern name
of the fortress there, Wijk by Duuerstede.   This
is the point at which that branch of the mouth of
the Rhine which alone flows to the sea under the
name Rhine, separates from the Lek and passes by
Utrecht to the North Sea.   It may be well to say
for the benefit of those who examine the map of
modern Holland, that the river Lek was originally
a canal dug by the Romans to connect the Rhine
and the Maas, Dorstat and Rotterdam, and their
fortress commanded the entrance.   In Boniface's
time it was still only a canal.   In the year 839
a great inundation occurred, the effect of which was
so much to enlarge the canal, by the fierce rush
of pent-up water, that since that time it has been
the bed of the main stream.   Up to 839 the full
Rhine flowed through Utrecht.

The political position was unfavourable to Win-

[1] Lundenwick.   [2] *Hist. Eccl.* ii. 3.
[3] *Annal.* xiv. 33.

frid's hopes of missionary success. A great rising
of the pagan Frisians, under their king Rathbod,
had taken place, and there was war between them
and Charles Martel, the duke of the Christian
Franks. Such churches of Christ as had been planted
in Frisia through the influence of the Franks were
devastated. Winfrid sought an interview with the
Frisian king, and retired to Trecht, now Utrecht,
where he awaited the arrival of Rathbod. Bede calls
Utrecht Wiltaburg, the town of the Wilts, a people
whom Alcuin mentions. After an unavailing attempt to obtain from him permission to carry on his
missionary work, he left Frisia and returned to his
monastery in Wessex till a way should be opened.
While he was waiting there, . the Abbat Winbercht died, and Winfrid was unanimously begged to
undertake the office of abbat. He declined to abandon
his missionary purpose, and as soon as opportunity
offered he sailed once more for the continent of Europe.

This enthusiasm for missionary work was no new
thing among the Anglo-Saxons, and Frisia was no
new field for their missionary enterprise. The work
had begun, and in Frisia, forty years before, within
eighty years of the first preaching of Christ to the
English themselves. Wilfrith of Ripon and York
and Hexham, when on his way to Rome in 678 to
make his appeal against the Northumbrian government, had been driven out of his course in the
Channel, and came at last to shore on the coast of
Frisia. The present Holland, it may be said in
passing, is all that now remains of Frisia, the rest
having been washed away by the sea and by floods
from the land. He obtained the favour of the
Frisian king, Adelgisus, and exercised for the benefit

of the nobles and common people the great missionary zeal which afterwards showed itself in the conversion of pagan Sussex.

Wilfrith had soon passed on southwards on his way to Rome, but his work was not to be left long without a successor. A noble Northumbrian, Egbert, five years younger than Wilfrith, sent out that successor in 690. It must be remembered that we are speaking of men who came very early in the Christian history of the Anglo-Saxon race. Thus Wilfrith was born in 634, only eight years after the first conversion of Northumbria, and Egbert was born only thirteen years after that conversion, so that it is certain that their parents had been pagans in the earlier part of their life. Egbert had left Northumbria for Ireland at a time of disturbance, in 659, when he was twenty years of age, with Ceadda[1] and others, for purposes of study and devotion; in my little book on Aldhelm of Malmesbury we saw much of the fashion of going to Ireland for those purposes. In the course of time, Egbert caught from the Irish the missionary zeal which sent them to wander over all parts of the Continent. It is sufficient to mention in this connexion two great Irishmen of earlier date, Columban and Gall, who went together in 585 from Ireland to Switzerland by way of the Rhine, Columban pushing on thirty years later to Bobbio. The year in which they left Ireland for this purpose was twelve years before that in which Augustine first landed in Thanet to bring the knowledge of Christ to our English ancestors.

---

[1] Chad. The Anglo-Saxon hard *Ce* was evidently pronounced so sharp that it sounded like the *Ch* in " church." Indeed, the word "church" is itself a double example of this.

Egbert, then, determined to leave his Irish home
and go to the pagan lands of Northern Europe.   In
the year 687, just a hundred years after the far-
reaching expedition of Columban and Gall, he proposed to sail round Britain, starting probably from
the mouth of the Moy in the north of Connaught,
to preach to the pagans in Germany.   These pagans
are described as Frisians, Danes, Old Saxons, and
others, from whom, so Bede says, the Angles and
Saxons are known to have derived their origin.[1]   If
he could not accomplish this, he would go to Rome,
to see and adore the thresholds of the blessed Apostles
and Martyrs of Christ.   It is needless to enlarge
upon that, as one of the many convincing evidences
that the claim of Rome upon the regard of our
ancestors of those early times was not the later
Petrine claim at all.   It was the claim given by the
repose in that city of the remains of the two joint
chiefs of the Apostles, Peter and Paul, or as Eusebius,
and the early Irish, and old Slavonic ritual books,
have it, Paul and Peter.

Retained in Ireland by the warnings of visions,
and physically by storms which convinced him that
the visions had shown to him the will of God, he
sent out in the year 690 one of his Northumbrian
students, Willibrord, who had been with him twelve
years, and with him a company of eleven others.
They landed in Frisia.   By this time Rathbod had
become king of the Frisians, in place of Wilfrith's
friend Adelgisus, and Pepin of Herstal, Charles
Martel's father, the duke of the Franks, had con-
quered him.   By Pepin's aid Willibrord was enabled

---

[1] *Hist. Eccl.* v. 9.

to make good his footing in Frisia, and Pepin gave to him Utrecht, which became under him an episcopal and archiepiscopal see. Here he worked for nearly fifty years, dying at a very advanced age about the year 738, twenty years after Boniface came to Frisia for the second time.

Of Egbert, who set in motion all this great missionary work, we may say in passing that he was obedient to the vision which warned him not himself to seek the mission field; but, it would seem, not till he had done his best to disobey, and his ships had been wrecked. The vision bade him labour for the good of the Church of the adoption nearer home. The message conveyed by his vision was quaint and graphic. " Let him go at once to Columba's Monastery of Hy, because their ploughs do not go straight and he will bring them into the right way." He went accordingly to Iona, and succeeded in bringing them into line with the wider Catholicity.

Two other Englishmen, the two Hewalds, the white Hewald and the black Hewald, had gone out from Ireland to labour among the Old Saxons, pagan cousins of the Anglo-Saxons. These fierce pagans, who gave endless trouble to the Frankish dukes and later to King Pepin and Charlemagne, occupied a vast territory, including the mouth of the Elbe to the north and Westphalia and Hanover to the south. Of this people, so interesting to us from their near kinship to our own ancestors, Bede tells us that they had no king, only a number of chieftains; and when it became necessary to go to war they drew lots to decide which of the chieftains should lead the people. Him they obeyed as long as the war lasted, and when peace came he returned to his former equality with

the other chieftains. The steward of one of these
chieftains received the two English missionaries into
his house for some days, till such time as he could
send them on to his lord. The natives, however,
looked with great suspicion upon the strangers and
their religious rites, which Bede describes as follows :
"They spent their time in hymns and psalms and
prayers; and they daily offered to God the sacrifice
of the saving victim, for they had with them sacred
vessels and a tabula [1] consecrated in place of an altar."
The natives were determined not to allow the Hewalds
to reach their chief, fearing that if they got speech
with him they would convert him to the new faith,
and thus by degrees the whole province would be compelled to change its religion. So they took Hewald
the White and killed him at once with the sword, but
Hewald the Black they subjected to long torture,
tearing him at length limb from limb.

We can scarcely help noticing here the curious fact
that in all the detailed history of the conversion of
the English in this island of ours, there is not recorded
one single martyrdom. Roman missionaries, it is
true, fled away, and did not stay to be in danger of
losing their lives. If they had stayed, our record

[1] In my *Theodore and Wilfrith*, S.P.C.K. 1897, a description
will be found, with an illustration, of the little portable altar
found on the breast of St. Cuthbert when his tomb was opened
early in last century. It is of embossed silver fitted on to a
piece of old oak 6 inches square, the oak itself having originally
been used as a portable altar. A similar little altar-slab was
found some 800 or 900 years ago on the breast of Bishop Acca
of Hexham, with the inscription *almae trinitati, hagiae sophiae,
sanctae mariae*. The inscription on Cuthbert's altar-slab is
probably Greek. The great basilica at York, which Archbishop
Albert built after the fire of 741, was dedicated to fostering
wisdom, *almae sophiae*.

might not have been so clean. But the fact remains
that our ancestors did not martyr those who endeavoured to convert them, and their cousins on the
continent of Europe did. The fact and its possible
explanations will bear consideration for which here
there is no place.

Yet another English missionary must be mentioned,
besides a figure which flits unsuccessful across the page,
one Wictbert, who also came from Ireland, tried the
missionary life in Frisia for two years, found no fruit
among his barbarous hearers, and returned from failure
abroad to show forth a high example at home. This
other whom we must name is Suidbert, one of the
twelve Englishmen whom Egbert sent out from
Ireland. When Willibrord was absent from the
mission field on a visit to Rome, Suidbert was chosen
by his companions and sent to England to be consecrated bishop. Theodore of Canterbury being dead,
and the archbishopric being not as yet filled up,
Suidbert followed Wilfrith into his retreat in Mercia,
and was by him consecrated on June 21, 693. We
may wonder how Wilfrith, so great a stickler for
Catholic practice, effected this consecration without
irregularity, what bishops he found as coadjutors,
what valid appointment Suidbert could show, to what
see and district he consecrated him, and by what
right he consecrated any one to the foreign field.
His own resort to Paris for consecration to an
English see bears in the same direction. Suidbert
returned to the Continent and went to work among
the Bructeri, to the north of the Rhine and the
Lippe. After a time the Old Saxons drove out
the Bructeri, and Pepin of Herstal, at the instigation
of his wife Blythryda, gave Suidbert the island in

the Rhine called by Bede *In litore,* "near the shore."
There he built a monastery, and died in 713, a year
or two before Boniface went out.   The island called
In litore is the well-known Kaiserswerth, some six
miles from Düsseldorf.

As is suggested above, we do not know what lies
behind this resort of the missionary party to England
for episcopal consecration, when the head of the
party so soon after sought and received consecration
at Rome.   Bede's phrase is that during the absence
of Willibrord in Rome, the brethren that were in
Frisia chose Suidbert from among themselves and
sent him to Britain to be consecrated bishop.   Of
Willibrord he says that Pepin with the consent of all
sent Willibrord to Rome, where Sergius was still
Pope, desiring that he might be consecrated archbishop of the Frisian nation.   It would seem that for
episcopal consecration to missionary work any regular
bishop or bishops would suffice; but when it came to
the consecration and authorization of an archbishop
in the parts of north Europe, the Pope was regarded
as the only ecclesiastical authority adequate for the
occasion.   At Willibrord's consecration, Pope Sergius
gave to him the name of Clemens, as a later Pope
gave to Winfrid the name of Boniface.   There
had only been one Bishop of Rome called Clement,
and he dated from the first century, and there was
not another till near the Norman Conquest.   Of
Bonifaces, on the other hand, there had already been
five in the list of Popes when the Pope gave that
name to Winfrid.

It may be mentioned here, for it illustrates a fact
in the history of Boniface to which reference will eventually be made, that a main purpose of Willibrord's

first visit to Rome is thus stated by Bede,[1]—"he hoped to receive some relics of the blessed Apostles and Martyrs of Christ, in order that when he destroyed idols and erected churches he might have ready the relics of saints which he could place in them; for then he could dedicate the churches in honour of those whose relics were deposited in them."

We have seen that Egbert had desired to convert the people of the lands from which the Angles and Saxons came to Britain. This sense of cousinship was strong, and it was kept alive among the Anglo-Saxons. King Alfred, in his great gift to his people of his own version of the reports of travels by Ohthere and Wulfstan, called special attention to the interest which the English ought to feel in the countries that were the cradle of their race. This part of his great geographical work he wrote himself, and this is what he says,—"West of the Old Saxons is Friesland; from thence north-west is the country called Anglen and Zealand." "The Angles dwelt in these lands before they came into this country." Procopius, in his history of the Gothic war, written about the year 553, says that Britain was peopled by three nations, the Britons, Angles, and Frisians.[2] The Frisians themselves, as represented by the early Dutch, claimed our Saxon Hengist as one of themselves.[3] Thus we must under-

---

[1] *H. E.* v. 11.

[2] The authority of Procopius is very great. He accompanied Belisarius in his many wars in the capacity of secretary.

[3] A Dutch Chronicle in verse of about the year 1270, based upon an earlier work of 1245, speaks of him as having been driven into exile from Frisia :—

> Een hiet Engistus, een Vriese, een Sas,
> Die uten lande verdreven was.

stand that the sense of kinship directed the missionary ardour of the Anglo-Saxons to Frisia and the
neighbouring districts.

As regards the ardour itself, we must bear in mind
that our early Christian ancestors had an advantage
which we do not possess.   They could contrast Christianity with paganism in their own lands, in their
own families, even in themselves.   The more picturesque sides of paganism have come down to us
in story and in legend ; they saw it in its full un-
cleanness and degradation.

Another consideration is worth mentioning.   The
modern missionary desires to win the heathen into
the loving fold of Christ.   The early Anglo-Saxon
desired to save his distant kinsmen from damnation ;
sure, certain, eternal.   " Without doubt "—the words
are not unfamiliar—" they shall perish everlast-
ingly."   Rathbod of Frisia was told this very plainly.
In the language of the pseudo-Athanasius, he was
assured that the souls of his ancestors were neces-
sarily among the damned.   He replied that he would
rather be with them there than with a handful of
beggars in heaven.

We must also, in estimating the forces which
drove our early ancestors with such earnestness to
the mission field, remember that in the most marked
of the earlier cases they had caught the Celtic fire.
We trace the inspiration of passionate fervour to
their residence in Ireland.   They went there in the
first instance for study, Ireland being the only land
where devotion to deep study was a characteristic of
the native race.   How the love of study passed from
Ireland to England we saw in our examination into
the life and labours of our own St. Aldhelm some

seven years ago.[1] But, being there for study, they
were caught by the force of the other racial characteristic of that strange island, a characteristic so
closely akin to the moving force in their own Anglo-
Saxon nature. They caught that restless passion
for pushing into distant and strange lands, which
made the itinerant Irish missionaries, so many of
them claiming to be bishops, almost all of them
disregarding ecclesiastical order and the rights of
dioceses, made them a nuisance which more than one
Council of European Churches sought by stringent
rules to abate.

Add to this the fact that religious men in England
found life in the world beset by many temptations,
and found religious fervour impeded by many obstacles
and subjected to many shocks. They retired to the
cloister, and there for a time found the hoped-for
relief from the obvious difficulties of a secular life
in times such as theirs. But cloister prayer, and
cloister meditation, and cloister study, could not long
satisfy the racial force that pulsed in the very nature
of the vigorous Anglo-Saxons. They must be up and
doing; and as their impulse had already, in the step
which they had taken, been religious, it must be
religious work that they must go forth to do. The
inherent love of adventure, the inherent craving for
difficulties to overcome, the inherent sense that a life
of comparative ease is a life comparatively unworthy
of a man; given all this—which I trust we have in
us still—given all this, guided in the direction it shall
take by the primary impulse of religion, the only
kind of work that could satisfy their aspirations was

---

[1] *Life and Times of St. Aldhelm*, S.P.C.K., 1903.

missionary work, and that in dangerous places. For this they eagerly discarded the cloister stage to which they had first risen, and sprang into a higher range of thought and labour.

And there was a dark side, too. The vices of the world had gained entrance by back ways into the seclusion of the cloister. Each man who came in, and each woman too, for there were more convents of nuns than of monks, and in many cases one monastery had within its enclosures two separate parts, the nuns' quarters and the monks' quarters, each man and each woman brought into cloister life all the natural passions; and it is not in seclusion, but in the busy work of life, that those passions are best kept in a subordinate place. In Bede's time the monasteries had sunk very low in the moral scale, so that he advocated a large measure of the treatment which exactly 800 years after, to the very year, their successors received at the hands of a Tudor Parliament of Lords and Commons of the unreformed religion. We are enabled by some of the letters addressed to Boniface, to realize how far from peaceful the life in an English monastery could be in his time, and how far from spiritual. We can imagine how a high-souled man would recoil from the discovery that a cloister wall did not shut out vice, and with what keenness of joy he would find himself fighting, in the free air, the battle of the Lord against the open abominations of heathen races, powerful and dangerous.

CHAPTER II

THE earliest letter of Winfrid which we possess
was written in 716 or 717. As it is the earliest of
a very long series, it may be given in full. He was
about thirty-six or thirty-seven years of age when he
wrote it, and we may regard it as the direct reflection
of his literary education, before he had developed a
style of his own under pressure of business and cir-
cumstance. His letters afford evidence of the influence
of Aldhelm in thought and in phrase, and it is very
tempting—and not improbably true—to suggest that
either at Malmesbury or at Sherborne he did come
under the personal teaching of that most learned
saint, named by William of Malmesbury as one of the
two most learned of the English, the other being Bede.
Next to these two, William named Alcuin of York
as the third most learned Englishman before the
Norman times. The quotations from Aldhelm's letter
to Acircius (King Aldfrith of Northumbria) on
grammar, and from his Praise of Virgins, are given
in notes, and the subject of Winfrid's literary indebtedness to Aldhelm in his early years will not be
carried further. He completely emancipated himself

from the stilted style of his instructor. At a later period we shall find his relative Leoba even more directly using Aldhelm's phrases.

[1] "To my dearest companion and most loved friend, whom not any perishable gift of temporal gold nor any honeyed urbanity of wit by the blandishments of flattering words has bound to me, but the renowned affinity of spiritual intimacy, the bond of charity that cannot fade away, has of late joined us together; to Nithard, Wynfreth suppliant in Christ Jesus wishes the health of perpetual safety.[2]

"In most humble words of my mediocrity I pray the illustrious ability of your youthful manhood, dearest brother, that it never weary you to call to mind the words of the most wise Solomon (Ecclus. vii. 36), 'In all thy matters remember thy last end, and thou shalt never do amiss,' and elsewhere (St. John xii. 35), 'Walk while ye have the light, lest darkness come upon you, for he that walketh in darkness knoweth not whither he goeth;' for all things present will soon pass away, and the things that are to abide will quickly be with us. And all the precious things of this world, whether under the species of gold and silver, or in the variety of sparkling gems, or in the acquired diversity of ornamental dress, in a most apt similitude pass away like a shadow, as smoke they fade away, as froth they disappear,[3] according to the true saying of the psalmi-

---

[1] Ep. 9 ; 716-717.

[2] "Spiritalis necessitudinis ... inmarcescibilis catena caritatis nuper copulavit ... perpetuae sospitatis salutem." In Aldhelm's Letter to Acircius we find "mihi spiritalis clientelae catenis connexo . . . immarcescibilem sempiternae sospitatis salutem."

[3] "Simillima collatione ut umbra praetereunt, ut fumus

grafist,[1] 'The days of man are but as grass, for he flourisheth as a flower of the field,' or again, 'My days are gone like a shadow, and I am withered like grass.'"

He urges Nithard to study the Scriptures. "Strive to follow with intentness of mind the study of the Holy letters, and to acquire thence the comeliness of glorious and true beauty, that is, divine wisdom. It is more splendid than gold, more fair than silver, more burning than the carbuncle, more clear than crystal, more precious than the topaz, and we have it on the authority of the gifted preacher[2] that every precious thing is not worthy of it. For what, my dearest brother, is more fittingly sought by the young, or what is at length more soberly possessed by the old, than knowledge of the Holy Scriptures? Guiding the ship of our soul without any wreck of dangerous storm, this knowledge will bring it to the shore of most delightful paradise[3] and to the perpetual joys of the angels on high."

After more in the same style, the letter ends with twenty-eight lines of eight syllables, each pair of lines more or less rhyming, with difficult accents, beginning and ending thus :—

fatiscunt, ut spuma marcescunt." In Aldhelm's Letter we find "simillima collatione ut somnium evanescit, ut fumus fatescit, ut spuma marcessit."

[1] This coining of words from the Greek is a marked note of Aldhelm's style. In his next sentence Wynfrith uses Greek words in Latin letters, "apo ton grammaton agiis fiustratis," and "cata psalmistam"; all savouring of Aldhelm.

[2] Proverbs viii. 11.

[3] "Scientia sanctarum scripturarum deducit ad amoenissimi litus paradisi." Aldhelm's Letter has "de amoenissimo scripturarum paradiso".

Vale, frater, florentibus
Iuventutis cum viribus
Ut floreas cum Domino
In sempiterno solio.

.   .   .   .   .

.   .   .   .   .

Inque throno aethereo
Christum laudes praeconio.

It is almost unnecessary to say that nine con-
secutive lines of the poem begin with the letters of
the word Nithardus.

The concluding words of the letter itself, which
are simple and natural, appear to show that Wynfrith was in England, on his one short return from
the mission field, and that Nithard, whose name does
not appear again, was himself living in the parts to
which Wynfrith hoped soon to return :—

"If the Lord Omnipotent will that I reach again,
as I purpose, those parts of yours, I vow that I will
be to you in all these matters a faithful friend,
and in the study of the divine Scriptures, so far
as my ability enables me, your most devoted
helper."

The simple straightforwardness of this ending of so
turgid a letter may remind us of the description which
Willibald gives of the successful results of Winfrid's
diligent studies under Abbat Winbercht,—"he shone
in very great knowledge of the Scriptures, in eloquence
of grammatical art, in the modulation of richly-
flowing metres, as also in the simple exposition of
history, in the tripartite exposition of spiritual meaning, and in skill in dictating." This first letter of
his illustrates the second, third and fourth of these—

the fourth, best of all. Othlon, in place of all this, simply says that he acquired the desired knowledge of grammatical art, of metrical subtlety, and of spiritual meaning.

Winfrid must of course have letters commendatory from his own bishop. In this year, 718, Daniel was Bishop of Winchester, the great see of Wessex having been divided into the two sees of Winchester and Sherborne in 705, on the death of Haedde. Daniel was appointed to the former, Aldhelm to the latter of these two sees, Sherborne being very much the larger in area, but Winchester the more important, on account of the intimate relations between the kings and the bishops. There might have been some question as to whether the Bishop of Sherborne should commend Winfrid, when we remember where his infancy and boyhood were spent, how very important the ecclesiastical foundations at Malmesbury and Glastonbury and Wimborne were, and how completely, so far as we are informed, Boniface drew his English helpers, men and women, from those foundations. But Aldhelm was dead some nine years and we do not know that his successor was a man of much mark. As monk and as presbyter Winfrid was of Daniel's diocese. And Daniel himself was a man of mark by character and by learning. Bede testifies to his learning and to his ability by coupling his name with that of Aldhelm on terms of equality. In speaking of the subdivision of the Wessex see, he says of the two bishops, Aldhelm and Daniel, "both of them sufficiently instructed, alike in ecclesiastical affairs and in knowledge of the Scriptures." To Daniel, who survived Bede by many years (died 746), Bede handsomely acknowledges his indebtedness for information given, in the preface to his Church History of the English race.

Daniel's letter of commendation has been preserved, and may now be given. It will be seen that Daniel carefully abstains from making any reference at all to Winfrid's purposes or wishes. When Anselm was on his way to Rome, at one of the many times when the ecclesiastical world was divided between two sole and infallible popes, sometimes even three, he was a very great man in the realms that recognized Urban; through Clement's districts he had to pass as far as might be unmarked and unknown. Wynfrith's difficulties would have been of the same kind if his purposes had been set forth. All would on each occasion depend upon which of the two kings, which of the several dukes, nay, which of the bishops and abbats, he had· at the time reached. Inasmuch as rulers temporal and spiritual had a much more inquiring eye for persons travelling through their districts than they have now, Daniel must have known full well that Winfrid would time after time have to state his purpose. We must suppose that he could trust him to make diplomatic statements.

It is not necessary to point out how completely the wayfarer had to trust to free hospitality on his slow way through those distant parts to which Winfrid's steps were directed, where there was no very beaten track. On the direct road to Rome accommodation more approaching to the inns of later times was gradually provided.

[1] " To the most pious and clement kings, to all dukes, to the most reverend and most loved bishops, to the

---

[1] Ep. 11; A D. 718.

religious abbats also, to the presbyters and spiritual sons sealed in the name of Christ, Daniel, servant of the servants of God.

"Whereas the mandates of God are by all the faithful to be observed with sincerest devotion, it is demonstrated by the attestation of holy Scripture how great is the gift of hospitality, and how acceptable to God it is to show to wayfarers the office of humanity. By reason of the mercy of hospitality, the blessed Abraham was held worthy to receive the presence of angels and to enjoy their venerable discourse. Lot also, by the ministration of a like piety, was snatched out of the flames of Sodom; the grace of hospitality saved him from death by fire, because it was obedience to the commands of heaven. Thus also will it tend to the welfare of your dilection, that you receive the bearer of these, the religious presbyter and servant of the Omnipotent God, and show to him that charity which God loves and teaches. In receiving the servants of God you receive Him whose majesty they serve, who promises thus—'He that receiveth you receiveth Me.' Doing this, then, with devotion of heart, you carry out the commands of God, and trusting in the oracle of the divine promise you shall have with Him eternal reward.

"May grace from on high keep safe your eminence."

We may now follow Winfrid on his course from London when he left his native land in 718 never to return. It may be remarked here that in the great basilica of St. Boniface, a very disappointing building, founded by King Ludwig of Bavaria in 1835, the saint is represented in one of the frescoes

as setting sail from Southampton.[1]   Willibald says
with express clearness that he again embarked at
London.   He carried with him the commendatory
letter from the Wessex bishop, Daniel, which we
have just seen.   His plan was to do the whole thing
thoroughly, by going first to Rome to see the Pope.
He landed at the usual port for those who meditated
a journey to Rome by way of the Alps and Lombardy,
namely Quentavic, at the mouth of the river Canche,
corresponding to the modern Étaples.   He and his
party arrived safely at "the thresholds of the Blessed
Peter the Apostle", "and with great joy entered the
Church of Saint Peter, chief of the Apostles."   Thus
Willibald puts it.   The change of phrase from the
usual Anglo-Saxon phrase "the thresholds of the
blessed Apostles", that is, Peter and Paul, is an
interesting note of the growth of the Petrine claim.
Willibald was writing a quarter of a century later
than Bede, but Boniface had begun the change of
phrase long before that.   In a letter and reply which
passed between Boniface and his correspondent
Eadburga, two of the large number of Bonifatian
letters which have so close a personal interest for
English people, the English lady spoke of visiting
the thresholds of St. Peter and St. Paul, Boniface in
his reply spoke of Rome as the threshold of St. Peter.

It is very easy in these days to say that Boniface
and his party landed on the shores of France and
reached Rome safely.   Willibald had more to say
about it than that.   Boniface landed at Quentavic.

[1] Richard, Willibald, and Wunnibald, sailed from near
Southampton.   The attention of Bavaria being fixed locally
on Willibald and Wunnibald, we may understand how the
mistake was made.

There he formed a camp and waited till companions by degrees joined him. It was like the gradual formation of a caravan in the East. When at length all the multitude had collected together, they set out. Day by day the cold of winter came upon them more severely. Many churches of the saints they visited, to offer prayer to the throne on high for their safe passage over the summits of the Alps. They prayed also that the Lombards on the other side of the Alps might be moved by feelings of humanity towards them. They prayed also that they might evade the malicious ferocity of the pride of the soldiery. And when they reached Rome, they offered up unmeasured thanks to Christ for their safety. Clearly it was a very serious matter indeed in those days.

In going to Rome to obtain the sanction of the Pope for his missionary work, and not the sanction only but a commission to carry it on, there can be no doubt that Winfrid took a right step. Some great ecclesiastical sanction he must have. He could not be a free-lance; there were too many ecclesiastical free-lances, especially from Ireland. The secular government of the territories where he proposed to work, nominally a Frankish government, was in a very unsettled state, as we shall have to see, and the ecclesiastical supporters of that secular government were far from being what they ought to be. Winfrid desired to have behind him a spiritual authority which no one dared call in question in the lands of the Franks, in order that he might be unhampered in his work among the neighbouring heathen. The Pope at that time was the second Gregory.

We have a pleasant account of the first interview of Winfrid with Pope Gregory. Not many days after his arrival in Rome he saw the Pope. He described to him in full order the events of his journey and the occasion of his arrival in Rome, and with what anxious desire he had laboured long. The Pope suddenly interrupted his narrative, looking at him with a glad countenance and smiling eyes, and asked if he had brought with him commendatory letters from his own bishop. Winfrid opened his cloak and brought out and gave to the Pope a sealed document and an open or general letter. The Pope took them at once and nodded to him to go away. The Pope read the letter and went through the commendatory document; and afterwards had daily conferences with him till the time came for him to leave Rome again. When that time came, the Pope gave to him a letter to the following effect [1] :—

Gregory, servant of the servants of God, to Boniface the religious priest.

The Pope has learned that from a youth Boniface has studied the Holy Scriptures and has striven to increase the talent specially committed to him, namely the desire to make known, to the nations that do not believe, the mystery of the faith. He rejoices in the fact, and desires to aid the undertaking. Therefore, in the name of the Indivisible Trinity and by the unshaken authority of the blessed Peter, chief of the Apostles, whose office of teaching he exercises by dispensation, the place of whose holy see he administers, he gives him power to hasten to any peoples that are held in the error of unbelief, to set

[1] Ep. 12 ; May 15, 719.

before them the ministry of the kingdom of God by
introducing with the persuasiveness of truth the
name of Christ our Lord God, to put into their
untutored minds in an intelligent manner the preaching of the Old and the New Testaments by the
spirit of power and love and soberness. Lastly, he
is to be intent upon maintaining the discipline of
the Sacrament for initiating those who are to believe,
according to the formula of the holy apostolic see,
which has been set forth for his instruction.

The letter is dated on the Ides of May in the third
year of the reign of the most pious lord Augustus Leo,
crowned of God great emperor.

Willibrord had in the same manner sought the
authority of the Pope for his work. The lands in
which he as well as Winfrid desired to work had
formed part of a province of old Rome, and so were
naturally the care of the Bishop of Rome. Pope
Sergius had received Willibrord when Pepin of Herstal
had given him the city and fortress of Trajectum or
Ultrajectum, now Utrecht; and in 696 Willibrord
had again visited Rome, received the pall from the
same Sergius, and been made Archbishop with the
fullest authority to rule his new see.

Boniface left Rome, still a presbyter, armed with
Pope Gregory's letter. After a restful and enjoyable
visit to the excellent King of the Lombards, Liutprand,
no doubt at Pavia, he crossed the Alps, probably by way
of Tyrol, passed through the eastern parts of Bavaria,
and reached Thuringia. We may take modern Saxony
as roughly representing Thuringia. Here he found a
double difficulty. There were the pagans to deal with,
and there were bishops and priests. The bishops and
priests appear to have been the more difficult of the

two, and throughout Boniface's time this was so.
There were two kinds of bishops and priests who came
in his way, and both were difficult. The Frankish
bishops and priests were many of them men of bad
lives, with nothing spiritual about them; and the
wandering bishops and priests of the Irish school
were queer in their practices and their ways. Neither
kind cared much for spiritual authority, or for the
pope, as Boniface in one of his letters very frankly
states. With the lay people of Thuringia he took
special pains, calling together the senators and the
chief men, delivering to them spiritual addresses, and
instructing them in the right way of truth. He then
passed on into Frankish territory, but hearing of the
death of Rathbod he hastened to Frisia by the water-
way, joined Archbishop Willibrord at Utrecht, and
for three years worked with him.

By this time Willibrord was feeling old. Bede
has a very touching little entry about him, written
near the end of Bede's own life. "Willibrord himself," he says,[1] "surnamed Clement, is still living,
venerable in old age, having been thirty-six years
a bishop, sighing for the rewards of the heavenly life,
after the manifold conflicts of his heavenly warfare."
Willibrord begged Winfrid to become his episcopal
coadjutor, to succeed to the archbishopric on his
death. Winfrid steadfastly refused, pleading among
other reasons for refusal that he was not yet of the
canonical age of fifty. We do not know of any canon
imposing that as the lower limit of age for the consecration of a bishop, and it has been suggested that
Winfrid referred to the age at which Levites retired

[1] *H. E.* v. 11.

from active work (Num. viii. 24). However that may have been, he persisted in his refusal, and to rid himself of Willibrord's insistence took a long journey to the south-east, halting at last on the river Ohm, in the district now called Hesse Cassel. Here he found two Hessian chiefs, Detdic and Dierolf, who worshipped idols and yet called themselves some kind of Christian. We in England may remember that we had a similar example in our own land. Bede tells us that in his time King Aldwulf of East Anglia used to relate an experience of his own youth. He had seen when a boy the temple of his great-uncle Redwald, the first Christian King of East Anglia, and in it Redwald had a large altar for Christ and a small altar for demons, which remained till Aldwulf's days.

Winfrid's teaching met with great success among the Hessians, and he established a monastery at Amanaburg, Amana being the ancient or the Latin name of the river Ohm. The place is now called Amöneburg. He then proceeded to the northern districts of the Hessians, near the frontier of the Saxons, that is towards the modern Hanover, and met with like success, many thousands consenting to be baptized. This multitudinous conversion reminds us of similar accounts in the early days of the preaching of Christianity to the Northumbrian cousins of these German peoples.

Winfrid thought it right to report his successes to the Pope, and he sent a trusty messenger, Binna, to Rome, bearing letters of narrative and inquiry. There is every reason to believe that Binna was an Englishman. We find one of the same name filling a large secular position in Mercia towards the end of the century. This later Binna was specially connected

D

with us of the diocese of Bristol, inasmuch as he signs, as *Bynna dux*, a document restoring lands at Aust to the Bishop of Worcester, which had been held without right by Bynna, *comes regis*, probably himself. King Offa was present and confirmed the deed with the sign of the Cross.[1] The Pope, the same Gregory II who had received Winfrid some five years before, sent Binna back to Winfrid very promptly, with letters inviting him to come to Rome. Though shorter than the journey from Quentavic, it was a serious journey in those days, a journey of danger and labour. Willibald tells us that the great English missionary went on his way to Rome accompanied by a crowd of retainers and surrounded by a band of brethren. They crossed over the heights of the Alps of the Franks and the Burgundians and of Italy, the mention of the Burgundians indicating that they crossed the Alps by one of the western passes. The mention of the Bavarians, on the occasion of his previous journey from Rome, indicated one of the eastern passes, the Bavarians of those times not reaching so far west as Bavaria does now. They halted when they came in sight of the walls of Rome and offered condign thanks to the Throne on high; then they went to the Church of St. Peter and fortified themselves by prayer; and then they were quiet for a time to rest their weary limbs.

The Pope soon heard of the arrival of Winfrid. He was well received, and was conducted to an hostel. As soon as a convenient day was found, the Pope and he met at the basilica of St. Peter and saluted one another in a few pacific words. The apostolic pontiff

---

[1] Haddan and Stubbs, iii. 484-5.

then questioned Winfrid on the Creed and on the handing down of the faith of the Church. The man of God humbly made reply as follows :—" My Lord Apostolic, I have not the skill, a mere stranger, to answer by word in intimate discourse. I beg that thou wilt give me time and leisure to write a statement of my faith, that the unspoken letters may set it forth in orderly manner." This was at once granted, but with an order that the thing must be done quickly. Without loss of time Winfrid wrote out an account of his belief in regard to the Holy Trinity, and it was delivered to the Pope. He had to wait some days for a second invitation, and this time he was summoned to the Lateran, the real seat of the Bishops of Rome, the Mother Church of the ancient city. His face humbly bent towards the ground, he knelt at the feet of the apostolic pontiff and begged his blessing. The Pope raised him up, gave back to him the paper on which his confession of faith was written, bade him sit by his side, and instructed him always himself to keep firm this faith, and to teach it to others to the utmost of his powers. I do not know if it has been noticed by those who have written on the so-called Creed of Athanasius that Willibald describes Winfrid's statement as *integra et incorrupta,* " whole and uncorrupted," the words in the so-called Athanasian formulary, in the prefatory part which the document itself declares to be not part of the Catholic Faith, being *integra inviolataque,* "whole and undefiled." We may, I think, not unfairly imagine that what Winfrid did was to write out from memory—or possibly from a manuscript, for we are not told what supervision of his examination there was—verses 3 to 27 of the Athanasian Creed, already well known in the Gallican

Churches.   The Pope asked him a great many more
questions about the holiness of religion and the verity
of the faith, and indeed they spent nearly the whole
day in discussing these matters.   It is very pleasant
to read of this care for the soundness and fullness of
the faith on the part of Gregory II.   He was the
strong Pope who withstood the Emperor Leo when
the Emperor forbade the use of images; rescued
Rome from the Lombards when King Liutprand was
actually at the gates; and eventually worked so
successfully in the direction of freeing Italy from the
tyranny of Constantinople, that the complete separation came to pass in the next half-century.

The close examination of a priest before his consecration as bishop, now fortunately for some bishops
obsolete, was a serious reality at some times in the
middle ages.   There is an echo of it in our Form for
the Consecration of Bishops, wherein the archbishop is
bidden to say " I will examine you in certain articles ".
More than one person elected to the Archbishopric of
Canterbury has been rejected in Rome for ignorance,
and another has had to be elected in his place.   This
was by agreement between the King and the Pope,
as a canonical way of voiding an unsuitable election.   Thus in 1228, on Stephen Langton's death,
a Canterbury monk, one Walter de Hempsham, was
elected by the monks.   Against him the king and
the prelates appealed to Rome.   Pope Gregory IX
had him examined.   The cardinals asked him about
the Descent into Hell, and reported *male respondit*,
his answer was bad.   They asked him about the
Real Presence, *male respondit* again.   On the whole
they reported that he had not only not done well,
he had done *pessime*, very badly; and he was rejected.

The method was not only canonical, it was also
simoniacal in its application.　The result in this
case was brought about by the promise of a tenth
of all movable property in England and Ireland to
the Pope for the war against the Emperor.　A few
years later another Canterbury election was cancelled
by a like quaint process.

No obstacle to the consecration of Winfrid was
interposed on this or on any other ground.　The Pope
intimated to him that he proposed to advance him to
the episcopate, and fixed as the day for the ceremony
St. Andrew's Day, November 30.　The young priest
did not withstand the prelate's purpose, and on the
day appointed he received the dignity of the episcopate, and the additional name of Boniface.　So
say both of the Lives.　The statement about the confirming of the additional name of Boniface is not
at all inconsistent with his having used that name
before.　The Pope's act made it his lawful name.
Bishops in these modern days frequently regularize
the use of a name other than the baptismal name, by
using it in the act of Confirmation.

Suggestions that the name Bonifacius was a pedantic
play upon the *Wyn* in the name of the young priest,
whence came the Anglo-Saxon *wynsum*, our "win-
some", and that Wynfried and the modern Welsh
Gwynfryd are the same word, may be left to those
who delight in such things.

CHAPTER III

On this visit to Rome, Boniface took the oath to the Bishop of Rome, his consecrator, on which much has been written. It is generally said to have been the oath regularly taken to the Bishop of Rome, as Bishop and Patriarch of Rome, by the bishops specially under his patriarchal jurisdiction, namely the suburbicarian bishops. That phrase has been the subject of almost endless discussion. It is certainly taken from the phraseology of the civil government of the Western Empire. An apt example is to be found in a decree of the Emperor Julian—"not only throughout all Italy but also in the suburbicarian regions"—where "Italy" means the province or vicariate so called, corresponding to northern Italy, and "the suburbicarian regions" mean the Roman vicariate, which included the territories from Campania and Umbria to Apulia, Calabria, &c., and the islands of Sicily, Sardinia, and Corsica. The Nicene Council arranged that the ancient custom—which apparently must mean the civil custom—should continue, and the Patriarch of Alexandria should govern the churches throughout Egypt, the Metropolitan of Rome governing the suburbicarian churches. Whatever else may be in doubt in the meaning of the phrase, it is at least certain that it did not include Britain.

The oath was taken on November 30, in the year 722 or 723. Into the discussions as to which of

these years is indicated by the date given it is not
necessary to enter; the weight of opinion seems to
be with 722.[1]   The oath is as follows[2]:—

"In the name of the Lord God and our Saviour
Jesus Christ, in the reign[3] of the Lord Leo, crowned
of God great Emperor, in the sixth year of his reign,
and the sixth year after his Consulship, and in the
fourth year of the reign of his son Constantine, great
Emperor, Indiction VI.

"I Boniface, by the grace of God bishop, do
promise to thee, blessed Peter, chief of the apostles,
and to thy vicar, blessed Pope Gregory and his
successors, by the Father, the Son, and the Holy
Spirit, the indivisible Trinity, and by this thy most
sacred body, that I show the holy catholic faith in
all fidelity and purity, and persist by God's help in
the unity of the same faith, in which the whole
safety of Christians is acknowledged to be, that in no
way will I, on the instigation of any one, give consent
to anything contrary to the unity of the common
and universal Church, but, as I have said, I will show
forth in all things my fidelity, purity, and aid, to
thee and to the profit of thy Church, to whom has
been given by the Lord God the power of binding and
loosing, and to thy foresaid vicar and his successors.
And if I shall become aware that prelates walk
contrary to the ancient institutes of the holy Fathers,
with them I will have no communion or fellowship;
nay more, if I shall have strength to forbid them,
I will forbid them, and if I have not, I will immedi-

---

[1] Ep. 16; Nov. 30, 722.   [2] Dümmler, Ep. 16, p. 265.
[3] The joint Emperors were Leo III and Constantine IV.
The words *piissimo augusto* in connexion with the name of Leo
appear to have been erased in the MS.

ately make a faithful report thereupon to my lord
the apostolic.[1]   But if, which be far from me,
I shall attempt to do anything contrary to this my
profession, in any way, whether intentionally or
accidentally[2], may I find myself accused in the
eternal judgment, may I incur the punishment of
Ananias and Sapphira who presumed to lie to you
about their property.   This transcript of my oath,
I Boniface, humble bishop, have written with my
own hand, and placing it over the most sacred body
of the holy Peter as is prescribed, God being my
witness and judge, I have taken the oath, which also
I promise to keep."

This oath has some slight variations from the
form of the oath taken to the Bishop of Rome by
the suburbicarian bishops, as set forth in the *Liber
Diurnus*.   The only variation of importance is in the
words: "if I shall become aware that prelates walk
contrary to the ancient institutes of the holy Fathers";
where the suburbicarian bishop swore thus—"if I shall
become aware that anything is being done contrary
to the public weal or our most pious prince."   The
reason for the variation is obvious, and the change
made goes deep and far.   The suburbicarian bishops
must not infrequently have wondered who their "most
pious prince" actually was.

The day after Boniface had laid the document
containing this transcript of his oath on the tomb of
St. Peter, the Pope gave to him the following
letter[3] :—

---

[1] Wurdtwein states that this was at first the title of all
bishops, but afterwards of the Pope alone.   He refers to Greg.
Mag. epp., v. 37.

[2] Ingenio vel occasione.   [3] Ep. 17 ; Dec. 1, 722.

"Gregory, bishop, servant of the servants of God, to all most reverent and most holy brethren his fellow-bishops, religious presbyters or deacons, glorious dukes, magnificent chiefs, counts also, and all God-fearing Christians.

"We are very anxious on account of a report which we have received and believe. There are some races in the parts of Germany and on the east side of the Rhine, who under the suasion of the old enemy live in error, in the shadow of death. We have learned that some, under cover of the Christian religion, worship idols. Others, not as yet having knowledge of God, nor washed in the water of holy baptism, do not recognize their Maker. For the illumination of both, we have thought it right to send the bearer of this letter, Boniface, our most reverend brother bishop, to preach the word of the right faith in those parts, so that by preaching the word of salvation he may provide for them eternal life, and if anywhere he should find those who have left the path of true faith, or by suasion of the devil are in error, he may correct them, and by his teaching may bring them back to the harbour of safety, and inform them from the doctrine of this apostolic see, and may establish them so that they continue in the same catholic faith.

"For the love of our Lord Jesus Christ, and for reverence of His Apostles, we exhort you in all ways to support him in his efforts, and to receive him in the name of Jesus Christ, as it is written: 'he who receiveth you, receiveth Me.' Further, we exhort you to provide things necessary for his journey, give him companions, food, drink, everything he requires, that by the favour of God he may succeed in the work of piety and the business of salvation entrusted

to him, and you may be found worthy to receive
a return for your labour, and from the conversion of
those who err a reward may be granted you in
heaven.   May any who favour or further the work
of this servant of God, sent from this Apostolic and
Catholic Church of God for the enlightening of the
Gentiles, be held worthy, by the prayers of the chiefs [1]
of the Apostles, of the fellowship of the sacred
martyrs of Jesus Christ.   But if any—we desire it
not—should attempt to hinder his work, or to oppose
the ministry entrusted to him or his successors
entering upon the same labour, may he be smitten by
the divine sentence of anathema, may he lie under
perpetual damnation."

A second letter, addressed to all clerics and people,
Boniface received from Gregory on the same day.
It is merely a common form from the *Liber Diurnus*,
the "synodal which a bishop receives", and has no
local or personal reference beyond the insertion of the
name, Bonifatius.   It is the letter in which the Popes
forbad the reception of Africans to holy orders, on
the ground that some of them were Manicheans and
many of them had been re-baptized.   It also contains
the well-known order about the application of the
rents of church property and the offerings of the
faithful : the bishop is to divide the whole into four
portions, one for himself, one for the ministering
clergy, one for the poor and the stranger, and one
for the fabrics of the churches.

In the same month, December 722 or 723, Gregory
wrote three other letters of commendation, one to the
Thuringian Christians,[2] one to Karl Martel, and one

---

[1] Apostolorum principibus.   [2] Ep. 19; Dec. 722.

to the Altsaxons. Two of them are short, and all of
them should be given here as documents of primary
importance at the beginning of Boniface's episcopal
career :—

" To the magnificent men, our sons Asulf, Godolaf,
Willar, Gundhar, Alvold, and all Thuringians loved
of God, faithful Christians, Gregory the Pope.

'· Being informed of the constancy of your magnificent faith in Christ, that when the pagans would
have compelled you to the worship of idols, you replied
in full faith that you would rather die than in any
way violate the faith in Christ once received, full of
great exultation we gave due thanks to our God and
Redeemer, the Giver of all good things. Whose
grace accompanying you, we desire that you should
proceed to better and higher things, and for the
confirmation of your faith should adhere with religious
mind to the holy apostolic see, and, as the work of
sacred religion shall demand, should seek solace from
the said holy see, the spiritual mother of all faithful
people, as the sons and coheirs of a kingdom ought to
seek from their royal parent, and from the ministry
of our present most dear brother Boniface. Him we
have sent to you, ordained bishop for the purpose of
preaching, instructed in the apostolical institutions,
for building up your faith. In all things we will and
exhort that you obediently consent to him for the
completing of your salvation in the Lord."

It will have been noticed how the Popes in their
letters asserted, iterated, and re-iterated, the headship
of the see of Rome. It will be remembered that
until Boniface's time this was, in the case of many of
the converted heathen, a new and large idea. The
Popes represented it as a fundamental doctrine of the

Christian faith, and as such it was received by the
new believers.   So far as the history of the middle
ages is concerned, that is the most important creative
feature of the Pope's letters :—.

"To the glorious lord our son Karl the duke,
Gregory the Pope.[1]

"Being well assured that you, most loved in Christ,
bear among many fitnesses a mind well-disposed
towards religion, we make known to your dignity,
loved of God, that we have felt it necessary to send
our present brother Boniface to preach to the people
of the German race, and to various persons dwelling to
the east of the Rhine, held in the error of heathenism,
or up to this time fettered in the darkness of ignorance.   He is a man approved in faith and morals,
consecrated bishop by us, instructed in the institutions
of the apostolic see, over which by God's favour we
preside in care of the Church at large.   For the sake
of those to whom he is to minister we commend him
in all ways to your glorious benevolence, that you
assist him in all his needs, and most firmly defend
him against all adversaries, over whom in the Lord
you prevail.   When God sent out His Apostles,
a light to lighten the Gentiles, He said, ' Whosoever
receiveth you, receiveth Me.'   Instructed by us in
the institutions of the Apostles, the said prelate goes
forth in the function of preaching."

With regard to the next letter,[2] the question has
been much discussed whether it is to be attributed to
Gregory II or Gregory III.   In either case it seems
a little early in Boniface's episcopal career for such
a letter to the Altsaxons.   But the documentary

---

[1] Ep. 20 ; Dec. 722.   [2] Ep. 21.

evidence is in favour of it; and in Boniface's letter to England (ep. 46) asking prayers for the conversion of this very pagan race, he informs his English friends that he has had the consent and blessing of two Popes for his work among them. As this was written in or about 737, the two Popes must have been Gregory II and Gregory III. The numeration of the Gregorys is rather confusing at this point. The Pope whom we have so far called Gregory II was known in his own time as Gregory Junior, no doubt out of special consideration for Gregorius Magnus, our own Pope Gregory. When he was succeeded by yet another Gregory, the new Pope was quaintly described as Gregorius Junior Secundus, a roundabout way of saying Gregory the Third. Later on, Willibald excels himself by getting seven words into Gregory's title: *Gregorius a Secundo Iuniore cum primo Tertius* (ch. x).

Though the attribution of the letter in question to Gregory II appears to be incorrect, the letter will come in better connexion here than later on.

"Gregory the Pope to the whole people of the province of the Altsaxons."

The letter itself is a *cento* of texts of Scripture appropriate to an exhortation against idolatry. At least twenty passages of Scripture are directly quoted or evidently referred to; the Psalms three times (it might well have been more), Isaiah once, St. Luke three times, the Epistle to the Romans twice, to the Corinthians once, to the Colossians seven times, to Timothy once. It may be permitted to suppose that the popes must have felt the difficulty of having always to quote St. Paul and never St. Peter. Dümmler is most careful to give in the margin the

actual reference to each text quoted or referred to in
the letters of the Bonifatian period. I cannot find one
quotation from the Epistles of St. Peter in the letters
of the Popes. Dümmler carefully notes, in the margin
of the two hundred large pages of letters of the Bonifatian period, the places of Scripture from which
quotations are found in the text. In no case, unless
the inquiring eye has failed, does any Pope quote
from St. Peter's Epistles.

Boniface, who made a special appeal that a copy
of St. Peter's Epistles might be sent to him, only
quotes from them three times in all his many letters.
The passages which he quotes are (Ep. 73) 1 Pet. iv. 3,
' The time past of our life may suffice us to have
wrought the will of the Gentiles,' &c. ; (Ep. 78) 1 Pet.
v. 8, 9, ' Be sober, be vigilant ; because your adversary
the devil,' &c.; (Ep. 106) 1 Pet. iv. 8, ' Above all things
have fervent charity,' &c.

The Pope's letter concludes thus :—

" Dearest ones, the faithful minister and fellow
servant in the Lord, Boniface, my brother and fellow
bishop, I have sent to you for this purpose, that he
may learn your circumstances, and console your
hearts with the word of exhortation in Christ Jesus
our Lord ; that being freed from the fraud of the
devil, you may be found worthy to be placed among
the sons of adoption, and, freed from eternal damnation, may have eternal life."

The Thuringians were a remarkable people, and the
origin of their name is curious. They appeared in
history as Düringer or Thüringer in the beginning of
the fifth century. They took their name from the
second part of the name of the Hermundüren, of whom
they were a branch. Domitius Ahenobarbus had

settled the Hermundüren, a Suevian race, shortly
before the birth of Christ, in the territory between
the Main and the Danube.   They were firm allies of
Rome, and they prospered and enlarged their territory, expelling the Chatti from the salt springs in the
neighbourhood of their boundary to the north, the river
Werra.   In A.D. 152 they are mentioned, with the
Marcomanni and others, as threatening the northern
boundaries of the Roman empire, and then in the
absence of history they are lost.   They emerge as
Düringer about A.D. 500, when they had the Saxons
on the north, the Alemanni on the south, and the
Franks on the west.   They then spread north to the
lower Elbe and south to the Danube.   Under an
ambitious duke they fell foul of the Franks, and from
that time they cease to be shadowy and begin to have
a personal history, and not a fortunate one.   Her-
manfried, Berthar, and Badrich, three brothers, were
the dukes of the Thuringians. The first named made
away with his brothers, became sole duke, and married
Amalaberg, daughter of Theoderich I of Austrasia,
son of Clovis the first Christian king of the Franks.
He did not carry out his promises to that king, but
he had become so strong that Theoderich did not deal
with him alone, but called in the aid of his brother,
Chlotar I of Neustria, and in A.D. 530 or 531 he was
killed under the walls of Zülpich.   The north-east
part of his enlarged territory went to the Saxons, the
south went to Austrasia.   This south part from the
Main to the Danube became completely Frankish and
lost its old name, which was used only for the territory
between the Werra and the Saale.   Over this limited
territory Dagobert I of Austrasia appointed a duke,
Radolf, in 630, who ten years later rebelled against

Sigebert III of Austrasia, and Thuringia lost its independence in 640. Under Pepin the ducal dignity was set aside, and the country was administered by counts of the Helmengau, Altgau, Eichsfeld, Westgau, Ostgau, Lancwiza, and Arnstadt. Gregory III in addressing the great men of Thuringia names six districts, but the names are quite different from these. The German historians of modern time, in speaking of Boniface's work in Thuringia, say that in 725 he founded the Johanniskirche on the Alte Berg by Georgenthal, the monastery of Ohrdruf, and the Marienkirche in Erfurt. The monastery of Ohrdruf, ten or eleven miles from Gotha, was certainly founded by him, but not so early as 725. In Erfurt he placed a bishop much later than 725. We have no record of his connexion with the Church of St. John at Altenberg near Georgenthal, which is eight miles from Gotha. Altenberg claims to be, and may well be, the oldest village in Thuringia, and it claims that the Johanniskirche was founded by Boniface. The church has ceased to exist; but a century ago, the people, proud of its antiquity, erected on its site a stone monument thirty feet high in the shape of a church candlestick, to indicate the fact that from very early times the light of the Gospel shone forth from the Alte Berg; the monument is known far and wide as the Candelabrum, or Candelaber.

The name of Thuringia survives now only in the Thüringer Wald. Even here the ruin of former greatness is evident on the modern map. The long line of Wald country running south-east from Eisenach is marked in its northern part as Thüringer Wald, in its southern part as Franken-Wald.

On December 4, 724, Gregory II informed Boniface that he had written[1] to Charles Martel, the Thuringians, and the people of Germany : —

" Moved by the evangelic precept, Pray ye the lord of the harvest that he send forth labourers into his harvest, we have bid you Go preach the Gospel of the Kingdom in the parts of the west[2] for the illumination of the people of Germany seated in the shadow of death, that you may make gain of them as is written of the servant to whom the talents were given. You have told us that by the ministry of preach- ing the unbelieving people are being converted. We give thanks to the Lord of power, from whom come all good things, who willeth every man to come to the truth, and pray that He will aid thee to bring out of darkness unto light that people by the in- spiration of His power. Be able to say with the apostle, I have fought a good fight, I have finished my course, I have kept the faith. Persist, that thou mayest receive the crown of thy labour, for God promises salvation in the end[3] to them that persevere. Let not threats terrify thee, nor terrors cast thee down ; holding firm your trust in God, speak out the word of truth.

" With regard to that bishop [4] who up to this time has slothfully neglected to preach to the people of whom we speak, and now claims it as his right, as of his diocese, we have written a fatherly letter to our most excellent son the patrician Charles, asking him to restrain the bishop, and we believe that he will

[1] Ep. 24.

[2] West from Rome, but to the eastward of the parts with which we are concerned.

[3] *In fine*, not *in finem*.

[4] The circumstances suit the case of Gerold of Mainz, who held that bishopric from about 720 to about 741.

order the difficulty to be avoided.   But do not you
cease to preach the things that make for salvation, in
season and out of season.

   " To the Thuringians and the people of Germany
we have not failed to write of practical and spiritual
things, among other advice bidding them construct
dwellings for the bishop and build churches."

   It has been said, in connexion with a remark of
Willibald's,[1] that the Thuringians were converted to
Christianity long before, in the time of the sons of
Clovis, and that this is stated by Gregory of Tours
in the third book of his history of the Franks, which
was written about the year 575.   But all that he
there says is that Lothaire carried off, from the conquest of Thuringia by himself and his brother Thierry,
a daughter of the Thuringian king, whom he married,
and that she became a Christian.   She was the well-
known St. Rhadegund.   There is not anything in
Gregory's letter to suggest that the Thuringians in
general had ever been Christians, or that Christianity
had been planted there two hundred years before.[2]
Gregory desires that the Christian religion should be
placed on a firmer footing among them, and sends
his dearest Boniface to be their bishop.

   To the whole people of the Thuringians, that is, to
a nation of pagans, Pope Gregory wrote, on the same
day as to Boniface, a very interesting and curious
letter.[3]   He tells them, with an air of complete
authority, that he is sending his brother the most
holy bishop Boniface to them, with instructions to

---

[1] And see Ep. 19 ; A D. 722.
[2] Rhadegund was born in 519, and was carried off by Lothaire
at the age of 10.
[3] Ep. 25 ; Dec. 724.

baptize them, to teach them the faith of Christ, to
bring them out of error into the way of salvation,
that they may have eternal life.   They are bidden,
therefore, to obey him in all things, to honour him as
their father, and to incline their hearts to his teaching.
It was not for gain of money but for gain of souls
that he was sent.   They must love the Lord, and
receive baptism in His name; for the Lord our God
hath prepared for them that love Him that which eye
of man hath not seen nor heart of man conceived.
They must leave off from evil works and do well;
they must not worship idols, or offer sacrifices of
flesh, for such God does not accept.   They must
observe and do in all things what Boniface teaches,
and then they will be safe, they and those that come
after them, for ever.   They must build a house in
which their bishop should live, and churches in which
they must pray, that God may pardon their sins and
grant them eternal life.

It is a remarkable letter to be addressed by the
Pope to a distant nation of pagans, of whom there
was no reason to suppose that they knew anything
at all about the person who addressed them, or about
his office and authority.   The character of Pope
Gregory II was a fine one, wherever we have
the opportunity of testing it in the story of
Boniface.

The next letter [1] from Gregory II to Boniface contains detailed answers to twelve questions of a practical
character which Boniface had sent, much as Augustine
of Canterbury consulted Gregory the Great and received his answers.   We need only notice the answer

---

[1] Ep. 26; Nov. 22, 726.

to the concluding question, a delightfully human
answer :—

"The religious presbyter Denual[1] has brought
desirable news. He tells us that you are well, and
that God furthers the ministry for which you are
sent. He has brought also your letter, from which
we learn that the Lord's field, which lay uncultivated,
bristling with the thorns of unbelief, has been brought
under your plough, sown with the seed of the Word,
and is now bringing forth a fruitful harvest of
belief.

"In this same letter you have asked what this
holy apostolic Church of Rome holds and teaches
under several heads. You know well that the blessed
Apostle Peter stands as the beginning both of apostleship and of episcopacy. When you consult us about
the state of the Church, we teach with the doctrine of apostolic vigour, not of ourselves as of
ourselves, but by His favour who openeth the
dumb mouth and maketh the tongues of infants
eloquent.

.   .   .   .

"At the end of your letter you tell us that there are
certain presbyters or bishops enmeshed in many vices,
whose life is a stain upon the priestly office, and ask
if it is lawful for you to eat and speak with them, if
they be not heretical. We reply that you admonish
and convince them by apostolic authority and bring
them to the purity of ecclesiastical discipline; if any
of them are obedient, they will save their souls and
you will have earned your reward. Do not refuse to

---

[1] This no doubt represents the ordinary pronunciation of the
name Denewald. Denewald was one of Boniface's most trusted
helpers.

have conversation with them, and a common table. It frequently happens that those whom disciplinary methods make slow to observe the rule of truth, the civilities of the table and kindly admonition bring into the just way. You should observe this same principle in the case of important laymen who give you help."

While Boniface thus sought and obtained the advice of the Pope on many points of importance and of detail, we have a remarkable example of his appeal to English knowledge against Roman advice. It will be found set out in Appendix B, page 357.

CHAPTER IV

WHEN we speak of Boniface as the Apostle of Germany, we use a misleading expression. The word Germany, used in that sense, is specially misleading, because at the same time we find Boniface supported by the armed forces of the Franks. This tends to produce the idea that there were then, as there are now, two countries, the one called France and the other called by the general name of Germany. Instead of this, there was in fact one great kingdom or group of kingdoms, the kingdom of the Franks, who were originally a collection of Teutonic tribes. This kingdom, or these kingdoms, included roughly the territories we know as Northern France and Western Germany. Lorch, on the Danube, was about the easternmost point reached by the territory of the Franks; beyond that to the east came Pannonia and the kingdom of the Avars. The modern Bohemia, for example, lies outside the territory of the Franks.

This vast area was in the main divided into two parts, the eastern, called from its eastward position, Austrasia, practically the same word as our Austria though meaning a very different territory, and the western, called curiously enough "not-eastern", that is Neustria. There was a like arrangement of names at that time in North Italy. The line of division between the Frank kingdom of Neustria and the Frank kingdom of Austrasia did not follow any natural or modern line. The simplest way of indicating its direction is by taking the two main lines by which English people travel to Switzerland. Those who go to Amiens, and take the line thence by Laon and Reims and Châlon, travel just to the east of the boundary, that is, are in Austrasia. Those who pass from Amiens by Paris and Lyon travel to the west of the boundary, and are in Neustria. This description, which is confined to our present purpose, disregards the boundaries of the Burgundian Franks and says nothing of the Frank kingdom of Aquitaine.

It is very common knowledge that Clovis, the sole King of the Franks before the splitting up of his dominion into four separate parts for the sake of his sons, became a Christian after the battle of Tolbiac in 497. This was exactly a hundred years before our Kentish king, Ethelbert, who had married the Christian great-granddaughter of Clovis, took a like step. Clovis gave a kingdom to each of his four sons, and the position of their respective territories may be gathered from the seats of government, naming them from the west eastward, Orleans, Paris, Soissons, Metz. When Winfrid landed in Neustria in 717, there were only three males of the once large house of Clovis known to be alive, two of them being kings respectively of the Neustrian and Austrasian Franks. Four years before the death of Boniface, the line of Clovis became practically extinct, in the twelfth generation.

It is also very common knowledge that for many of these twelve generations the kings of the several Frank kingdoms were not allowed to do anything real

as kings. The power was entirely in the hands of
their chief officer, the Mayor, or Major, or greater
personage, of their palace. The English people of
those times knew too much of the tyranny of the
mayors of the Neustrian kings, in whose territory
they landed when they crossed the Channel. The
territory of Austrasia did not reach to the North
Sea, the Old Saxons and the Frisians lying between
the northern boundary of Austrasia and the sea. Thus
all English people who crossed the Channel, by any
of the ordinary routes, on the way to Rome and elsewhere, had to land in Neustria, and in one form or
another they were pillaged on landing. We hear of
this in the Life of Wilfrith of Ripon and York, when
Ebroin, the Neustrian mayor of the palace, had very
evil designs upon him, and pillaged the wrong man
by mistake.[1] Soon after Wilfrith's time, the rival
armies of the Neustrian and the Austrasian Franks
met in battle, under their respective mayors, and the
Austrasian mayor and army completely defeated
the Neustrian mayor and army. Thereupon all
Neustria and Austrasia were united under one mayor,
the Mayor of Austrasia, though for a time the
two secluded kings, who were first cousins, were
allowed to continue their nominal sovereignty. It
was the battle of Testry, just within the Neustrian
border, in the year 687, that effected this great political change. The seat of government of Neustria
was transferred to Austrasia, and the whole of the
two kingdoms was governed from Cologne as the
official residence of the mayor, sometimes from

---

[1] By a fortunate mistake of one letter, as Wilfrith's biographer
tells us, Ebroin pillaged one Winfrid, a Mercian bishop, not the
same as our Winfrid or Boniface.

Herstal his family residence.   These splittings up of the Franks into Neustrian and Austrasian, and southwards into Aquitainian and Burgundian, and their amalgamations, have to be kept carefully in mind by all who study the after-history of the several parts of the great empire founded by Charlemagne, the great-grandson of the Mayor of Austrasia who won the battle of Testry.

The great Mayor of the Palace who won that victory was Pepin, of Herstal on the Meuse.   He came of a noble family, famous for great ecclesiastics among its members, ecclesiastics who after the fashion of those early times were often married men with families. Such men, in many cases, had entered religion, or taken holy orders, in middle life, having married and had children born to them in earlier life.   A similar explanation accounts for abbesses writing about their sons and daughters.   It was this Pepin who received Willibrord and gave him Utrecht, and received Suidbert and gave him Kaiserswerth.   It was the disturbances which followed upon his death, until such time as Charles Martel, his son, had showed his strength, that drove Winfrid back to England, as we have seen, on his first attempt at missionary work.[1]

The rapid decay of the kingly power, and the corresponding rise of the power of the mayor, now called duke, may be seen by comparing two facts. When Wilfrith of York and Ripon passed through Austrasia on his way to Rome, some years before the battle of Testry, he was received by the Austrasian

[1] All the very many persons among us who can trace their descent to Scottish kings, or to Plantagenets, have this Pepin as an ancestor, through his less than lawful son Charles Martel, the grandfather of Charlemagne.

king Dagobert, and the king pressed him to give up
England and settle in Austrasia, offering him the
bishopric of Strassburg. The other fact is this—
all through the life of Boniface the mere existence
of such a person as the King of the Franks is never
even referred to; everything depends upon Charles
Martel and his son the other Pepin, the Short. Thus
Willibald tells us that the Pope put Boniface under
the protection of the reign, or the kingdom, of the
glorious Duke Charles. His letter is addressed thus—
" Gregory the Pope to the glorious lord, his son,
Duke Charles ", and no mention is made in it of the
Austrasian king. His successor Gregory III, nine
of whose letters have been preserved, addressed two
letters to Charles Martel, in each of which he describes
him as subregulus, sub-king, but addresses him as
all-powerful, with no reference to a king. In a letter
to Boniface he speaks of Charles as Prince of the
Franks, and it is by that title that Willibald speaks
of him when he carries on his biography with an
account of the return of Boniface, as bishop, from
Rome.

The Pope defines in his letter to Charles Martel
the area over which the powers he had given to
Boniface were to range. He was to preach to the
people of the race or nation of Germany, and to
the various heathen races settled on the east side of
the Rhine. A list of these races or tribes is given
in one of the letters[1] of Pope Gregory III, referred
to above. It is of sufficient interest to be inserted
here.

" Gregory the Pope to the great men and the whole
people of the provinces of Germany, the Thuringians

[1] Ep. 43 : A.D. 737.

and Hessians, the Borthars and Nistresians, the Wedrechs and Lognais, the Suduods and Graffelts, and all
who are settled in the eastern quarter."

Another reading has *Thesis* in place of *Hessis* and
Unedredis for *Wedrechs*. It is not difficult to see how
this may have been due to careless writing or careless
copying. The districts are most of them identifiable;
especially the Graffelts, inasmuch as Fulda was in the
district of Grabfeld. The other districts are supposed
to be Boroctra (of the Bructeri), Nifthars on the
river Diemel, Wetterau, and Lahngau. The Suduods
cause a good deal of discussion.

After the usual preface declaratory of Boniface's
soundness in the faith and fidelity to the see of Rome,
but with the significant addition of the statement
that he presented himself with a view to prayer at
the thresholds of the blessed apostles [1], the Pope ex-
horts them " to accept worthily from him the word
of exhortation, and to receive in the ministry of the
Church the bishops and priests whom he shall ordain
on the authority given him from the holy see. And
when he prohibits any whom he finds wandering from
the path of the right faith or from canonical doctrine,
let him in no way be hindered by you ; what he shall
lay upon them let them carry out from fear of God,
for he who refuses obedience earns for himself
damnation. And do you, dearest ones, who have
been baptized in the name of Christ, put on Christ ;
abstain and prohibit your own selves from every rite
of the pagans, and not your own selves only, dearest
ones, but those also who are subject to you. Diviners
and soothsayers, the sacrifices of the dead, auguries of
groves or springs, filacteries, enchanters and sorcerers,

[1] Apostolorum.

and sacrilegious observances which were practised in your district, contemn and cast away, the whole intent of your mind being turned to God."

The rest of the letter consists of a string of seven passages from the Gospels and one from the Epistle to the Romans.

Roughly speaking, the territory which the Popes called Germany included not only that which the Franks called the Austrasian or Eastern Kingdom of the Franks, but also the contiguous countries of the pagan barbarians; and thus it came curiously near to the modern idea of Germany. Tacitus had given one of his clear definitions of Germany in the first words of his book, so invaluable for all Teutonic peoples, the *De Germania* as it is called for short. Its full title sets forth its special value, " Of the site, peoples, and manners, of Germany." All Germany, he says, is separated from the Gauls and Rhoetians (roughly Switzerland) by the river Rhine, and from the Pannonians by the river Danube; from the Sarmatians and Dacians, by mountains and by mutual fear. The Germany of the Popes of Boniface's time was larger than the Austrasia of the Franks. Austrasia may be put as the territory between the Rhine and the Danube, not extending further north than the southern boundary of the modern Hanover. This was in the main the settled part of the Germany over which Boniface's influence was felt; the contiguous territories to the east were his mission field. To the north he worked at the beginning and at the end of his career in Frisia. We have no definite information that he worked among the Old Saxons. It is said in the Life of St. Ledger that Charles Martel gave a cold reception to Winfrid at the time when he came from England and sought permission to exercise his missionary function in Frisia. There is no hint of that in Willibald's account, nor in Othlon's. If there was foundation for the statement, a change came now. Charles Martel, on receipt of the Papal letters which Boniface handed to him, at once acted vigorously. He addressed a letter[1] to all and sundry, charging them to do all they could for the missionary bishop, whom he had taken under his protection. The letter was a careful and prudent one, and it deserves to be given in full:—

" To the holy lords and apostolic Fathers in Christ the bishops; to the dukes, counts, deputies[2], stewards, agents, officers, messengers, and friends; the illustrious Charles, mayor of the palace[3], your well-wisher.

" Know that the apostolic Father in Christ, Boniface the bishop, has come to us, and has begged that we should take him under our protection[4] and defence. Know that we have with glad mind done this. We have given to him the strength of our hand. Wheresoever he goes he must be preserved quiet and safe in our love, protection, and defence; on this condition, that he does justice, and receives justice likewise. And if any difficulty arise which cannot be decided

[1] Ep. 22; A.D. 723-4.
[2] Vicarii. To render it "Vicars" would seem misleading.
[3] Major domus.
[4] *Munde burgium*, or *mamburgium*. A low-Latin word of Teutonic origin, from *mund*, or *munt*, in the sense of protection. The Anglo-Saxon form was *mundbora*. Mambourg (or main bourg) was the title of a regent in the Low Countries; thus Maximilian the Emperor was Mambourg for his little son Philip, the father of Emperor Charles V, and Charles's aunt Marguerite of Austria, who was regent for Charles as a child, speaks of his position as *Mambournie* in French, "je vous ay durant vostre mambournie servi bien et léalement," *Marguerite of Austria*, by Christopher Hare, 1907, p. 232.

by the law, he must be left quiet and safe to our judgment, both he and his, so that no one shall do anything contrarious or harmful to him. And that the surer credence may be given to this, I have confirmed it at the foot with my own hand and we have sealed it with our ring."

In connexion with this letter of the secular power a general remark must be made. Boniface made no scruple of expressing the opinion, that however necessary it was to have proper ecclesiastical authority behind him, the authority namely of the Pope, the possibility of doing his work, whether that of conversion of the heathen or that of reforming the abuses which were rife among the Christian priests and bishops of the Frankish Church, depended upon the authority of the Mayor of the Palace, not upon that of the Pope. In a letter [1] to his friend Daniel, Bishop of Wessex, to which we shall have later to give some attention, he writes thus—" Without the patronage of the Prince of the Franks, I could neither rule the people, nor defend [2] the priests or deacons, the monks or nuns; nor without his mandate, and the awe which he inspires, could I put a stop to the rites of the pagans and the sacrileges of idol-worship."

Armed with Charles Martel's letters, Boniface returned to his work among the Hessians, who in one of the letters which have been preserved are described correctly by the ancient name of Catti, or Chatti. Here he at once exercised episcopal functions. Many of the Hessians had already accepted the Christian

---

[1] Ep. 63; A.D. 742–746.

[2] Another reading omits *defendere*, and thus makes Boniface say that he could not rule people, priests, deacons, monks, or nuns, without the help of Charles.

faith; they were now confirmed by the grace of the sevenfold Spirit, and received the laying on of hand. Willibald properly uses the singular, hand, not the plural, hands, in speaking of the rite of confirmation. Some of the Hessians refused to accept completely the evidences of the faith undefiled. Some sacrificed secretly to trees and springs of water; others sacrificed openly. Some practised, unseen, soothsayings and divinations, magic arts and incantations; others, without attempt at concealment. Some occupied themselves in auspices and auguries, and cultivated divers rites of sacrifices. Some, who were of healthier mind, threw off all gentile profanation, and did none of these things. It was by the advice of these last that Boniface now took a very bold and important step.

There was at Geismar, in lower Hessia, a mighty tree, called the Thunderer's Oak in the ancient language of the people of the country. We might have supposed that this meant the Oak of Thunor. But the best information which has come to us makes it dedicated to Wotan, our Woden. It is clear that with these peoples Woden was the chief god, and Thunor and Saxnot the second and third gods of their trinity. This noble object of pagan worship, sacred throughout the land, he determined to fell. He made no secret of his purpose. When he came to the spot, with his Christian attendants, he found a large number of pagans assembled. Not intimidated, he began to ply his axe, the pagans most diligently cursing him within themselves, and vowing him to perdition as an enemy of the gods. He had got but little way made towards the heart of the tree, when a great rush of mighty wind struck the immense mass of trunk and branches,

and brought the whole to the ground. The trunk
was split into four pieces. The astonished pagans
recognized the hand of a higher power; they ceased
to curse; they turned to blessing, and became believers
in the Lord.

We have curious and interesting evidences of the
effect produced by the destruction of objects of super-
stitious adoration in ages much nearer to our own
time. The most curious and interesting of these evidences are to be found in the history of the beginnings
of the Reformation in the Engadine, written by a
contemporary historian. At Campfer there was a
celebrated image of St. Roche, with a shrine of the
highest sanctity. One winter's night three men
passed with sleighs; they seized the huge image,
fastened it to the tail of the sleigh, and dragged it
with scoffs and jeers to Cresta. Some prudent people
got it put back for one day, but an accident which
happened to one of its most devoted worshippers that
day turned him against it; the image was expelled,
and the Roman Mass went with it. At Celerina the
assistant priest was a man of the new views, and he
used to go at night and drive wedges into the cracks
in their famous images. When his nefarious devices
produced their contemplated effects, and the images
fell to ruin, the Reformation came in at once. At
Pontresina they were persuaded to test the powers
of their images. They carried them in procession
from the church to the high bridge, and threw them
over the parapet into the swift glacier stream. They
never saw them again; and the reformed service replaced the Mass. In all such cases we see in the
more modern times that the destruction of the objects
of superstition is, at least with the more thoughtful,

the effect of a change of feeling, not the cause of such change. We may perhaps risk the opinion that in the early times of the Christian missionaries a good many people were not unready to be convinced, and secretly hailed an open opportunity of adopting the new views. Probably Boniface's advisers among the Hessians had an instinct that what in modern phrase is called the psychical moment had arrived. It would not have done to attack the Thunderer's Oak prematurely.

The great oak, as we have seen, split into four pieces. Boniface's men set to work upon these pieces, and split them further, so that they were able to build a little oratory of wood on the plateau where the tree had stood, and this was dedicated by Boniface to the honour of St. Peter. When the saint some little time later built a church on the spot, he attached to it a monastery dedicated to the twin princes of the Apostles, Peter and Paul. The oak was in the place called Geismare, variously spelled, probably the name of a small district. The church and monastery were in Fridislar, now Fritzlar.

Fritzlar is reached to-day by a short light railway from Wabern, forty minutes from Cassel. Fritzlar is now a considerable town, enclosed for the most part by ancient walls with a wealth of round towers at intervals. An old drawing of the place shows twenty towers in the year 1640, conically capped like the Irish round towers and the two round towers in Scotland, Abernethy and Brechin. When the system of watch-towers on the neighbouring and the more distant hills is seen as a whole, dating no doubt from the time of the Celtic inhabitants of the district, it is difficult to resist the conclusion that here we have the origin of the round towers of Celtic Ireland.

Besides ancient walls and round towers, Fritzlar is a place of beautiful houses, brick set in framework of wood of the most varied and complicated designs, *Holzbau*, in the local phrase. Houses of this most interesting type abound in the whole of a large district here. They are no doubt the glorified descendants of original framework huts made good with mud and clay. Whether Boniface and his Crediton companions took with them to Fritzlar the local style of " cob " walls, is a question worth considering.

The bishopric founded by Boniface for these parts was called Büraburg, or Bierburg, and some of the biographies of the saint make curious assertions as to the position of Bierburg in modern times. As a matter of fact, the *burg* on the Buraberg is only a half-hour's walk from Fritzlar. On that *berg* Boniface set the seat of the bishop ; but it very soon ceased to hold the honour. The Fritzlar story is that the first bishop and his people fled to the safety of Fritzlar to escape from an inroad of pagans, and when the danger was over the Fritzlar people kept the bishop and called him Bishop of Fritzlar. This, in turn, did not last long, for Charlemagne transferred the bishopric to Paderborn, a place very well worth visiting for its own sake. To this day, they say, Wildungen, near Fritzlar, still belongs to Paderborn. There was only one bishop of Fritzlar, Megingoz, or Megingot, a man well known in another capacity. To rule the primitive monastery and serve its church, Boniface appointed his countryman, Wigbert.

The abbey church of Fritzlar is a very interesting Romanesque building. The earlier church was destroyed

Fig. 1. In the Treasury, Fritzlar.

by the Saxons in 1078, only a small piece of it being now traceable, and the present building dates from 1171. The passage to the *confessio* has been walled up, and a rough way into the crypt of 850 has been cut right through an ancient pier, the original arch of entrance being visible on the west wall of the crypt. Here the relics of St. Wigbert lay till they were removed to Hersfeld, where they perished in the destruction of that beautiful monastery. An arm in a silver shrine in the treasury is the only relic left of this great Englishman from Dorset, the first Abbat of Fritzlar, the close friend of Boniface, the trainer of Sturmi of Fulda. His day is still kept with great rejoicings on August 13, when a service is held in the crypt. The arm and hand, in their silver case, will be seen near the extreme left in fig. 1.

The treasury is full of remarkable things. They are recently described by a Marburg professor in three large volumes.[1] Fig. 1 shows the outlines of a group of them. The greatest treasure is the noble jewelled cross, given to the church by the Emperor Henry the Saint, the husband of St. Cunigonde, in or about 1020. Many of the more important objects are of the twelfth century. There is a handsome Gospel-book of that date in silver gilt and enamel, with the Evangelists in the corners and the Apostles by threes. The only early parchment is a beautiful folio page of Latin grammar, of Boniface's time and of English style; it begins with "argutus malorum facinorum et futurum arguturus et derivativum ex hoc verbum argutor argutaris". In the choir, on the north side, is a reliquary with the names Liborius (Bishop of Paderborn) Wihtbertus Gotthardus.

[1] Elwert, Marburg, price 40 marks.

F 2

The road from Fritzlar to Geismar is short and pretty. You pass along one of five avenues of trees parallel to one another and to the old wall of the city, with some of its round towers still standing. Then the road winds between English hedges and orchards to an open plain, rich in clover and oats and potatoes, with hills in the distance topped with round towers. Then down a steep hill into a pretty village with remarkably fine *Holzbau* houses. This is Geismar. The church stands on a slight eminence, a spur from a higher hill, and is contained within a strong ancient wall, with solid round towers at the angles, each face of the wall being about seventy yards long. The houses hug the wall on the side towards the road; on the other sides the wall is being picked to pieces, or has already disappeared. There is nothing commanding or striking in the site, though no doubt a great oak, standing where the church now stands, would be visible from considerable distances. There does not appear to be any tradition in the place as to the position—or, indeed, as to the fact—of the famous tree of Pagan worship. This favours the claim of Fritzlar that the oak stood on the elevated spot where now is the sanctuary of the Abbey Church. Standing on that spot, it would indeed be seen far and wide.

The Life of St. Wigbert was written by Servatus Lupus, the Abbat of Ferrières; the date of the Life is therefore about 836. He wrote it at the instance of Abbat Bun and his brethren; this no doubt means Bruno Abbat of Fritzlar and the community of that monastery. Bruno was the abbat who with Raban laid the foundations of the new church in honour of St. Wigbert on July 10, 831. It was dedicated by

Raban, who had in the interval become Archbishop of Mainz, on October 28, 850.

Dorset has the credit of having produced Wigbert. He had from early youth shown great promise of religious zeal and study. Lupus informs us that Boniface knew of his fame, and secured his assistance not long after he got to work in Germany. There are several indications that Wigbert was of considerable age, and it has been supposed by some that he was the same as the Abbat of Nutschel who was Boniface's instructor; that idea, however, must be abandoned.

Soon after his elevation to the archbishopric of Mainz, Boniface appointed Wigbert to the abbey of Fritzlar. Lupus describes Wigbert as a priest, *sacerdos*, "of the second order." This description has been understood to be due to the fact that *sacerdos* meant either bishop or priest, the latter being the *sacerdos* of the second order; the idea that a second order of bishop is meant, that is a *chorepiscopus*, appears to be less well founded. At Fritzlar he became intimate with Megingoz, who afterwards became Bishop of Würzburg, and between them they raised to a high pitch the standard of the monastery, which had before been "lax and fluid". Finding him so successful a disciplinarian, Boniface gave him a second monastery to rule, Ortdorff (Ohrdruf in Gotha, on the Ohre), and here again he brought about a great and satisfactory change. Ill health coming upon him, he obtained leave from Boniface to return to Fulda, and there he died. The letter which Boniface wrote to Fulda on the occasion of his death will be found below.

Lupus tells us in particular a marked habit of Wigbert, and an interesting action. His habit was, when he was on his way to hear the confession of

a sick monk, to decline to enter into conversation
with any one, or to salute any one whom he met on
his way. The one action which Lupus says he cannot
pass over without mention is certainly very interesting, and it has a direct bearing on a question much
discussed in distant parts of the world and at the
Lambeth Conference, the question of the necessity
of using only the fermented juice of the grape in
the Holy Eucharist. Wigbert was one day engaged
in celebrating, and he found that by some accident
there was no wine. He hastened from the church
in search of wine, and seeing a bunch of grapes
hanging on a vine, he plucked it and squeezed the
juice into the chalice with his hands. Finding that
a grape-stone had got into the chalice, he quickly—
and as he thought unseen—planted it at the entrance
to the church, and then forthwith completed the
consecration. An inquisitive brother, who had closely
noticed what was done, asked him afterwards why
he did this. Seeing that he was caught, he replied,
"If the Lord cares for what I do, in the course of
nine years you will know." And so it was. Shoots
sprang up from the seed. They were trained on
props. Within the time stated they formed a charming porch to the church.

The saint's relics were not allowed to rest. The
wild Saxons attacked Fritzlar. The relics were taken
to Buriburch (Büraburg) for greater safety. Then
they found themselves at Geismar. Then they got
back to Fritzlar. Then a divine messenger came to
Albuin (said by the editors to mean Witta, white,
albus), Bishop of Büraburg, and bade him remove
the bones to Hersfeld (Herolfes felt). The bishop
informed Lul, the Archbishop of Mainz, of this

injunction; Lul informed the great Karl; Karl
gave assent. By Lul's instructions, Albuin and
three of the monks, Ernust, Baturich, and Wolff,
conveyed the relics to Hersfeld secretly and by night,
lest the people of Fritzlar should raise a tumult.
This was probably in the year 780. The precious
treasure was received with great joy at Hersfeld,
and was magnificently housed in the most important
place in the church. Again with the assent of Karl,
Lul provided a shrine decorated with gold and silver
and other suitable metals, as had come to be the
custom throughout Gaul and Germany. This was
all completed on the Ides of August, whence
August 13 is St. Wigbert's day.

The remains of St. Wigbert, as was said above,
were dispersed when the beautiful Abbey of Hersfeld
was destroyed.

It is interesting for English people to claim one of
the most remarkable—if not, architecturally, the most
remarkable—of Christian buildings in Germany as
dedicated to St. Wigbert, and that through a direct
English influence. The building referred to is the
Wipertigruft, the Wipert-crypt, at Quedlinburg.
It is the earliest example of massive rectangular piers
alternating with comparatively slender cylindrical
columns with simple capitals and Attic bases. These
are so early that they support not arches but an
architrave of solid slabs of stone, from which the
barrel vault springs. The crypt is only some twenty-
two feet long, sixteen [1] wide, and seven to eight high.
German architects agree that it does not show any
trace of Romanesque work in its construction; the
Romanesque basilicas with a similar arrangement of

[1] The central portion is only about 10 ft. wide.

pier and column succeeded this piece of work, did not precede it. The pillars and architrave are covered with stucco. The history of this crypt does not concern us, but it must be referred to in order to bring in the later English connexion.

Henry the Fowler (afterwards the Emperor Henry I) had a property outside the village of the Quitlinga, long before he built the "Burg" there. This Pfalz of his had a chapel attached to it, which was built about 900, and was dedicated first to St. James and afterwards to St. Wigbert.

Matilda, widow of Henry the Fowler, received the Pfalz and chapel as her legacy on her husband's death in 936. Her son the Emperor Otto confirmed the gift. Over the chapel she built in 961 a conventual church, which she eventually handed over to the abbesses of the Burg founded by herself and her husband. The whole is now a farm building, to which the Wiperti-Strasse leads.

Besides the Life of St. Wigbert by Servatus Lupus, an account of St. Wigbert's miracles was written by an anonymous monk under the Emperor Otto I, the son of Matilda. This led to a great growth of reverence for the saint throughout Saxony. When Otto married the English Edith, the daughter of Edward the Elder and granddaughter of Alfred the Great, there was twofold reason for a dedication to the English Wigbert.

Before we leave Wigbert and Fritzlar, it may be well to give the letter from Boniface to Tatwin, the new abbat, and the monks of Fritzlar, on the death of the first abbat. It has some interesting domestic details. There is much uncertainty as to the year of Wigbert's death. There is another letter written to a number of brethren and sisters, including two of those to whom the letter under consideration is addressed, presumably later, in which Boniface speaks of himself as being in Rome with Pope Gregory and uncertain when he can return to them. This must have been written in 737 or 738,[1] and the date of Wigbert's death given in the Annals would appear to be too early by some years.

"To my dearest sons Tatwin and Wigbert priests, to Bernhard and Hiedde, Hunfrith and Stirme, Boniface the servant of the servants of God perennial health in the Lord.

"With fatherly love I beseech your dilection that because our father Wigbert is dead you study to keep with the greater care the rule of monastic life. Let Wigbert the priest and Megingot the deacon teach you the rule, and keep the canonical hours and the church's course, and admonish the rest, and be 'master' of the children and preach the word of God to the brethren. Let Hiedde be provost and admonish our slaves; and let Hunfrith help him when necessary. Let Styrme be in the kitchen, and Bernhard be the workman and build our little dwellings when needed. About everything necessary ask Tatwin the abbat, and whatever he advises, do. And let each study according to his power both to keep his own life in chastity, and in your common life to help other, and in brotherly love to abide until our return by God's will. And then let us all together praise God and in all things give thanks to Him. Fare ye well in Christ."

This is the picture of a very small society, in which each individual person is an important element.

[1] Ep. 40; 735-737.

Small as it was, it bred men who came to fill important positions. Megingot the deacon was afterwards bishop of Würzburg in succession to Burchardt, and Styrme, who was a pupil of Abbat Wigbert, became abbat of Fulda. In the cases of Wigbert the priest and Styrme the cook. it will be observed how usual it was for early workers to have the same name, and how unsafe it is to build identity upon identity of name. Between Styrme the cook of Fritzlar and Sturmi the abbat of Fulda there could not be at the time any confusion, though the fact of a Styrmi becoming abbat of Fulda might cause some confusion in the Annals. But at Fritzlar we cannot but suppose that between Wigbert the abbat and Wigbert the priest there must at times have been confusion.

CHAPTER V

WE may now look to the biographer Willibald to give us the order of Boniface's proceedings after felling the oak at Fritzlar, among the Hessians.

On his way to Thuringia Boniface is said to have thrown down idols in various places, in the region of Eichsfeld, and near Hildesheim, and near Bielem. There could be no doubt among the Thuringians as to what his business was with them. He at once called together the seniors and the principal men, and addressed them in terms which showed that the Pope had omitted to use a powerful argument in his letter, probably through ignorance of the facts. Though it had never been general, Christianity had not long before existed in Thuringia on a not incon-siderable scale. He entreated them to return to the Christian faith, which they had once accepted and in the blindness of ignorance had deserted. There had been great tyranny exercised over them some time before by two of their rulers, Theobald and Beden (or Heden), and in despair a large number of them had put themselves under the Saxons, the people occupying the territory to the north, roughly speaking the region of Hanover. False brethren had brought in heretical depravity; four of them, prominent in Boniface's time, are named, and their names are

suspiciously English, Torchtwine, Berchthere, Ean-
bercht, and Hunred, described by Willibald as
fornicators and adulterers, which often means only
that there were married priests. They stirred up a
great strife against the man of God, but he prevailed,
and they were worthily punished. With great de-
privations and but few helpers, the reaping of the
harvest went on ; till at length success brought its
reward and the number of the preachers was multiplied. Churches were built, and Boniface founded
a monastery at Ohrdruf, near Erfurt, where the
brethren laboured with their own hands to procure
food and clothing. Willibald does not name the
dedication of this monastery, but two chapters
further on he remarks of another monastery, "this
also he dedicated to the honour of St. Michael the
Archangel." It is typical of the growth of miraculous
stories that Othlon, who gives the dedication of
Ordorf to St. Michael, states the reason of that
dedication as follows :—

"Why that monastery was dedicated in honour
of the holy Michael must be briefly told. The
holy Boniface, preaching and baptizing, crossed into
Thuringia, and having fixed his tents near the river
Oraha, spent the night there. The whole night
through a great light from heaven shone round the
place where the bishop was. In that light the holy
Archangel Michael came ; he appeared to the bishop,
spoke to him, and strengthened him in the Lord.
When morning came, praising and blessing God,
the bishop celebrated there the solemnities of the
Mass. Then he bade prepare breakfast on the same
spot; but his attendant told him there was nothing
to eat. He replied, 'Cannot He who fed the mul-

titude of the people with manna in the desert for
forty years provide for one day's refection for me
His unworthy servant?' He bade them set a table.
A bird flying by dropped upon the table a fish large
enough for one day's food. The holy prelate gave
thanks to God, and bade them cook the fish at once.
It was cooked and eaten, and he bade them throw
the remains into the river."

The report of the successes in Thuringia spread
far and wide through most part of Europe. From
Britain there came to him, when the good news
reached that land, a multitude of readers and writers,
and men learned and skilled in various arts. By
far the greatest part of these put themselves regularly
under Boniface, and laboured to bring the people
over to the true faith; others travelled about in
the towns and country parts of Hessia and Thuringia,
preaching the word of God. So far Willibald.

Othlon had collected the names of some of the
helpers who came from Britain, and he tells us that
Boniface had sent to ask them to come. The chief
men were Burchardt and Lul, Willibald and his
brother Wunnibald, Witta and Gregorius. The
religious women whose names he records were Chuni-
hild (the maternal aunt of Lul) and her daughter
Berathgid, Chunitrud and Tecla, Leoba and Waltpurgis
the sister of Willibald and Wunnibald. The first
two of these ladies were very erudite in liberal knowledge, and were established as the heads of monastic
institutions [1] in Thuringia; Chunitrud was dispatched
to Bavaria, to sow there the seed of the divine word;
Tecla settled near the river Main, at Kitzingen, and

---

[1] Magistrae.

at Ochsenfurt, near Würzburg ; Leoba was set to
preside over a large number of nuns at Bischofsheim,
and there for a year or two Walburgis worked with
her.   So far Othlon.   We have a good deal to say
about most of them, and we have one or two letters
connected with their coming out which it will be well
to give here.

We have a letter of Boniface addressed to Leoba
and Tecla and Cynehild and all the sisters, loved in
Christ, dwelling with them.   This letter is dated by
Dümmler between 742 and 746.   The date usually
given for the arrival of the large party of English
workers is 748.   It seems clear from the address of the
letter and from its contents, that Boniface was writing
to them in their religious house in England, and not
in any abode in Germany.   It is probable that this
letter first put into their minds the idea of going out
to the mission field, where he so earnestly desired to
leave behind him spiritual sons and daughters.[1]

" To my dearest sisters, to be venerated and loved,
Leobgytha, Tecla, and Cynehild, and all the lovable
sisters dwelling with you, greeting of eternal dearness."

He begs for their prayers lest he—the last and worst
of all the legates sent by the catholic and apostolic
Roman Church to preach the Gospel—should have no
fruit of his labour, and should pass away not leaving
behind him spiritual sons and daughters in his stead.
Nay, worse than that, some of whom he had felt
sure as sheep having in the end a place on the right
hand of Christ, had turned out to be stinking butting
goats, who must be placed on the left hand.   There

---

[1] Ep. 67 ; 742-6.

is nothing else in the letter which has any bearing on the circumstances of their position or of his work.

Another letter of Boniface to Leoba, here as in the other cases under her full name of Leobgytha, is evidently written to her after her arrival,[1] and when she was acting as a teacher of doctrine, though the Germans do not seem to take that view :—

" To Leobgytha, the venerated handmaid of Christ, perennially to be kept in sincerest dearness, Boniface, servant of the servants of God, health desirable in Christ.

" Be it known to the dilection of your sanctity, that our brother and fellow-presbyter Torhthat has told us that you have acceded to his request, and have agreed, if my consent gives licence, to commit the labour of teaching to a certain young woman, for a time. Know without doubt, that our will gives consent and approval to the course which your dilection thinks fitting in this matter for the increase of result. Fare thee well in Christ."

We may suppose that this letter was written late in Boniface's life, when Leoba was feeling less young than she had been; or at some time when she was feeling the work too much for her health. We find an interesting link between Leoba and this priest Torhthat in the Life of Leoba,[2] in a similar connexion. " When she saw that the time of her falling asleep was drawing near, she sent for the venerable presbyter Torahtbraht, an Englishman, and he stayed by her the whole time, serving her with reverence and affection."

We have by fortunate chance the letter in which

---

[1] Ep. 96. [2] See p. 171.

Leoba first introduced herself to the notice of her relative Boniface. The address of the letter makes it most probable that it was written after he became archbishop.[1] It was the first step in a friendship which proved to be of the closest and most lasting character; and we may fairly regard it as the real beginning of the flow of English sympathy and English help to the greatest of English missionaries.

"I ask of your clemency that you would deign to remember the former friendship which you made long ago with my father, by name Dynne, in the west country,[2] now dead for seven years, and would not refuse your prayers to God for his soul. I commend also to you the recollection of my mother, whose name is Aebbe; she, as you know well, is bound in consanguinity to you. She still lives, greatly burdened, and long grievously oppressed by ill health. I am the only daughter of my parents; and I would that I might, though quite unworthy, take you in place of a brother; for in no man of my family do I place such confidence of hope as in thee. I send a little gift to you, not that it is worth your looking at, but that you may retain some memory of my littleness, and not forget me by reason of distance; nay, that some bond of love may be formed for the rest of time. My. brother, whom I must love, earnestly see to it that the shield of your prayers defend me against the poisoned darts of the hidden

---

[1] "Bonifatio, summe dignitatis infula predito." Dümmler says that the argument to this effect has convinced him.

[2] If she wrote from Wimborne, *occiduis regionibus* must probably refer to an early acquaintance at Exeter, if not at Crediton. But if the mention of Eadburga in the letter has reference to Lul's correspondent Eadburga, Abbess of Thanet, *occiduis regionibus* may refer to Boniface's residence at Nutschal.

foe. I beg, too, that you will correct the rusticity of this letter, and will send me some words of your affability by way of pattern.

"These verses under-written I have tried to compose in accordance with the rules of poetic tradition, not audaciously, but in the desire to exercise the rudiments of a slender and feeble intellect, and needing thy assistance. This art I learned under the tuition of Eadburga, who never ceases to investigate the divine law.

> "Arbiter omnipotens, solus qui cuncta creavit,
> In regno patris semper qui lumine fulget,
> Qua iugiter flagrans sic regnat gloria Christi,
> Inlesum servet semper te iure perenni."

It is sad to have to say that although Leoba declares she has not done this audaciously, it is an audacious piece of copying, from the treatise on the construction of Latin verse by Aldhelm of Malmesbury. Both in her prose letter, and in her verse, she copies wholesale.

Lul, Denehard, and Burchardt, after their arrival in Germany, wrote a letter to Abbess Cuniburga,[1] which is on various accounts of interest. Its interest perhaps especially lies in the fact that it gives a reason for their having accepted the call to foreign service.[2]

"To the most loved lady and most religious abbess of Christ, Cuniburga, of royal race, Denehard, Lul,

---

[1] No doubt of Wimborne, a sister of King Ine, usually called Cuenburg. The Cuneburga who is named on the Bewcastle Cross in 670, a daughter of Penda and Abbess of Caistor, was too early to be the lady addressed by Lul and his companions.

[2] Ep. 49; between 732 and 742.

and Burghard, thy sons and slaves, wish the everlasting health of safety.

"We desire the clemency of your kindliness to know that we embrace thee with love in the chamber of the heart beyond all other persons of the female sex.[1] By reason of the death of father and mother and other near relations, we have come to the German races. We have been received under the rule of monastic life by the venerated Archbishop Boniface, and are partakers in his labours so far as our poor abilities allow. Now, therefore, from the inmost recesses of our hearts we pray thee deign to hold us in communion with thy sacred congregation. Refuse not to bring our vessel, tossed on the stormy waves of the world, to a harbour of safety by the protection of thy prayers; even as we, sinners as we are, pray every moment for the divine estate of your highness. This, if we had been present, we should have hoped to obtain by loving petition, with bent knees and salt showers of tears; and now though absent we beg it of you with earnest prayer. This also we desire your sagacity to know, that if it happens to any one of us to visit again the realms of Britain, we seek no man's rule and aid before we have submitted ourselves to your benevolence. For in thee we place the firmest hope of our mind.

"We pray further with regard to two youths, named Beiloc and Man, whom I Lul and our father have set free and sent to Rome and commended to our uncle, that if they are free of will, and if it be their wish, and if they are in your holding, you will for the

---

[1] This is quoted from Aldhelm of Malmesbury, the founder of the school and style of these three monks.

gain of your soul send them to us by the bearer of this letter. If any one should unjustly attempt to stay them, we pray that you will deign to defend them.

"Three little things by way of small gifts accompany this letter, frankincense, pepper, and cinnamon; minute portions, but sent with all affection of mind. Weigh not the smallness of the gift, but we pray thee have regard to the love of spiritual dearness. And, we further pray, pardon the rusticity of this little epistle, and deny not to send to us some words of thy sweetness; we wait breathlessly for the pleasure of hearing them."

Here is a letter to the community of Glastonbury, evidently from one who had very recently gone forth from the community to work with Boniface [1] :—

"To the lords holy and to be desired in Christ the fathers and brethren set in the monastery of Glestinga-burg, Wiehtberht the presbyter, your assured servant and suppliant of the servants of God, wishes health in the Lord.

"Blessed be God, who will have all men to be saved and to come to the knowledge of the truth, who has also by His will guided our journey into these districts, that is, to the confines of the pagan Hessians and Saxons, prosperously beyond sea and through perils of this world, by no merit of ours but by your licence and prayers, and of His mercy. You know, brethren, that no expanse of country divides us whom the love of Christ binds together. Always therefore your brotherliness and regard and my prayers to God for you abide in me. I wish moreover that you should know, dearest ones, that our

---

[1] Ep. 101.

Archbishop Boniface, when he heard of our arrival, deigned himself to come a long way to meet us and received us very kindly. Believe now, most loved ones, that our labour is not in vain in the Lord to us, and is of profit to you. For the Almighty God by His mercy and your merits accomplishes our work to a good sufficiency, though it be very perilous and laborious in almost every respect, in hunger and in thirst, in cold and in pagan incursions. I beg you, therefore, pray diligently for us that there may be given us power of speech and persistence in work and fruit of our labours. Fare ye well in the Lord. Salute the brethren all round, first Ingeld the abbat and our society. And inform my mother Tetta and her society of our prosperous journey. I entreat you all in common, with strenuous prayers, to give me your earnest prayers in return for mine. And may the divine clemency protect your blessedness, praying for me."

Glestingaburg is of course Glastonbury, and the name of Abbat Ingeld gives the extreme limits of date of the letter. Tetta was the Abbess of Wimborne; here as elsewhere the Anglo-Saxon writers in Latin put the English names of persons into the Anglo-Saxon oblique case when the construction of the Latin requires it. It is very tempting to suppose that this Wiehtbert is the same as the first Abbat of Fritzlar, of whom something is said in connexion with the mention of that place. Mabillon in the *Acta Sanctorum* naturally takes him to be the same, but Dümmler dissents. There is no decided evidence in favour of the conjecture, beyond the similarity or identity of name. But the whole tone is that of an important person, come with a party, however small, to do an important work, a man of some considerable age and position, considering his message to Tetta, a royal lady. The pagan incursions, also, exactly suit the district upon which Wigbert entered when at Boniface's request he came out to help him.

The Wiehtbert who wrote this letter was a man who yearned for sympathy. We have a scrap of a letter of his to an unnamed "most dear brother and fellow-presbyter" [1] :—

"With strenuous prayers of inmost love I entreat that you will deign to remember me in your holy prayers; for I am smitten with the hammer of worldly trial, vain things disturbing me."

He was also a man held in high regard by others, as witness this most interesting letter to him before he left England for Germany [2] :—

"To our most dear brethren the Abbats Coengils and Ingeld, and separately to our relative Wiehtbert the priest, the whole congregation of three monasteries, that of the most reverend Father Aldhun, and those of the Abbesses Cneuburg the handmaid of Christ and Coenburg, health in the Lord, perennial and indissoluble.

"Gladly and thankfully have we received the gifts of your salutation, and with God's help we desire to recompense them worthily. That communion which you have written that you have in your prayers with regard to us, we agree to have with regard to you, unceasingly, with goodwill and pure faith, at the hours which you have mentioned. The names of our deceased sisters I Cneuburg pray thee, O Wiehtberht, faithful priest, to have in

[1] Ep. 102.   [2] Ep. 55.

memory, and to send round to all friends. The first
was Quoengyth, my own sister, and Edlu, who was
mother of Eta, the kinswoman of Aldhun, formerly
your abbat. The *depositio* of both was on one day,
the 13th of September. May the Lord omnipotent
deign to keep safe your beatitude, praying for us,
dearest brothers and lords. Emmanuel through the
age. Salute all the servants of Christ about you
with our most true words, dearest brothers."

This touching letter of Cneuburga was written,
we suppose, by the sister of King Ine of that name.
If so, she was probably Abbess of Wimborne, which
her sister Cuthburga had founded. The Eta of
this letter can scarcely be Tetta, who was a sister
of Ine and also Abbess of Wimborne; under her
St. Leoba and St. Agatha were educated. King
Ine had a brother Ingild, but he died in 718. There
was another Ingeld, who is believed to have been
Abbat of Glastonbury. Coengils is third among
the names of Abbats of Glastonbury after Ine's
restoration of the ruined monastery. Aldhun is said
to have been Abbat of Wimborne, but without solid
ground. There was an abbat of St. Augustine's,
Canterbury, of that name from 748 to 760, but he
is too late. Wiehtbert may have been addressed
separately as a relative; but more probably as the
one of the three who was a priest and was thus
concerned with arranging the special prayers at the
celebrations of masses.

The Abbey of Wimborne, as is said above, was
founded by Ine's sister Cuthburga. She married
Ealdfrith, king of Northumbria 685-705. She
became a nun at Barking, the double monastery
which Bishop Erkenwald's sister ruled so successfully,

and she founded a similar institution in her native kingdom. Her sister Cuenburh, or Cneuburh, became Abbess of Wimborne. As the Saxon fashion was to give to ladies long names of form and short and easy names for common use, as in the case of Ethelburga of Kent, the wife of King Edwin of Northumbria, whose pet name was Tate, Tetta may have been Cneuburh, a less easy word.

While Boniface was winning thousands to the spiritual life, Gregory II was dying in Rome. He was succeeded by a third Gregory, and Boniface sent messengers to lay before the new Pope the evidences of the close relations of the mission with Gregory II, to promise humble submission to the apostolic see, and to beg for the friendship and communion of the holy pontiff and of the whole apostolic see. The Pope at once gave a pacific reply; granted his friendship and communion and that of the apostolic see to Boniface and those under him; and sent to him, with gifts and relics, the archiepiscopal pallium.

We have the letter of Pope Gregory which accompanied the gift of the pall. The date is uncertain, and hence some have maintained that it was written by Gregory II and therefore the pall was given by him. But Willibald, in his Life of Boniface, says distinctly that the pall was given by Gregory III, and that definite statement forces us to decide the dispute as to the date and authorship of the letter in favour of Gregory III and the year 732 or thereabouts. Gregory II died 11th February, 731, Gregory III was elected 16th February and consecrated 18th March; he held the papacy ten years, eight months, and twenty-four days. This letter opens thus [1] :—

[1] Ep. 28 ; 731-2.

" To our most reverend and most holy brother Boniface our fellow-bishop, sent by this apostolic church of God for the illumination of the people of Germany or wheresover gentiles abide in the shadow of death, fixed in error, Gregory the servant of the servants of God.

" Great thankfulness possessed us when we read in the letter of your most holy brotherliness that by the grace of our Lord Jesus Christ you had turned very many from heathenism and error to the knowledge of the true faith. Since by divine institution we are taught in parables, that to whom five talents were entrusted five more were given as gain, so the gain of a like commerce we applaud with the whole Church. Hence we rightly send to thee the gift of the sacred pall, which you are to receive and wear by the authority of the blessed Peter the Apostle, and we direct that you be counted one among the archbishops, by the guidance of God. How you are to use it we inform you by apostolic mandate,—only when you perform the solemnities of masses, and when it falls to you to consecrate a bishop.

" You have informed us that the crowds of those who are converted, and the distances, are so great that you cannot go to all, to teach them that which tends to salvation. We therefore instruct you that in accordance with the decrees of the sacred canons, where the multitude of the faithful has grown large, it behoves you, relying on the force of the apostolic see, to ordain bishops, but only after pious considera-tion, that the dignity of bishop be not lowered.

" With regard to the presbyter who, as you tell us, came to us last year and was absolved of his nefarious doings, he neither confessed here nor was absolved. If you find him devoted to error, correct him according to the canons by the force of this apostolic see, and any others of like kind. He came to us and said, ' I am a presbyter,' and asked commendatory letters to our son Charles. We gave him nothing else.

" Those who, you tell us, have been baptized by pagans, if it is really so, baptize in the name of the Trinity."

The Pope then proceeds to deal with a number of questions which Boniface had addressed to him. One of these drew a curious distinction. Some, Boniface reported, ate wild horse, and many ate the domestic horse; what was he to do ? To eat either, the Pope replied, was unclean and execrable. We have heard a good deal in this year of grace 1910 of the importation from England of decrepit samples of the *caballus domesticus* for the eating of the same German race.

Boniface was now an archbishop. He had been a bishop without a defined diocese ; he was now an archbishop without a defined province, ranging over large regions beyond the bounds of other arch-bishoprics. He began to take larger steps. He built a church at Fritzlar, which he dedicated to the honour of St. Peter and St. Paul, that most usual dedication, setting forth in so many countries the equality of importance which the earliest ages assigned to the two princes of the Apostles, and another at Hamanaburg, dedicated to St. Michael the Archangel. This was on a hill, as is usually the case with churches of this dedication. He founded also two small monasteries, attached to these churches, and placed a considerable number of monks in them. He then passed down into Bavaria, in the time of Duke Hucpert, and had there his wonted success. He came across a schismatic called Eremuulf, and in accordance with the canons condemned him and drove him away, converting the people from the idolatry of his perverse sect. This visit to Bavaria was to bear large fruit in three years' time. Meanwhile he went north again to control his own diocese. The meaning of that phrase of Willibald's is seen later, when we find that there was already a bishop in Bavaria.

It was now time for him to go for a third time to Rome. Among other reasons, Willibald tells us that Boniface felt himself to be advanced in years, and desired to commend himself to the prayers of the saints. The year was 738, and he was probably not yet sixty years of age. He was received very kindly by the Pope, Gregory III. Boniface's success in Rome is described as remarkable. Not the Romans only, but strangers in Rome, flocked to hear him. A great multitude of Franks, and Bavarians, and Saxons from Britain, and visitors from other provinces, diligently followed his teaching. Where he taught, we do not know. How perpetually we have to notice with regret that the chroniclers of past ages did not set down that which to them was matter of common knowledge, the obvious as we should say ; it is just the matter of common knowledge, the obvious to the then world, that would enable us to really understand things as they were.

Boniface spent a considerable part of a year in Rome, visiting the relics of the saints and praying at their shrines. He then paid a parting visit to the Pope, and set out on his return journey with many gifts and a collection of relics. The output of relics from Rome would appear to have been practically inexhaustible. Some quaint estimates have been made of the superabundance of bones which important saints must have possessed, the number of nails on the Cross, and the immense masses of timber the Cross would appear to have contained. The demand for relics in the case of one in the position of Boniface was very great, for each new altar set up in the course of his conversions and organizations required for its full hallowing the insertion of some relic or relics of a saint. We have this set out at full length in the order for consecrating a church in our earliest English Pontifical, which dates from exactly the date of which we are speaking, the Pontifical of Ecgbert the Archbishop of York. The main structure was called the altar. In the middle of the top a hole was left, in which incense, and the consecrated element of bread, and the relics of saints, were placed. Over them was laid and fixed the table (tabula) on which the elements were for the future to be consecrated. It is well to bear in mind, in the employment of ecclesiastical nomenclature, that the "Table" was regarded as the most hallowed part of the "Altar".

Boniface went by way of Pavia, the capital of the Lombard kingdom of North Italy. It must be remembered that we are dealing with a time when as yet the Pope was not a great temporal prince, though the time when that great error of judgement on the part of the spiritual Papacy took effect was not far distant. He rested his weary limbs under the hospitality of the Lombard King Liutprand. This king, so famous in history, was very closely concerned with the provinces in which Boniface's work lay. He had in his early youth been driven from Lombardy, and had found shelter among the Bavarians. Three years before Boniface's visit, he had adopted Pepin, the son of Charles Martel. And in the year following Boniface's visit he joined forces with Charles Martel, and enabled him to secure his final victory over the Saracens.

From Pavia Boniface passed to Bavaria, by invitation of the Bavarian Duke Odilo. Here he spent a long time in restoring to soundness and health the debased form of Christianity which existed in the land. There were men who claimed falsely to be of episcopal order. Others had appointed themselves to the office of priesthood. Others practised all manner of like deceptions, and led the people away from the truth. Boniface dealt promptly with all such, and then took an important step, the results of which in the Middle Ages were great. With the consent of the Duke Odilo, he divided the province of Bavaria into four bishoprics, and ordained four bishops to preside over them. John became Bishop of Salzburg; Erembercht, Bishop of Freisingen, now Freysing; Goibald or Gaibald, Bishop of Ratisbon, at that time called Regina, whence its modern German name of Regensburg;[1] and Vivilo,[2] Bishop of Passau, then called Patavia. Othlon tells us that Vivilo was already a bishop, having been consecrated by the apostolic prelate (praesul, the Pope pre-

---

[1] The little river Regen runs into the Danube nearly opposite to Regensburg. It is not improbable that the Romans found the name indigenous, and thence called the place Regina and Reginum.

[2] We shall have more to say of this bishop.

sumably). We find his name among those of the
bishops of Bavaria and Alemannia to whom Pope
Gregory addressed letters commendatory of Boniface.
The name Patavia carries us back into the time of
the Romans. They, with their sound military instinct,
seized upon this most remarkable of natural fortresses,
commanding alike the Inn and the Ill and the
Danube, and having garrisoned it with picked
Batavian troops from our modern Holland, they
called it Batāva Castra.

CHAPTER VI

GREGORY III gave to Boniface a letter of commendation to ecclesiastics in the widest. possible terms [1]:—

"Gregory, bishop, servant of the servants of God, to all our most loved bishops, most venerable presbyters, religious abbats, of all provinces.

"The Lord going before and confirming the word of truth by this present most holy man Boniface, our brother and fellow bishop, sent by our predecessor of holy memory the prelate Gregory to preach the word of God in those parts, after long time, God favouring his earnest desire, he came for the sake of prayer to the sacred thresholds of the blessed chiefs of the Apostles, Peter and Paul. When his prayer was accomplished, we sent him out to his accepted task, the angel of the Lord going before. To him may the love, and reverence, and religion of you all deign to give assistance, for you know what our Lord Jesus Christ saith, 'He that receiveth a prophet in the name of a prophet shall receive a prophet's reward, and he that receiveth a righteous man in the name of a righteous man shall receive a righteous man's reward.' And if by chance any of your ministers

---

[1] Ep. 42 ; A.D. 787.

shall wish to join this most holy man in the ministry of exhortation of the holy catholic faith, in no way prevent him, dearest ones. Out of your own flock give him helpers who by the grace of God may adequately minister the word of preaching, that they may make gain of souls to our Omnipotent God, that your community may have a portion in the good work, and that they may merit to hear the voice of the Lord saying, ' Ye who have left all and followed me shall receive an hundredfold and shall have eternal life.' "

After some time spent in active work in Bavaria, Boniface received the following letter [1] :—

" To the most reverend and most holy brother Boniface our fellow bishop, Gregory the servant of the servants of God.

" The teacher of all the gentiles, the illustrious apostle the blessed Paul, says, ' To them that love God all things work together for good.' In the letters of your brotherliness you have told us of the heathen people of Germany whom our God of His pity has freed from the power of the pagans and to the number of a hundred thousand souls has gathered into the bosom of holy mother church by means of your efforts and the help of Karl prince of the Franks. You have told us also of what you have done in the province of the Bavarians. Raising our hands to heaven, we give thanks to our Lord God, who has opened a door of mercy and pity in those western parts for the knowledge of the way of salvation, has opened the door of mercy and sent His angel to prepare your way before you. To Him be glory for ever and ever.

[1] Ep. 45 ; 29 Oct. 739.

" You have informed us that you have reached the people of Bavaria and have found them living out of ecclesiastical order, having no bishops in the province except one, by name Vivilo, whom we some time ago [1] ordained ; and that with the assent of Otilo, duke of those same Bavarians, and of the chief men of the province, you have ordained three other bishops and have divided the province into four parts, that is, into four dioceses, that each bishop may have his own diocese. You have done well and adequately, my brother, for you have in our place fulfilled the apostolic precept and done as we told you. Cease not, father most reverend, to teach to them the holy catholic tradition of the Roman See, that the ignorant may be illumined and may hold the way of salvation, by which they may pass to their eternal rewards.

" With regard to the presbyters whom you have found there, if it is not known who ordained them or whether those who ordained them were bishops or not, if those presbyters are men of good life and catholic, trained in the ministry of Christ and in the holy law, let them receive the blessing of the priesthood from their own bishop and be consecrated and thus let them perform the sacred ministry.

"Those who have been baptized with various imperfections of gentile tongues, if they were baptized in the name of the Trinity, let them be confirmed by the laying on of the hand and the sacred chrism.

" Now Vivilo was ordained by us. If he in some ways goes beyond canonical rule, teach and correct

---

[1] Vivilo is dated " about 728 " in the list of bishops of Passau. He is the first on the list. If the dates are correct, he was consecrated by Gregory II. not Gregory III.

him according to the tradition of the Roman Church which you have received from us.

"With regard to the Council which you are to hold in our stead near the banks of the Danube, we instruct your brotherliness that you are there by apostolical authority. So far as the Lord gives you strength, cease not to preach the word of salvation, that the Christian religion may in the name of God grow and multiply.

"You are not free, brother, to remain in one place of the labour you have undertaken. Confirm the hearts of the brethren and all the faithful in the western parts where God has opened a way of salvation; desist not from preaching. Where you find a suitable place, ordain in our stead according to canonical rule bishops, and teach them to hold canonical tradition. By this you will prepare for yourself a reward of great price, for you will make for our Omnipotent God a perfect people. Be not reluctant, most loved brother, to undertake rough and diverse journeys, that the Christian faith may be spread far and wide by your efforts."

The date of the following letter from the Pope to certain bishops in Alemannia and Bavaria is uncertain. The letter appears to come in best at the point which we have now reached [1] :—

"To our most loved bishops seated in the province of the Bavarians and in Alemannia, Wigg Liudo Rydolt Phyphylus Adda, Gregory, Pope.

"Catholic authority of the holy Fathers enjoins that twice in a year synodals should be celebrated, for the well-being of Christian folk and for exhorta-

---

[1] Ep. 44.

H

tion of the adoption of sons,[1] and that the examination of canonical causes should go forward, that the necessities of each may be aided by pious instruction. Wherefore, in accordance with the teaching of the apostle, I admonish you, my dearest ones, by the mercy of God, that ye walk worthy of the vocation wherewith ye are called, that your ministry may be perfected in the sight of God.

"It is fitting that you should know to receive our brother and fellow bishop Boniface, present as our vicegerent, with honour worthy and due for Christ's name. From him, as appointed by us, receive and keep worthily the ecclesiastical ministry with the catholic faith, according to the custom and rule of the holy catholic and apostolic church, over which by the guidance of the mercy of God we are seen to preside. Deny, prohibit, cast away pagan rites, and the doctrine either of Brittons [2] who come to you or of false heretical priests, or adulterers, wherever they come from. Teach thoroughly the people of God committed unto you with pious admonitions, and altogether keep clear of the sacrifices of the dead. And as you shall be instructed by our said fellow bishop, so keep the catholic and apostolic doctrine, and make haste to please the Lord God and our Saviour. And in whatever place he shall command you to meet for holding councils, whether by the Danube, or at the city Augusta, or wherever he shall appoint, there for the name of Christ be

---

[1] Rom. viii. 15, "Ye have received the spirit of the adoption of sons."

[2] "Britto" had become a term of reproach as meaning the Celtic inhabitants of these islands of ours, whose ways were often very queer.

found ready as you may learn from his mandate for
your meeting, that in the day of Christ's coming
ye may be found worthy to stand at His tribunal
with the fruit of good work and to say 'Behold, we
and the children whom Thou hast given us, of
them we have not lost one'; and that you may be
worthy to hear the voice of the Lord saying, 'Come,
ye blessed of my Father, receive the kingdom prepared
for you from the foundation of the world.' Fare ye
well."

It is not easy to account for the choice of bishops
to whom this letter should be addressed, or for their
names or sees. Wig is said by Dümmler to be the
same as Wicterp, Bishop of Augusta or of Ratisbon.
Augusta is not infrequently puzzling as the name
of a see. Before the Romans came into the part
of Europe with which we are dealing, the Celtic
Vindelici occupied the district which was afterwards
Bavaria. They had important towns, Bregenz,
Kempten, Straubing, and a town on the Inn afterwards Passau. When the Romans overthrew the
Vindelici, they founded two colonies, one, Augusta
Vindelicorum, now Augsburg, the other, Batava
Castra, at the junction of the Inn and the Danube,
where the town of the Vindelici was situated, called later
Patavia, now Passau. This colony derived its name
from the fact that the Romans settled there a body
of picked Batavian troops, from Holland as we should
say. Augsburg claims that it had a bishop, Nar-
cissus, as early as 304. Half a century later, the
Alemanni seized it and bishops ceased to be. In
534–6 the Franco-Galli seized the territory and in
the time of Justinian I restored the bishopric, as
appears from the address of the Synod of Aquileia

H 2

to the Emperor Maurice.[1]   Zosimus was the bishop
of Augusta next before the Synod.   After a long
gap, filled in the twelfth century by seven dummy
names, we come to Wicterp (Wigbert) about 736 to
740.   The bishops were called episcopi Augustani.

But there was another Augusta sufficiently near
to cause confusion, Augusta Rauracorum, represented
now by Basel, or Basle.   It also had bishops from
early times, the first mentioned being Justinianus,
who signed the decrees of Sardica in 344 and of the
Synod of Colonia in 346.   The bishop of 650, Rag-
nacharius, signed as Augustanae et Basiliae.   Thus
there were two Episcopi Augustani.   More than
that, down to 1648 both Augsburg and Basel were
in the archbishopric of Mainz.   There can, however,
be no doubt that the Pope on this occasion was not
concerned with Basel, and it is practically certain
that he could not omit the Bishop of Augsburg
from his address.   Further, the fact that he names
Wig first may be taken as an indication that Wig
held the premier see.   We are driven to look for him
in the lists of bishops of Augsburg, and Wicterp,
known to be also Wigbert, who was bishop at the
time, is the only name like Wig.

But why should the see of Wig be stated by
Dümmler as Augusta or Ratisbona?   Ratisbona was
the old Celtic name of the town settled at the
junction of the Regen with the Danube, called by
the Romans, probably from the name of the river,
Regina Castra, and by the Germans, certainly for the
same reason, Regensburg.   Turning to the Bishops

---

[1] "In tribus ecclesiis nostri concilii, Beconensi, Tiburnensi,
et Augustana, Galliarum episcopi constituerant sacerdotes."
The sees named are Pettau, Lurn, and Augsburg.

of Regensburg, we find the list headed by four or
five great names, described not as bishops but as
having preached in the city of Regensburg, St. Rupert
about 536, St. Emmeram about 549, then a long
gap. At last we come to the bishops. About 730–9
we find Wikpert "qui et Augustanus episcopus.
Episcopatum hunc restituit S. Bonifacius circa 739".
This explains Dümmler's alternative. It was not
Wikpert but Goibald or Gaibald that Boniface appointed to the bishopric of Regensburg in 739. He
comes next to Wikpert in the list of Regensburg
bishops, and before Wikpert Ratharius appears, as
the first actual bishop, about 720. This throws
doubt upon the accepted statement that Boniface
restored the line of bishops in Gaibald.

With regard to Liudo, there is in the list of Bishops
of Speyer or Spires a bishop of that name in 739,
and as far as can be ascertained nowhere else. At
first sight it would appear that Speyer is too far off,
but that is not so. Speyer, Augsburg, Eichstätt,
Würzburg, were all in the same archbishopric (Mainz)
before 1648, and Speyer is now in the archbishopric
of Bamberg, with Würzburg and Eichstätt as its
only companions.

Rydoltus is not found in any list of bishops. But
Rudolf became Bishop of Constanz in 736, and
Constanz was in the archbishopric of Mainz at the
date mentioned above.

About Phyphylus there is no difficulty. It was a
Greek Pope's way of pronouncing Vivilo, the name of
the bishop whom Boniface appointed to Passau, the
first bishop there.

There remains Adda. In the lists of Argenti-
nensian bishops, so called from Argentoratum, the

old name of Strassburg, we find in 739 Eddo, with
the variants Heddo, Hetti. This is the only known
name of a bishop of the time which corresponds to
Adda, and it is no doubt the same man. Strassburg,
too, was in the archbishopric of Mainz at the date
named above.

These identifications being accepted, it becomes
easy to see the magnitude of the area within which
the Pope directed the bishops to act in common—
Augsburg (or Regensburg), Speyer, Constanz, Passau,
Strassburg. The omission of bishoprics so completely
Bavarian as Freising still is and Salzburg was, is
due to the fact that Boniface had not as yet developed the episcopacy of Bavaria. John of Salzburg's
bishopric dates from 739, but the dates of Corbinian
of Freising present considerable difficulty.

The history of Bavaria, Baiern, is another example
of the acquisitive energy of the old Frankish race. At
the time of Folk-wandering, Germanic people from
their home in the land of the Boii, Boiohaemum,
Böhmen, Bohemia, had taken the name of Baiuvarii.
Baiwaren [1] had taken possession of parts of Noricum
and Rhaetia, with the exception of the part west of the
Lech, which the Alemanni held. That is, the Baiwaren
dwelt from the Fichtelgebirge to the High Alps, from
the Lech to Carinthia and the Steiermark, Styria.
They, as usual at that period, were under dukes, who
were also called kings. The first of these of whom
we can really get hold is Garibald I, of the race of
the Agilolfings. In concert with the Lombard King
Authari, he endeavoured to free himself from the
overlordship which the Franks had established. He

[1] In the Bonifatian letters we have Baiuarii, Baiubarii,
Baiuaria.

was defeated, and died in 590. The Franks invaded the land, and set Tassilo I upon the throne, and Tassilo got rid of Garibald's son Grimoald. Under his successors, another Garibald and two Theodos, Christianity spread in Baiern, by means of the monks Eustachius and Agilus from the Burgundian monastery of Luxeuil, St. Emmeram, and St. Rupert of Worms. Theodo II and his sons were baptized. His grandson Heribert fought unsuccessfully against Charles Martel, and not only lost the whole north part of his kingdom, but became more dependent still upon the Franks for the part that remained. His son Odilo endeavoured to take advantage of the strife among the sons of Charles to free himself; but unluckily for him he took the wrong side, supporting his brother-in-law Gripho, and he was taken prisoner at the Lechfeld. As his ransom he had to give up all the land north of the Danube, and the Franks enrolled it in their kingdom as the Nordgau. It was under him, and with his consent, that Boniface founded the bishoprics of Passau, Freising, and Salzburg. The disasters of the ducal line did not end with him. Odilo's son was six years old at the time of his father's death, and was under the guardianship of his mother, the Frankish princess Chiltrudis. But he married Liutgard, the daughter of the Lombard King Desiderius, and she induced him to free himself from the Frank overlordship. He sent no troops to the Frank Heerbann, did not attend the Maifeld, issued all decrees in his own name. He allied himself with his brother-in-law, the Lombard King Adalgis, with the Court of Eastern Rome, with the Avars; but all did not avail against the great Karl. In 789 he had to attend at Worms, receive his duchy as a Frank fief,

and send hostages.   He did not, however, cease from
his attempts; he was tried in the royal court at
Ingelheim, and condemned to death; but he was sent
instead to the cloister.   In 794 Baiern was formally
made a Frank province.

The scene changes to 1180, when the duke, Henry
the Lion, the founder of Munich, for devoting himself
too exclusively to the interests of his other duchy
(Saxony), was outlawed by the Reichstag, and the
Pfalzgrave Otto IV of Wittelsbach, of an ancient
Baierisch race, was elected Duke of Baiern.   His
descendants are now Kings of Bavaria.

When we come to speak of Boniface's dealings
with the Frankish bishops and clergy in the western
parts, we shall see to what a low state many of them
had fallen.   As we are now concerned with Bavaria,
two cases of that character must be mentioned here.

In dealing with ignorant priests, Boniface got in
one case into serious difficulty.   A priest in Bavaria
was so ignorant of Latin that he used an impossible
form of words at the vital part of the Sacrament of
Baptism.   The case may remind us of the origin
of our phrase *hocus pocus* from the blurred Latin of
the ignorant English priests at the critical point
of the other great Sacrament, when they ought to
have said but did not say, *Hoc est Corpus*.   Boniface
ordered the baptisms to be repeated, with the proper
form of words.   The two men in charge of the ecclesiastical district wrote to the Pope on the subject, and
the Pope took their side.   This is his letter, dated
July 1, 746 (the twenty-sixth year of the then
Emperor Constantine)[1] :—

"To the most reverend and holy brother Boniface,

[1] Ep. 68.

our fellow bishop, Zacharias the servant of the servants of God.

" Virgilius and Sedonius,[1] religious persons dwelling in the province of the Baierians, have intimated to us by their letters that your reverend brotherliness has given them injunctions to re-baptize Christians. Hearing this we were greatly disturbed, and fell into wonderment if the thing is as is said. They have reported that a certain priest in the province, being completely ignorant of Latin, said the words of Baptism in broken Latin, ' Baptizo te in nomine patria et filia et spiritus sancti.' [2] And on this ground your reverend brotherliness has thought there should be re-baptism. But, most holy brother, if he who baptized did not introduce error or heresy, but from mere ignorance of the Roman speech said the words in broken Latin, we cannot agree that there should be re-baptism. For, as your holy brotherliness is well aware, any one baptized by heretics in the name of the Father and the Son and the Holy Ghost ought by no means to be re-baptized, but should be cleansed by simple imposition of hand. Thus, most holy brother, if the thing is as it has been related to us, do not give them further injunctions of this character, but let your sanctity study to conserve what the holy fathers teach and enjoin.

" May God keep thee safe, most reverend brother."

[3] " Your reverend brotherliness has written that you have found a certain priest, a Scot, Sampson by

---

[1] In a second letter, *Sydonius*.

[2] Instead of *patris et filii*. Migne (*Epp. Zachariae*, vii. col. 929) prints *et spiritu sancta*, which on the face of it is more consistent with the priest's complete ignorance of Latin. But Dummler does not give this as an alternative reading.

[3] Ep. 80.

name, erring from the way of truth, saying and
affirming that without any mystic invocation or any
laver of regeneration a man can be made a Catholic
Christian by the imposition of a bishop's hand.   He
who says this is void of the Holy Spirit, alien from
the grace of Christ, and to be rejected from the com-
panionship of priests. For who, if he be not baptized
according to the Lord's command, in the name of
Father, Son, and Holy Ghost, and then consecrated
by the imposition of the hand, can be a catholic?
This most wicked man who preaches such things
condemn, and drive him out from the holy Church
of God."

Boniface would appear to have had something
more to say against Virgilius and Sedonius, for on
the first of May three years later Zacharias wrote
a long letter in which, among much else that is
interesting, their names appear in an unfavourable
connexion. This is what the Pope says of the two
ecclesiastics [1] :—

" Your fraternal sanctity has intimated to us that
the man Virgilius—I know not if he is called priest—
is maligning you, because to his confusion you
proved him to be in error from the catholic doctrine,
seeking to sow enmity between you and Ottilo the
duke of the Bavarians ; saying that he was allowed by
me to have the diocese of one, now dead, of the four
bishops whom your brotherliness ordained there. This
is in no sense true. And with regard to the perverse

[1] Ep. 80 ; 1 May, 748.
The letter of Boniface to which this is an answer must
have been written some considerable time earlier, for, if the
date 748 is correct, Ottilo had been some time dead. Possibly
the offence of Virgilius did not become known to Boniface till
after Ottilo's death.

and iniquitous doctrine which he has uttered against
God and his own soul, if it is made clear that
he maintains that beneath this earth there is another
world, with other men and a sun and a moon, call
a council, drive him out of the Church, depose him
from the honour of priesthood. We are writing
to the duke, and are sending to Virgil letters of
evocation, summoning him to come to Rome and be
carefully examined, and if he is found to hold erro-
neous views, to be condemned canonically.

"We have learned what your holiness has written
about the priests Sydonius and Virgil. To them, as
was fitting, we have written letters of rebuke; we
give more credence to thy brotherliness than to
them. If it please God, and we live, we shall summon them by apostolic letters to the apostolic see."

The learned German, Ernest Dümmler, the most
recent editor of the Bonifatian letters, remarks that
he does not find any difficulty in the two references
to Virgil in these two paragraphs, because in each
place the Pope says he will call him to Rome. But
it seems impossible that Zacharias could in the second
paragraph distinctly call Virgil a priest,[1] and in the
first paragraph distinctly say that he does not know
whether he is called priest, if he is writing in the
two paragraphs of one and the same man called
Virgil. His manner of introducing his name in the
first paragraph is suspicious, *Virgilius ille—nescimus
si dicatur presbyter*. In the second paragraph, immediately following the first, he writes quite naturally,
Pro Sydonio autem supra dicto et Virgilio presbyteris.
To any one who has puzzled over the diverse appearance of Virgil on the stage, it is a great relief to feel

---

[1] In each case, *presbyter* is the word used, not *sacerdos*.

a fair amount of certainty that there were at least two prominent ecclesiastics of that name in Bavaria at the time which we have under·consideration. We have a Virgilius in charge of an ecclesiastical district in Bavaria, to whom Boniface gives orders about rebaptizing ; we have Virgilius, of whom the Pope does not know whether he is a priest, holding views at that time most strange, still in Bavaria ; we have Virgilius an evidently well-known priest, still in Bavaria, who has got into some serious ecclesiastical scrape, and we have Virgilius, Bishop of Salzburg, then in Bavaria, who curiously enough did succeed one of Boniface's Bavarian bishops who was dead, namely John of Salzburg, in 745. In the Verbrüderungsbuch at St. Peter's in Salzburg, the names of the bishops and abbats of Salzburg defunct, from Hrodpertus (St. Rupert), the first named, to John, the seventh named, are all written in the original hand. The next name, written in a later but still contemporary hand, is Virgilius. Gams[1] introduces yet another question by dating the succession of Virgilius as 745, adding that he was consecrated 767. He was succeeded in 785 by Arno, the dearest friend of Alcuin of York.

But that is not all. We have a religious man Sidonius, in Bavaria, to whom also Boniface gave orders about re-baptizing ; we have a Sidonius, still in Bavaria, who in 748 has got into some ecclesiastical scrape, and we have Sidonius, Bishop of Passau, succeeding to that see in 749, when Beatus, who in 745 had succeeded the first bishop, Vivilo, died.

Were there seven persons, or two ? As a calculated

[1] *Series Episcoporum*, Ratisbona, 1873.

guess, the first-named Virgilius was the same as the Bishop of Salzburg, the first-named Sidonius the same as the Bishop of Passau. The others were merely persons with the same names as the bishops.

It may be added here that while John Bishop of Salzburg is described as one of the bishops appointed by Boniface to new sees in Bavaria, there is in the contemporary Verbrüderungsbuch a list of eight earlier bishops. Gams solves this difficulty in the most probable manner; John was the first diocesan Bishop of Salzburg. The others, we are to suppose, as for instance St. Rupert and St. Vitalis, were regionary bishops whose head-quarters were in St. Peter's, Salzburg.

CHAPTER VII

Of the thousands of English tourists who pass each year through Eichstätt junction on the way to Munich, how few take the pretty little light railway from the junction to Eichstätt-Stadt. All who do so are liberally repaid. The approach to the town is unusual and attractive. They find hid among the hills a delightful little old-world cathedral town, entirely dominated by the English Willibald the Bishop and his sister the English Walpurgis the abbess; she had for many years presided over the great abbey of Heidenheim in succession to her other brother, Wunnibald. The cathedral church is dedicated to St. Willibald, the convent church to St. Walpurgis. A beautiful bronze statue of Willibald, in the full pontificals which are still preserved in his church, commands the town in a great square (fig. 2). The names of the English saints are household words in Eichstätt. The only three men whose Christian name this present writer asked gave their name as Willibald; the only lady as Walpurgis.

Fortunately, we know a good deal of these three important English people, much of it at first hand. There is in the Royal Library at Munich a parchment in small quarto, of date about the year 800, beauti-

FIG. 2. ST WILLIBALD.

fully and most carefully written, containing the Lives of St. Boniface (by the presbyter Willibald), St. Wynnibald, and St. Willibald, in that order. Of the 102 folios, forty-four are occupied by Boniface, twenty-eight by Wynnibald, thirty-two by Willibald. The MS. came from the Cathedral Church of St. Corbinian in Freising. The Lives of Willibald and Wunnibald [1] are printed with useful notes by Pertz, *Scriptores*, i. 86–117.

Taking first the Life of Willibald, we find ourselves in presence of one of the two, or three, most remarkable travellers of the century of greatest travel in early times. How far the extreme interest which was created in Northumbria by the travels of the Frank Arculfus had made itself felt in the South of England, we cannot say; but that Willibald's travels were either begun or finally extended by Arculf's example is at least highly probable. Arculf was blown by storms to Iona, on his return from the Holy Land, about the year 680. There he dictated to Adamnan a careful account of his travels, and copied onto parchment the ground-plans he had made on the spot, on wax tablets, of the round church and the other churches on the holy area at Jerusalem. This account Adamnan presented to Aldwulf, the great King of Northumbria, in 701. Bede popularized it in his treatise *On the Holy Places*, and in Bede's popularized form it went far and wide. Willibald's journeyings began some twenty years after

---

[1] The fact that this name occurs both as Wunnibald and Wynnibald in contemporary or practically contemporary times shows that the u was modified. The ordinary runic u was like an inverted v, and a short vertical stroke at the bottom was the mark of modification. This appears on the Bewcastle Cross and in other Northumbrian runic inscriptions.

Aldwulf received Adamnan and heard the marvellous tale.

Willibald, Wunnibald, and Walpurga, were the children of one Richard, supposed to be a son of Hlothere, the ninth King of Kent (673-85). Their mother was Winna, or Wuna, a sister—possibly not quite so close a relation—of Boniface. At Crediton they show you "St. Winnifrith's well", which suggests that in Boniface's own generation, as in Willibald's and Wynnibald's, the children of the family had names given them with one or two syllables in common. Hilda's family, with its Hildilith, Hildegyth, and Hild, probably itself shortened from a three-syllable name, is a good case in point. Winna was a relative of Ina, the King of Wessex. Thus the family, including Boniface himself, was really one of high position, and in their case the usual preface to a Life of the times, "So-and-so sprang from a noble family of the Angles, but his manner of life was more noble still," was no doubt true. This connexion with the royal family of Kent may throw special light upon Boniface's dealings with Ethelbert II, the thirteenth King of Kent, the supposed Richard's first cousin once removed.

The Lives of Willibald and Wunnibald were written by a self-deprecating religious lady of Anglo-Saxon birth who had gone out to Germany for divine work. She speaks of herself as a poor little creature, a little ignorant child plucking a few flowers here and there from numerous branches rich in foliage and in fruit. She describes herself as a blood relation, though distant, of the distinguished subjects of her narrative, "from the extreme points of the branches of the family tree." In the Carlsruhe MS. of the eleventh

century, there is written in the margin, in a feigned
hand some four centuries later, at the point where
she speaks of herself in the terms cited above, *Roswida
monialis*: possibly, but very improbably, some oral
tradition of her name had survived. She wrote at
the dictation of Willibald himself, or from notes of
his conversation, after the death of Wunnibald. A
marked evidence of this is found in the fact that she
often calls Wunnibald saint, Willibald never. Once
she forgets that she is putting Willibald's narrative
into the third person, and gives his actual words,
" The shepherds gave us sour milk to drink." This
kindness was done by the shepherds when the travellers
were spending the night between the two springs
called Jor and Dan, which flowed down a hill and
at its foot united to form the Jordan. Gregory of
Tours [1] had already told of the Jor and the Dan, and
had placed their union at Caesarea Philippi.

The youthful Willibald persuaded his father Richard
and his brother Wunnibald, with one other, Tidbert,
to leave England with him for a visit to Rome. They
took ship at Hamble-mouth, about six miles below
Southampton, and sailing up the Seine found themselves after long journeyings at Lucca. Here Richard
died, and was buried in the church of St. Frigidian.
This saint was an Irishman, who was Bishop of Lucca
560–78, and founded the Cathedral Church of St.
Martin there. San Frediano represents the church
of Richard's sepulture. His epitaph named him *Rex
Richardus*, and added *Rex fuit Anglorum*. The three
survivors spent some months in Rome, and in the
spring of the next year Willibald and Tidbert set off
for Syria. They met with extreme hardships, and

[1] " Miracula in gloria martyrum," i. 16.

1

were often in very serious danger. The description
of Constantinople is in some respects the most
interesting part of the narrative. Sometimes they
deserved to suffer more than they did suffer. The
smuggling story is probably the best known of their
adventures. Balsam was at that time about the most
precious product of hot climates that they could
procure. At Jerusalem Willibald obtained some, in a
short piece of hollow cane. This cane, full of balsam,
he fixed in a gourd, and he plugged the upper end of
the cane with petroleum[1], so arranging it that the
end of the cane looked like the orifice of the gourd.
When they approached Tyre, after being missed by
a large lion that ate people who went to gather olives,
the customs people stopped them, and examined their
poor little possessions. They pounced on the gourd,
but when they smelled the petroleum they gave it
back without question. The travellers eventually got
back somewhere about the year 729. Willibald and
Tidbert went to Monte Cassino, and there for ten
years Willibald lived with the brethren, acting in
turn as sacrist, dean (in charge of ten monks), and
porter, an interesting order of official promotion.
About the year 740, Willibald came again to Rome,
with Abbat Petronax, and recounted his adventures
to Pope Gregory III. His uncle Boniface begged
him of the Pope for the German mission. He went
by way of Lucca, Brescia, and Garda, came to
Eichstätt, and there in 741 Boniface settled him as
bishop. The Life tells us that he was aged forty-one
when he was consecrated, and the place of consecration was Sulzeprucge. He died in 786, at the age
of eighty-six. The *prucge* is written over an erasure,

---

[1] "de petre oleo." The nun's Latin is very curious.

but in the original hand : other MSS. have Sulzpurg
and Sallpurg. Salzburg would from these facts be
a natural guess; but the place was Sülzenbrücken, in
Gotha. The nun, who uses strange words, ends by
calling Willibald a "blessed barilion". Her smatter-
ings of Greek suggest παρήλιον, "another sun."

The Life of Wunnibald naturally gives us less of
journeyings than that of his brother, and more of his
work in Germany. He was nineteen years old when
he left home with his father and brother. When the
brothers parted in Rome, Wunnibald returned to
England, and the account of why he returned and
what he did is worth giving in full.

"The mind of this active hero formed the wish to
return to the land of his birth, for this reason chiefly,
that he might exhort any one of his relatives to the
sacred warfare of the divine service, and take him out
with him to the mission field. He went at once to
his own hereditary place, where he was received with
great joy. By conversation and instruction he exhorted his brothers and sisters and others of his
relations to walk in the right way, not to allow their
feet to wander from the solid path of truth, but to
aim at ascending from the thresholds of this world
to the narrow gate of paradise, by the strait and
rough way of the Christian warrior. Thus warning
and urging he visited the vills and houses of his
relatives, and carried the minds of many from the
cares of secular business to the study of divine affairs.
And then for a second time, leave having been obtained, with the advice of his friends and the
assistance of the younger members, he set out for
Rome, one of his brothers going with him." Who
this brother was, we do not know.

At Rome he appears to have fallen in with his uncle Boniface, who invited him to come and work with him.   He consulted the brother who was with him, and other relations and friends, and with their leave [1] he set out with a small party of colleagues. They passed up into Thuringia, and there Boniface ordained him priest, and gave him charge of seven churches—possibly a group of seven, Irish-fashion. While in charge of these seven churches, he was visited by Willibald, whom he had not seen for many years. Wunnibald soon obtained the friendship of Duke Otilo; after three years he went to Mainz, and worked in those parts; then he moved on to Eichstätt, and with Willibald sought a fitting place in that region.   Such a place they found at Heidanheim (Heidenheim), and there Wunnibald bought some land and got other land given.   It was all rough wood, but they cut down the trees, cleared away the nettles and thistles, and built some huts.   Of what character these were we gather from one of Walpurga's miracles here; she stopped a fire in the village, which was raging among the dwellings built of reeds and straw.

Wunnibald had never had good health, and he soon became crippled, so that he moved about with difficulty.   He managed to get as far as Fulda, and there he lay ill, almost dying, for three weeks. Feeling better he moved to another place, not named, and there he lay ill for a week.   Thence he went to visit Megingoz at Würzburg, and spent three days with him. Then he returned to Heidenheim. Crippled and ill as he was, he formed an earnest desire to go to St. Benedict (Monte Cassino), and die there.   The

[1] This twofold mention of a formal family permission (*licentia*) is interesting.

abbat and the whole community begged him to come
to them. He invited his brother and other wise
friends to come and advise him. Their advice was
that he should remain quietly at Heidenheim, and
not deprive his flock of his presence among them.
This advice he took.

Become too feeble to go out to church, he placed
an altar at one side of his room, and there daily, when
he was physically able, he celebrated Mass. When
his end was close at hand, he called Willibald from
Eichstätt, and they spent his last day together.
Then he called the brethren into his room, made
a touching address to them, and died sitting in front
of his bed. He had for many years had his coffin
ready, and in it he was placed. Some time after, his
remains were raised, for the purpose of being placed
in the only part of his church which he had built to
its full height, namely, the eastern porticus, or apse.
The body was found to be quite sound and fresh, so
that his brother the bishop, and his sister Walpurga
who had succeeded him in the government of the
monastery, kissed it, as did all who could press
through the crowd and reach the body.

The *Life of St. Walburga*, as written by the
presbyter Wolfhard and dedicated to the then Bishop
of Eichstätt, Erkenbald (884-916), is contained in
Vol. III of the Bollandist *Acta Sanctorum*, her day
being February 25. In the prefatory remarks the
learned editors quote a very interesting document
from Gretser's Catalogue of Bishops of Eichstätt,
under the head of William of Reichenau who was
bishop from 1464 to 1496. It was this same Gretser
that wrote on the Oil of St. Walpurga. This is the
document:—

"In the year 1492, on August 20, I, Bernard Adelmann, of Adelmansfeld, Canon of Eichstätt, was sent by the most reverend Father in Christ and Lord William of Reichenau to the Illustrious Henry VI,[1] King of England and France, and Duke of Ireland, with the histories and the relics of Saints Wilibald, Wunibald, Walpurgis, Richard. These the said king received from me with the greatest reverence and devotion in the City of Canterbury on the 22nd of September of the same year. The king promised that a Mass should be celebrated daily in honour of these saints, and on the day on which he received the relics a solemn office should each week be sung. Among all the relics, that which the king chiefly admired and venerated was the Oil of St. Walpurgis."

Wolfhard tells us that Bishop Otkar (Ottcar, sixth Bishop of Eichstätt, 817–81) sent to Heidenheim two archpresbyters, Vulto and Adalungus, also Ommo and Liubila a nun of Mowenheim, to find the body of Walpurgis and bring it to Eichstätt. This was successfully accomplished on the 21st of September. Liubila's share in the transaction was so highly resented by those who were deprived of the presence of the saint's relics that at length she was driven to beg of Erkenbald, the next bishop but one (Gottschalk only held the see 881–4), that some portion of the relics might be given to her, to be replaced in their former home. The bishop assented to this, and in the year 893 the mausoleum of the saint was opened, in the church in which Otkar had placed her remains. A portion of the remains was divided off with the greatest reverence, and Liubila carried

[1] The date is evidently that of Henry VII; the action is more like Henry VI.

FIG. 3. REREDOS, ST. WALPURGA.

away that portion with the greatest joy. But alas! the people of Eichstätt got the idea that the whole of the remains had been carried away, and they in turn were plunged into the deepest grief. In order that the actual facts might be clearly known, Wolfhard was bidden to write the true history. It was on this occasion that the curious exudation of moisture from the saint's bones was noticed. From that time to this the Oil of Saint Walpurga has been famous. It has for us a special interest, inasmuch as it was chosen by Cardinal Newman as an example of a miracle that is credible.

When Walpurgis first went on to Germany, Boniface sent her to work under Leoba at Tauber-Bischofsheim. From that monastery she passed on in the course of time to take charge of Heidenheim, where she worked until her death in about 780.

The great portal of the cathedral church of St. Willibald of Eichstätt, a very fine piece of work, contains statues of the saint's father and mother, Richard and Una. He wears a king's crown, and the sacristan introduces him to visitors as the Lionheart King of England; the leopards are there to identify him. He appears similarly as King Richard, with his queen-wife, on the remarkable reredos of the altar of St. Walpurga at the nuns' church (see fig. 3). A wise visitor does not try to upset rooted beliefs. The other statues of this tier in the portal are St. Wunnibald and St. Walpurga. The cathedral church itself used to consist of the portion now called Willibald's Chor, being the western part of the existing church, an annexe to the nave of the Romanesque church, rebuilt in Romanesque style on the foundation of the original church. In it are his

splendid altar and sarcophagus, the original high
altar, at the back of which, facing eastwards, the
saint sits in marble (fig. 4). The complete set of the
vestments which he wore in life are shown to persons
who ask for them ; they are immensely interesting,
but almost too wonderfully preserved to satisfy even
an optimist. They are reproduced with marvellous
fidelity on the marble statue and on the bronze in
the square, including the nine virtues. The bones
of the saint were preserved in a stone shrine, em-
bedded in the wall of his Chor. The exact spot was
lost sight of, but it was accidentally found. They
now repose in the great sarcophagus.

On the way from Willibald's church to Walpurga's
church you pass the house in which was born in
1470 Willibald Pirkheimer, described in a tablet on
the wall as Patricier and Rathsherr of Nuremberg
under Maximilian I and Karl V; imperial coun-
sellor ; general of the Nuremberg troops in the Swiss
war ; patron of classicalism. A tablet in the Haupt-
markt of Nuremberg records the residence there of
this celebrated humanist. How few critics know
why Pirkheimer was called Willibald ! To complete
the English atmosphere of the house, the copier of
the tablet having lost his pencil in the gutter, a lady
sitting at an open window in the house presented
him with an iridescent pencil; he begged to know
her name—Frau Stesl ; her Christian name ?—Walpurga.

The Walpurgis church has a charming window
high up on the north side of the sanctuary for the
prioress—no longer, they tell you with regret, abbess
—of the fifty sisters; and the enclosed singing
gallery of the nuns, at the west end of the church,

FIG. 4. ST. WILLIBALD.

.

is a beautiful piece of lacelike woodwork. The lady-chapel, as we should call it, has the remarkable reredos of the Walpurgis-altar shown in fig. 3. The altar itself, and the place where the bones of the saint rest, are below the floor on which the spectator stands. The statues are thus labelled : "Sct. Ricardus Pater Gloriosus; Sct. Willibaldus; Sancta Walburga; Sct. Wunnibaldus; Sct. Wuna Mater Benedicta." From the bones of the saint oil is said to flow in considerable quantities from October to February. The apple-blossom nun at the wicket sells you seductive little glass flagons of it, from an inch high upwards, at prices varying with the size, and you get with the phial a collection of prayers to be used when applying the oil for curative purposes, a *Gebet vor dem Gebrauch des hl. Walburgis-Oeles*, a *Gebet zur hl. Walburga*, and a *Gebet nach dem Gebrauch des hl. Oeles*. Heidenheim, where Wunnibald and Walpurga ruled, was the principal monastery of Willibald's see of Eichstatt. The actual place of Willibald's residence at Eichstätt was naturally on the promontory dominating the town, still called Willibaldsburg. It was, in fact, the home of the bishops down to 1730.

How few English people are aware that an English lady gives to the night of the great gathering of German witches the name made so familiar to us by Goethe. Our Lady Walpurga was canonized at Rome on the first of May, the day of the great spring festival of heathendom, and she was accordingly honoured as the protectress against magic arts; thus her name has ousted the name of the witches from the Walpurgis-Nacht dance.

CHAPTER VIII

Foundation of three bishoprics.—Care not to multiply bishoprics too rapidly.—Witta of Büraburg.—Burchardt of Würzburg.—The Pope's letters to the three new bishops.—Würzburg of to-day.—Life of St. Burchardt.—Life of St. Kilian.—The Kilianshuch.—St. Burchardt's Gospel-book.

WE have seen that in the letter by which Pope Gregory III informed Boniface that he created him archbishop and sent him the pallium,[1] the Pope had advised that inasmuch as the converted pagans were now far too numerous and spread over far too large an area for him to minister effectively to them, he should ordain bishops, in accordance with the decrees of the sacred canons that where the multitude of the faithful increases, bishops shall be ordained. But he adds that Boniface must only do this after much pious consideration, lest the episcopal dignity become lightly esteemed.

Some nine or ten years later, in the early part of 742, Boniface wrote his first letter to Pope Zacharias, Gregory III having died on November 29, 741. In this letter,[2] among many matters of the highest importance, he informed the Pope that he had founded three bishoprics and ordained three bishops:—

"We have to inform your paternity that by the grace of God the peoples of Germany are decidedly touched, and we have ordained three bishops and have decreed the division of the province into three dioceses. We beg that the three towns or cities[3] in which they have been appointed and ordained may be confirmed and stablished by the writings

---

[1] Ep. 28.   [2] Ep. 50; A.D. 742. See Appendix B.
[3] "Oppida sive urbes." Whether the distinction of towns and walled towns is intended we have no means of knowing.

of your authority. One seat of a bishopric we have decreed to be in the fortress[1] called Wirzaburg, another in the town[2] named Büraburg, the third in the place[3] called Erphesfurt, which was formerly a city[4] of rustic pagans. We earnestly beg you to confirm these three places by charter by the authority of your apostolate, that, if the Lord will, there be three episcopal sees in Germany founded and stablished by apostolic mandate through the authority and precept of Saint Peter, and that present and future generations presume not to break up the dioceses or violate the precept of the holy See."

On April 1, 743, Zacharias replied.[5] He took the same point with regard to lowering the dignity of the episcopate which his predecessor had taken :—

"We learn from your letter that you have ordained three bishops for three several places, who are to preside over the people whom the Lord our God hath deigned to gather to Himself by the instrumentality of your holiness. And you have requested that by the authority of our see episcopal sees be confirmed there. But your holy brotherliness should maturely consider, and examine with subtle care, the question whether this is expedient, and whether the places themselves or the numbers of the people are such that they are worthy to have bishops. For you remember, dearest one, that in the sacred canons we are bidden to take care that we by no means ordain bishops to villages or small towns[6], lest the name of bishop be lightly esteemed. But we, moved by your words most sincere and dear to us, are willing

---

[1] Castellum   [2] Oppidum.   [3] Locus.
[4] "Urbs paganorum rusticorum."
[5] Ep. 51 ; Apr. 1, 743.
[6] "Villulae aut modicae civitates."

to grant without delay that which you have asked. We decree by apostolic authority that there be there episcopal sees, to be held in succession by bishops, who shall preside over the people and shall preach the word to them: namely, in the fortress called Wirzaburg, and in the town which is called Büraburg, and in the place called Erpfesfurt, so that hereafter it shall not be lawful for any one in any way to violate that which has by us been sanctioned."

The remark about not making bishops too freely, or for places of small importance, lest the dignity of the episcopate be lowered, has reference to a principle represented by a decree given by Gratian (80 can. 3), "Episcopi non in castellis aut modicis civitatibus debent constitui, ne vilescat nomen episcopi," bishops are not to be appointed in *castella* or in small towns, lest the dignity of the episcopate be lowered. It was awkward that both Boniface and the Pope had to use the word *castellum* to describe Würzburg; but it is so well known that *castellum* in the case of the earliest Würzburg meant a fortress that we can safely take it to have a meaning different from that of *castellum* in Gratian's decree, where it probably meant a village, as the Romans of to-day speak of the villages in the neighbourhood as *Castelli Romani*. This suggestion receives confirmation from the fact that the Pope uses the phrase "in villulas vel in modicas civitates" where Gratian's form is "in castellis aut modicis civitatibus". So far as Büraburg is concerned, it is difficult to imagine that it was ever more than a *modica civitas*, if it was ever so large as that. But it is not safe to presume that we can estimate past probabilities by present appearances; and when we read that 100,000 pagans had been converted in these parts by Boniface, we must either frankly disbelieve it or frankly allow that Buraburg may well have been more than a *modica civitas*. Of Erfurt (not spelled by the Pope exactly as Boniface spells it) we have no difficulty in believing that it was a place of sufficient importance to meet the terms of the decree. Boniface's statement is clear; it was a great enclosed place of residence of pagan folk engaged in the cultivation of the land, no doubt for many miles round. It was a place easily defensible, the river Gera flowing round it in a semicircle, with the Petersberg at the centre. The name would appear to be formed as so many of our Anglo-Saxon names of places are in England. Boniface's rendering of the name would make it mean the ford of Erph. Of Würzburg there is more to say.

It seems clear that Erfurt was to serve Thuringia, Büraburg Hessia, and Würzburg that part of Franconia as it came to be called.

Of Büraburg mention was made in connexion with Fritzlar. Its first bishop was Witta, one of the large party of English men and women who went out to work with Boniface when his success had become assured. Inasmuch as all those whose English home has been recorded came from Crediton or from Malmesbury or from Dorset, we may assign to one or other of those localities the early training of Witta. He appears again at certain points in the Church history of the time, usually under the supposed equivalent of his name, Albuinus. We shall see interesting mention of him when we look into the details of the life of Lul.

The "fortress called Wirzaburg" was of course the modern Würzburg. Here Boniface set as bishop a student-monk from the great school of Malmesbury, Burchardt, the companion at Malmesbury of Boni-

face's successor at Mainz, Lul. We have the letters
of recognition which Pope Zacharias wrote in 743
to Burchardt and Witta in identical terms.

A letter of like character no doubt went to the new
bishop of Erfurt also, for Zacharias tells Boniface
that he has written to the three bishops; but it has
not come down to us. The disappearance of the
letter means in this case that we do not know the
name of this first bishop of Erfurt. A suggestion
as to his name will be found on page 181. The
letter to Witta of Büraburg is addressed *Wittane
sanctae aecclesiae Barbarane*; "Barbarane" must
mean Büraburg. In neither of the addresses does
the Pope designate the bishop by his title of bishop.
Possibly or probably the Pope did not think right to
address him as bishop before he had read the letter confirming him as such. The following is the letter [1] :—

"To Burchard, most dear to us, of the holy church
of Wirtziburg, Zacharias the Pope.

"The Lord confirming the word, for spreading
wide the law of Christianity and showing the way
of orthodox faith, for teaching as this holy Roman
Church over which by God's appointment we preside.[2]
Our most holy and reverend brother and fellow bishop
Boniface has made known to us that he has decreed
and ordained three episcopal sees in the parts of
Germany where your dilection presides, and has
divided the province into three parishes [3]. On learning
this, with great exultation we raised our palms to
the stars, giving thanks to the illuminator and giver
of all good things, the Lord God and our Saviour

---

[1] Ep. 58 ; Apr. 1, 743.

[2] The sentence is so constructed in the original. In the
second sentence the reading of the letter to Witta has been
preferred, *sanctissimus frater* instead of *sanctissime*.

[3] *Parrochiae*, "parishes" ; meaning of course dioceses.

Jesus Christ who maketh both one. The said most holy man has begged of us by his letters that your sees be confirmed by apostolical authority. Wherefore we with ardent mind and divine aid, by the authority of the blessed Peter the chief of the Apostles, to whom was given by our God and Saviour Jesus Christ the power of binding and loosing the sins of men in heaven and on earth, do confirm and make stable your episcopal sees, interdicting by the authority of the Chief of the Apostles himself all of present or future generations from daring anything contrary to your said ordination which by the favour of God has been by our precept made in you; interdicting also this, that in accordance with the tradition of the holy canons, no one dare to translate from another bishopric or to ordain as bishop after your summons from this world, other than he who shall represent in those parts our apostolic see. And let no one presume to invade the diocese of another, or to take away churches. For if, which we do not believe, there shall be any one who shall attempt temerariously to act against this our precept, let him know himself bound by the eternal judgment of God with the chain of anathema. May those who keep the apostolic precepts, and follow the rule of right and orthodox faith, attain to the grace of benediction. For the rest, we pray the divine clemency to confirm and strengthen that which the Lord hath wrought in you. And may the splendour [1] (? love) of God, grace, and true peace, be with your spirit, most holy ones and by us most loved. With all your effort labour for the faith of Christ and strive to perfect His ministry, that with the illustrious

---

[1] In each of the two letters this is written *claritas*. Later copies naturally replace it by *charitas*.

Apostle [Paul] ye may be worthy to say: ' I have
fought a good fight, I have finished my course, I have
kept the faith. Henceforth there is laid up for me
the crown of righteousness which the Lord the
righteous judge will give to me in that day.'

" We salute you and wish you strong in the Lord.
Farewell."

An Englishman naturally goes to Würzburg, in
search of some record of his countryman Burchardt.
The record is writ large. The portion of the city
which is enclosed within fortifications on the left bank
of the Main is the " Burkardus-quarter ". The great
fortress which was the beginning of Würzburg is
there still, on the Marienberg, the residence for centuries of the bishops, who became in time dukes of
Franconia and prince-bishops. The palace which the
later bishops built on the right bank of the Main,
now the royal residence, is, as the guide-books say,
one of the grandest and most effective of the eigh-
teenth-century edifices of the kind. There is a fine
statue of Burchardt on the bridge over the Main, the
last statue but one on the left side as you cross from
the right bank. The principal hostelry is emblazoned
with this proud quatrain :—

> Burkardus Hof bin ich genannt
> Glaub' Hoffnung Lieb' hier Wohnung fand
> Dies dreifach Gut mit Kraft zu wahren
> Ist Frankenstolz seit tausend Jahren.

There are still the Burkardus-Thor and the Burkardus-
Mühle. Tradition says that the stream used to hug
the hill, and the navigable channel was there, the
main channel of the river as it now is being stony
shallows. This would bring all ships of any size
immediately under the fortress, where the Romanesque church of St. Burchardt still stands. A deep,

low, dark channel of swift water now lies between the west end of the church and the steeply rising hill, and tradition points to this as the ancient passage for ships and boats, the original west end of the church being built over it, in the guise of a bridge abutting on the face of the fortress-hill. The Romanesque church faced eastwards onto the Burkardus-Strasse, with two very pretty towers. At a later period the church was continued across the street and carried far on the other side. The present transepts occupy the width of the old street, which was of necessity diverted, and the present choir is raised so high on steps that the new street passes under it. The Romanesque towers are incorporated in the present nave, each containing an altar. The whole arrangement suggests that the earliest church had its altar at the west end.

The earliest Life of St. Burchardt was written about a hundred years after his time. It is useless for historical purposes. Beyond the story of the discovery of the relics of Kilian and his fellow martyrs, the author neither knew nor cared to learn anything definite about him. A very different writer compiled a careful account of the saint at the request of Peregrinus, Abbat of the monastery of St. Burchardt at Würzburg, 1130-56. This writer was a man of humble mind, an excellent quality for the biographer of a saint; he calls himself in his prologue, *E., a sinner, not worthy of a name.*[1] He had a considerable amount of information at his disposal.

Burchardt is said to have had two brothers, Gotwin and Adelmar, and to have been a blood relation of Boniface. He was trained at the school

---

[1] From another source we learn that " E." meant Egilward.

K

of St. Aldhelm of Malmesbury. He was sent, E.
tells us, to Rome by Boniface and Pepin, to treat
with Pope Zacharias of the change of dynasty in
Gaul, the deposition of the *roi fainéant* Childeric III,
and the coronation of Pepin. On another occasion he
was chosen by Boniface as his messenger to Rome,
to inform the Pope of the important result of the
Council of 747, at which the Frankish bishops
acknowledged subordination to the see of Rome.
Carloman gave him considerable possessions, among
them Hohenberg (now Homburg) on the Main, and
Karlburg, opposite Karlstadt on the Main. His
favourite religious lady, Immina, described as the
daughter of Hetan, the son of the Duke Gozbert of
Kilian's time, occupied Karlburg and died there;
Burchardt himself, having secured Megingoz of
Fritzlar as his successor in the bishopric, went down
the river by boat to Hohenberg. He had intended
to retire to another of the possessions which Carloman
had given, Michelstadt in the Odenwald, but he was
taken ill at Hohenberg, and there he died in a
hermit's cave still to be seen about two miles from
Wertheim, on the railway from that place to Lohr.
Megingoz had the body of the saint conveyed to
Würzburg, and there placed near the remains of
Kilian, Colonat, and Totnan. His relics were dispersed in the Swedish War. E. makes Burchardt live
till 791, and brings the Emperor Charlemagne and
Archbishop Lul into his story; but, in fact, he died
in 754, the year before Boniface's death. Gams [1]
accepts the statement that Burchardt resigned the
see of Würzburg, and dates the accession of Megingoz as 753.

Though Burchardt was the first authentic bishop

[1] *Series Episcoporum.*

consecrated and designated as of Würzburg, he was
not the first Christian teacher there, nor was he the
first bishop associated with the place. A Scot, by
name Kilian, had laboured in those parts some
seventy years before the advent of Burchardt; with
so much success that the Pope is said to have sent
for him and consecrated him "regionary bishop" of
Eastern Franconia—Teutonic Francia as the Life of
St. Kilian describes the territory. This Life was
written about 836 by Servatus Lupus, Abbat of
Ferrières, about 150 years after Kilian's death, and
the story sounds like an echo of the early history of
Boniface himself.[1] Kilian returned to Franconia
a bishop, with Colonat as his presbyter and Totnan
as his deacon, and Würzburg in the Middle Ages
honoured him as its first bishop. As the Apostle of
the Franks he is honoured in Franconia on July 8,
the day of his martyrdom in or about the year 689.

The Life of Kilian gives an interesting hint of the
hesitation—or more than hesitation—that was felt
on the Continent as to the ministrations of Irish
wanderers. The usual cause of this was the doubt as
to the position of the episcopal order in Ireland. The
Life, on the other hand, refers it to the fact that the
Pelagian heresy had its origin with a Scot, Morgan,
whose name was graecized into Pelagius. Kilian,
we are told, felt that before he began to preach at
the place where he had ended his long journey from
Hibernia, he must purge himself from suspicion of
this heresy, and Rome was the only place where he

---

[1] In the next generation after Kilian, Corbinian, whose Life
was written by his successor Aribo, was consecrated by
Gregory II as regionary bishop of Bavaria; he settled at
Freising, which afterwards became one of Boniface's Bavarian
bishoprics.

could be absolved. To Pope John he therefore went. On his arrival at Rome he found that John was dead, and Conon, the new Pope, examined and approved him.

The names of Kilian's companions are variously spelled. The forms Colonat and Totnan are the forms used in the Würzburg Missal and in the Würzburg Breviary. An early Life tells us that the band of missionaries in its original dimensions consisted of twelve persons, Kilian and eleven others, described as his colleagues and disciples, the three priests Colonat, Gallus, and Arnuvale, the deacon Totnan, and seven others not named. The principal Life mentions incidentally that when Kilian returned to Würzburg from Rome he left Columbanus in Italy, Gallus having been left ill of fever in Germany when Kilian set out for Rome. This may suggest that Arnuvale and Columbanus are the same person. Admiration of Kilian has gone so far as to believe that the Columban and Gallus here named as companions of Kilian were the famous founder of Bobbio, who died in 615, and the famous founder of St. Gall, who died in 640. John and Conon were Popes in the years 685–687.

The number twelve was naturally a favourite number for a body of Christians, or twelve with a leader. Columba at the foundation of Hy is a palmary example. A provost and twelve monks formed a *kloster*. A metropolitan and twelve bishops was the constitution originally laid down for the provinces of London and York. A college of priests consisted of twelve capitulars and a Prelate. Distinguished teachers, as Finan and Aidan, had twelve scholars. Ecgbert, the Northumbrian trainer of missionaries in Ireland, sent out a band of twelve. A pilgrims' caravan consisted of twelve pilgrims. At Wilfrid's consecration in Paris there were twelve bishops.

There is a curious error in the Life, due evidently to a copyist who was ignorant of German. It can scarcely have been due to Servatus Lupus himself. The missionary band ended its journey from Hibernia at a town called by the natives " Wirziburg ", " which can be rendered in the Latin tongue the Castle of Men,"—*virorum castellum*. As the name was from early times taken to mean " the town of vegetables ", *virorum* is a misreading of some derivation of *viridis*, the town of green things; indeed the Bamberg MS. of the eleventh century reads *viridiariorum*.

When Kilian came back to the place called in the Life Herbipolis, a Latino-Greek version of Würzburg, he found that the Duke whom he had known had passed away, and Gozbert was now Duke. Gozbert's brother died, leaving a desirable widow, and, in accordance with gentile custom, Gozbert married her. Geilana was her name. Gozbert was a devoted worshipper of Diana, the Teutonic deity thus latinized : but after much hesitation he accepted Christ, under the guidance of Kilian. The saint then told him that his marriage was incestuous, and urged him to put away Geilana. He replied that he had not time to think how to do this, as he was called away by a military expedition.

Geilana heard of it, and raged furiously. She bribed men, who came upon the three Christian teachers engaged in worship in their chapel at night, slew them, buried them with their vestments and books that they might be supposed to have left the place, and built a stable over their grave. When the Duke came back he asked Geilana where they were, and she told him they had gone away, she did not know where.

In course of time Gozbert was slain by his soldiers,

his son was expelled, his relatives destroyed or dispersed, and the whole thing was forgotten.   But
a certain Burgunda, a religious woman, whose cell
was very near that of Kilian and his companions, had
heard the noise made by the murderers, had found
a bloody cloth, and had held her tongue till she was
dying, when she told secretly what she knew.   Ger-
trude, a daughter of King Pepin, had founded a
monastery at the place then called Karleburg, and ·
she and her presbyter Atalonga got hold of the story,
searched for the place, obtained the necessary evidence,
laid it before Boniface, then Archbishop of Mainz,
and begged him to seat one of his new bishoprics at
Würzburg in honour of Kilian.   This he did, about
the year 745.

The saint and his companions had been buried on
the level ground on the right bank of the Main, near
the centre of the present city, where now stands the
Neumünster.   When the grave was opened there was
found in it a book of the Gospels.   This interesting
relic was duly honoured.   It was put later into a binding with ivory of the tenth century, enamels, and
precious stones, the ivory representing the three saints
kneeling, the executioner with his sword having cut
off their heads apparently at one stroke.   In the air
above, the saints are ascending to heaven in a boat.
The whole is a very graceful composition.   Fig. 5
shows the cover of the book.   The altar and tomb
of the martyrs are in the west crypt of the Neumünster.   An examination of four pages of the book
shows a connexion of origin with early texts, such as
Amiatinus, and Ingoldstadt, and Canterbury as represented in libraries at Cambridge and Oxford; see fig. 6.

This costly reliquary, to call it still by the name
which it once deserved, was kept in the Cathedral

FIG. 5. ST. KILIAN'S BOOK.

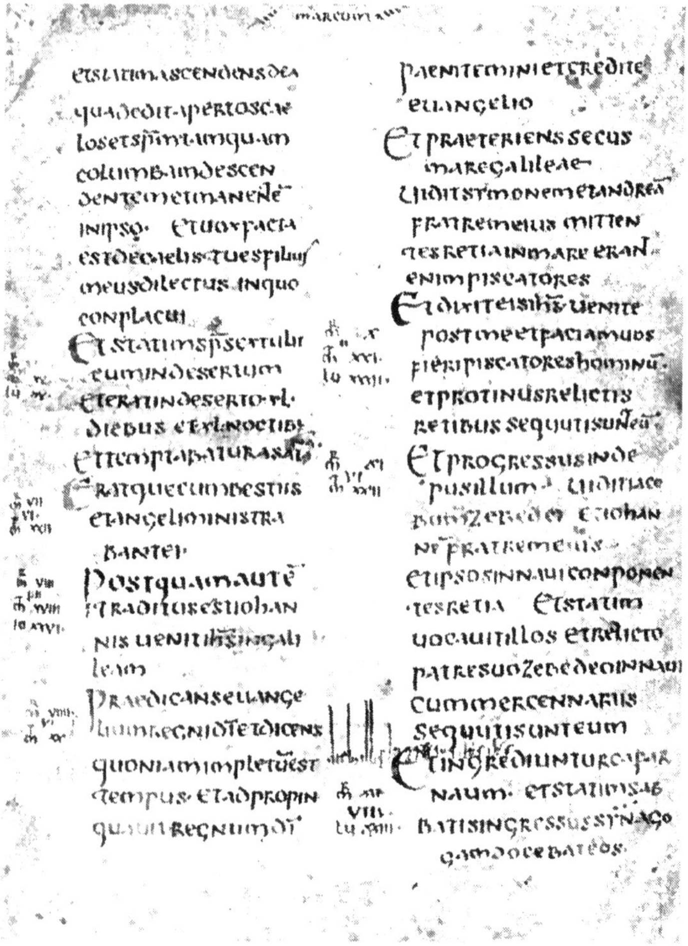

etsitim ascendens de
aquadedit apertos cæ
losetspmumqum
columbamdescen
dentemetmanene
inipso etuoxfacta
estdecælistuespfilus
meusdilectus inquo
conplacui
Et statimspsertulir
eumindeserium
eterat indeserto xl
diebus etxlnoctib;
ettemptabatura satan
Eratquecumbestus
etangeliministra
bant ei
Postquamaute
traditusestiohan
nis uenit ihsingali
leam
Praedicanseuange
liumregnideidicens
quoniam impletuest
tempus etadpropin
quauitregnumdi

paenitemini etcredite
euangelio
Et praeteriens secus
maregalileae
uiditsimonemetandrea
fratremeius mitten
tesretiainmare eran
enimpiscatores
Et dixiteishsuenite
postme etfaciamuos
fieripiscatoreshominu
etprotinusrelictis
retibus sequutisuntea
Et progressusinde
pusillum uiditiaco
bumzebedei etiohan
nefratremeius
etipsosinnaui componen
tesretia Etstatim
uocauitillos ettralicto
patresuozebedeoinnaui
cummercennariis
sequutisunteum
Etingrediunturcapar
naum etstatimsab
batisingressussynago
gamdocebateos

FIG. 6.   ST. KILIAN'S BOOK.

134

Church of Würzburg. It there served for taking the oath of homage to the prince-bishops. This, no doubt, and not, as might naturally have been supposed, its use as a Gospel book, accounts for the features of the saints being nearly worn away by centuries of kissing.

The enamels are understood to have replaced transparent rock-crystals, under which relics were placed originally. This original arrangement would naturally enhance the binding character of the oath taken.

The artist, having in mind Tertullian's words, "the blood of the martyr is the seed of the Church," makes a vine grow out of the blood of the three martyrs, on whose branches grapes hang. It is the emblem of the Church of Franconia, which grew out of their grave. We might almost suppose some connexion with the folk-saying of Franconia, "Was ist Franken?— Reben, Messgeläut, Main, und Bamberg; das ist Franken." But in early times Bamberg would not have held that position.

The ivory plaque is said to be of the tenth century, but might be of a later date. It has served as an ornament to Kilian's book since the early years of the eleventh century. The pillars and baldachin appear to have been fashioned on the Greek ivory cover of St. Burchardt's Gospel book, described below. They are exquisite pieces of work. The beautifully wrought silver borders were added in the fifteenth century under Rudolf von Scherenberg.

The handwriting is at least as early as the seventh century, which was the age of Kilian. The book shows signs of many wanderings, as would be its natural fate with a Hibernian Scot as its owner.

It may be added that in 1688 a leathern bag was found in a stone coffin in the Cathedral Church, with the inscription, *sacculus et sudarium S. Kiliani.* It contained a chalice, a reliquary, a vessel for the holy oil, and some small boxes made of bone, lead, and wood.

It has been remarked above that the ivory pillars and canopy on the cover of the Kiliansbuch appear to be fashioned on the Greek ivory cover of St. Burchardt's Gospel book. Fig. 7 shows that cover, sadly broken but evidently justifying the remark so far as the subject of the ivory is concerned, while the four Greek letters representing "Mother of God" sufficiently indicate the Greek character of the original from which the plaque is copied. This is further emphasized by a fact which the shadow of the raised work obscures. Besides the four Greek letters seen between the two figures, the name of the male saint is incised on the field at his right shoulder in four lines of two Greek letters each, Nikolaos.

There are some puzzling features in this plaque, which lead towards the conclusion that it is German work, not Greek work, and not earlier than the time of Henry the Saint and Kunigonde, if indeed it can be taken to be as early as their joint time. The Greek letters are cut with firmness and accuracy, the grouping resembles that of Greek emperors and empresses on ivory and enamel, the benediction given by the infant Christ is eastern. But the features of Mary and Nikolas, and the details of the nimbus in each case, are completely alien from any known Greek work. The vestures are decidedly well cut.

The silver plaque (fig. 8) on the rear cover is a fine piece of work, resembling a good deal of German work of 1200 or a little later. The main design, a lozenge enclosing a circle, with circles in the corners, is effective. The inscriptions, + HAIESTAS DNI, S. HATHEVS, &c., where H stands for M, are not mere

FIG. 7. BURCHARDT'S BOOK.

Fig. 8. Burchardt's Book.

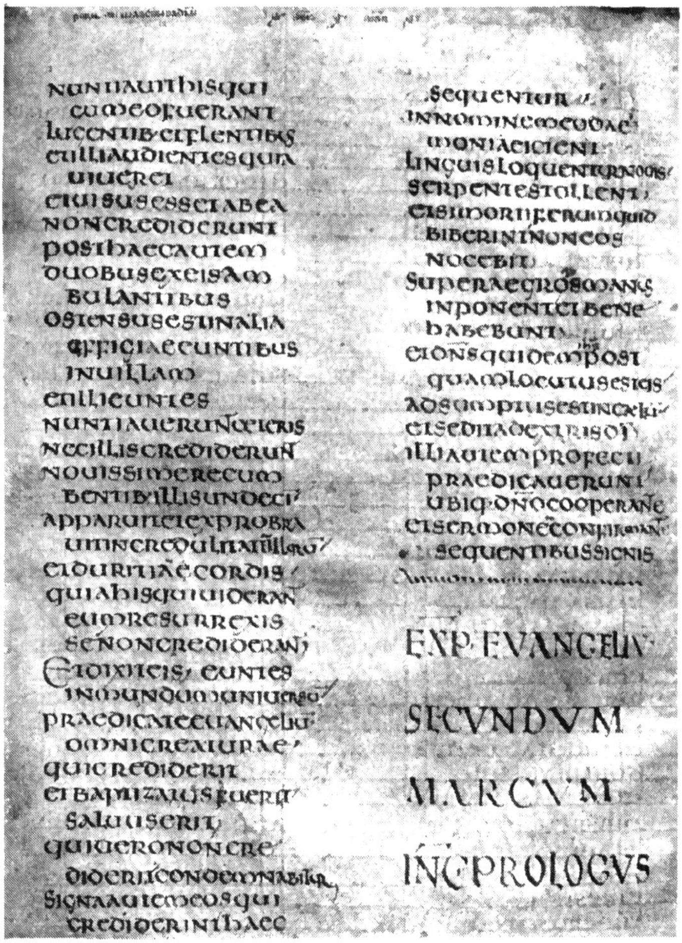
EXP EVANGELIV
SECVNDVM
MARCVM
INC PROLOGVS

Fig. 9. Burchardt's Book.

p. 137

blunders, this representation of M being not altogether unknown. Some of the earliest Gospels of the Lindisfarne and Irish types have curious forms of M; for instance, a vertical line with three short horizontal lines, and three vertical lines with a horizontal line running through them, an H in fact with a third vertical line in the middle. It may be remarked that the order of the evangelists St. Luke and St. Mark differs from the order on the cover of the Kiliansbuch. Much might be written on that, a subject in which Bede himself was interested.

While the main design and the arabesque fillings and borders are decidedly good, the cutting out of the interstices from the plate of silver on which it was incised is badly done, as will be seen at a glance. Here again the benediction is of the eastern type.

The text (fig. 9) appears at first sight to have been carelessly written, with erasures, insertions, and corrections. But it is in fact of the very highest interest. It was originally copied correctly, in a rough but good hand, from some early text of marked type. A later hand altered the readings to bring the text into accordance with one of a more generally accepted character.

The page shown in fig. 9 has several very interesting examples of this process of alteration. It begins with the third word of verse 10 of the last chapter of St. Mark, *nuntiavit*, "she told them." Taking the alterations in order, we have in line 12 the seventh letter, *a*, nearly erased with pumice, altering the original *effigioe* into correct Latin, *effigie*. The original reading is that of the Lindisfarne Gospels. The first letter of this line, *e*, is not an alteration, it is in the original hand, written over a letter erased by the first hand, and written when the whole was written,

not later.   What the erased letter was is not quite
certain; it ought to have been an *a, aeffigiae* being the
reading of one early text; *aecclesia* for *ecclesia* is of
common occurrence.   Lines 20 and 21 are of remarkable interest.   The English text is "He upbraided
them with their unbelief and hardness of heart".   The
original reading had "their unbelief and hardness of
heart" in the dative, *incredulitati illorum et duritiae
cordis*; this reading is that of the Corpus Christi text
which generally agrees with Amiatinus, and also that
of the Harleian text of the sixth or seventh century
with which this Würzburg text appears specially to
agree.   The alterer of the text had to put the dative
into the accusative.   To do this, he added three little
horizontal lines to the *i* of *incredulitati*, thus making
it into a very poor E, quite unlike the usual E,
and above it he placed a mark of the omission [1] of an
m, and so manufactured *incredulitatem*.   Going next
to *duritiae* he put the omission mark over the *a*, manu-
facturing *duritiam*, and instead of pumicing out the
now superfluous *e*, he put a dot above it and below, to
signify that it was to be treated as non-existent.   Those
who are curious in such matters will see that in the
mark of omission over the manufactured E there is
a round dot, half hid at the middle of the horizontal
stroke.   In line 9 of the second column *to* would
appear to have been omitted from *aegrotos*, "the sick."
But it is not so.   The original *aegros* was the reading

---

[1] It should be specially noted that the mark of omission used
by the first hand is quite different from that used by the alterer.
The two occur in the same line.   The older of the two is well
shown in lines 12 and 18 of column 2.   It must be added that
the mark of omission used in the single leaf agrees with that of
the alterer, not with that of the original hand.   It shows, however, the same tendency to lie more than is usually the case
over the place where the omitted letter would have been.

of the text copied by the first hand. It is the reading of the Book of Kells, of the Oxford Gospels of St. Augustine, and of other early texts. The alterer's favourite text had *aegrotos*. In line 12 of the second column, the original text has *dns, dominus*, without *Jesus*; the alterer's text had *Jesus* after *quidem*, "the Lord Jesus," the usual reading, and he wrote the *ihs* above the line. In line 19 of this column we have a curious reading in the original hand, *sermone* for *sermonem*, altered into correct Latin by the alterer, who placed his own mark of omission over the space where the *m* should come, that being his habit. On the face of it, one would say that the first hand had his attention occupied with ablatives at this point, and he unconsciously wrote an ablative here. But, curiously enough, we find *sermone* in the Harleian MS. already mentioned, and also in the famous St. Germain MS. Finally, with Kells, Lindisfarne, and others, again including the Harleian MS., our first hand did not end with *Amen*, and the alterer did not insert it ; probably he was working from a text which itself had it not.

We may venture to take a rather bold step here. The physically immense codex known as Amiatinus is the pandect (the whole Bible) taken from Wearmouth by Abbat Ceolfrid as a present to the Pope in the year 716. Bede saw him off, and wrote an account of the parting scene. The Amiatinus was only one of three great pandects belonging to the twin monasteries, and when it was taken away there remained one at Wearmouth and one at Jarrow. These have totally disappeared. But some time ago one great leaf of an old codex was found in Northumbria, and everything points to its being a leaf of one of the huge pandects. Now when the page

shown in fig. 9 is set side by side with this vast
page of old parchment, the sameness of hand and of
detail is so very evident that the observer is forced
to suppose that the Würzburg book is copied from
the pandect of which this is one page, and copied by
a hand trained under Bede in the scriptorium of the
monastery.[1]   Lul and Burchardt, two students trained
in the school of Malmesbury, went out together to
join Boniface.   Lul had some very close connexion
with Bede and his monastery.[2]   Burchardt, by Lul's
influence, obtained this Northumbrian treasure, kept
it always by him, took it with him to the cave in
which he ended his life, it went back to Würzburg
with his body, and it has ever since been treasured
there.   The writing, as noted above, is rough.

If this be so, then we have not only one leaf of
the great pandect, we have a complete and careful
copy of the four Gospels of the pandect, with all
their distinctive readings, written by one who learned
to write from the pandect itself and reproduced its
every letter. The connexion of other manuscripts of
the Bonifatian period with Wearmouth and Jarrow
is suggested in Chapter IX.

In order to see these beautiful and most interesting
books the visitor should present himself at the Old
Library in Würzburg, to the south of the Dom, at
nine o'clock in the morning.   He will be received
with a ready welcome, and will never regret his visit.

There are two quaint examples of stealing the
praises of Kilian and crediting them to other saints,

---

[1] Unfortunately the page of the pandect contains a portion of
the Third Book of Kings (in our nomenclature 1 Kings xi. 29 to
xii. 18), so that it cannot be tested by Burchardt's book, which
is not a pandect.

[2] See page 303, and the examples given in Chapter XIII of
requests for manuscripts from Wearmouth, &c.

robbing Peter to pay Paul as did Horatio Pallavicini of Babraham. The Breviary of the monastery of Lambach had these lines :—

> Longe ab insulis pars bona maris
> Ad fontem rediit teque requirit,
> Iesu, viventium fontem aquarum.
> Maris fons est Deus, pars *Kilianus*,
> Quem procul patriis sitit ab oris,
> Cervi more suum tendit ad haustum
> *Scotorum* insulae felix alumnus.

The Breviary of the monastery of St. Florian, specially honouring Kilian's presbyter Colonat, another form of whose name is Coloman, boldly reads *Colomannus* in place of *Kilianus*. The Breviary of the Cathedral Church of Eichstätt is more than bold, it is audacious. For *Kilianus* it reads *Willibaldus*, and for *Scotorum* it reads *Anglorum*. An Englishman rejoices in the honour done to Willibald, but regrets the theft.

CHAPTER IX

Foundation of Fulda.—Life of Sturmi.—Boniface's application to the Pope for confirmation of Fulda.—The Pope's
assent.—Fulda of to-day.—The Codex Fuldensis and other
MSS.—The Life of Leoba.—Care bestowed on relics by Rabanus.

Some considerable time after Boniface had by
means of Wigbert's skilled labours brought the
monastery of Fritzlar into an exemplary state of
discipline, he desired to extend his monastic machinery,
and determined to operate towards the south-east, in
the direction of his Bavarian work. This brings us
to the foundation of the greatest and most famous
of his ecclesiastical institutions, the renowned Abbey
of Fulda. As we pass in imagination from Fritzlar
to Fulda, we naturally follow the course which
Boniface's pioneers took under the guidance of a man
who was to make a deep mark upon the history of
Christianity in those parts. This was Sturmi.

The *Life of Sturmi*, the first abbat of Fulda, is
a work of the utmost value and interest. It tells
in contemporary language, and with full local detail,
the story of the foundation of the most important
of Boniface's ecclesiastical establishments.

Sturmi was one of the boys who had been entrusted
to Boniface's care by Bavarian families, when he was
leaving that district after setting its ecclesiastical
affairs in order. He put the boy Sturmi under the
charge of the Anglo-Saxon Wigbert, the first abbat
of Fritzlar. There the boy learned his letters and

Holy Scripture, and in due course was ordained deacon and priest. He was set to work at the evangelization of the pagans. After some three years of this work as priest, he confided to Boniface that his mind was bent upon a cloistered life. This gave Boniface an opportunity. He approved of Sturmi's desire, and made practical use of it. He determined to make Sturmi the means of founding a great monastery further to the south-east than Fritzlar, to serve as a centre of energy for the districts towards Bavaria. With this in view, Boniface bade Sturmi proceed to investigate the recesses of the great beech-forest called from the prevailing trees Buchonia. This beech-forest occupied a large part of Central Germany, and there was more than one trade route through it. Sturmi's business was to find a place where there was good water and a large expanse of fairly level ground, fit for being brought under cultivation when the trees had been removed. A picturesque French writer[1] on the life of Boniface, who has also written on the legends of the early Merovingians, reminds us that the forest of Buchonia was celebrated in Germanic legends, and also in the legends of the Franks; it was the scene of the assassination of Sigebert, the King of Cologne, on the instigation of his son.

The two rivers, Edder and Fulda, meet at a point not very far above Cassel, through which city they run as the Fulda, to become eventually the Weser. The valleys of these two rivers are divided by the range of hills called the Rhön-Gebirge. Fritzlar was connected with the valley of the Edder, and Boniface aimed at finding a site in the valley of the

[1] Professor G. Kurth, of Liège.

Fulda, on the other side of the Rhön-Gebirge. Sturmi, with two companions, no doubt went down the Edder to the spot where it joined the Fulda, and then turned up the course of the latter river and pushed his way, in a boat, through the dense forest of beech, of which the Rhón-Gebirge formed the west boundary. After three days' journey through the forest, they came upon a place which seemed exactly suited to their purpose. The two companions remained there while Sturmi went back to Boniface to report their success. The saint, however, thought it was too near to the Saxons, so dangerous to Christian enterprise, and he bade them carry their exploration further. They obeyed, and pushed on up stream for another three days, when they reached the spot where a little stream, the Lüder,[1] joined the Fulda. Not having found anything suitable, they returned to the place which they had previously selected. Boniface summoned Sturmi to Fritzlar and received him with special kindness; dispensed him from fasting and gave him a dinner; and then told him he was quite sure that there would be found a place prepared by God in the forest, and he must go and find it. Sturmi returned to his companions, who had remained in the place of their first selection. That selection, it may be remarked, was in itself a very good one, for on that very site was founded as early as 769 the great and famous abbey of Hersfeld. From this place Sturmi went on alone; no longer, therefore, in a boat, but riding an ass. On his way he crossed one of the trade tracks through the forest, leading from Thuringia to Mainz,

[1] There is still a village called Lüdermund, a few leagues short of the present Fulda.

and at the point where this track crossed the river Fulda he found some Slavs bathing in the stream. They were rude and menacing, but they did him no real harm; the worst that he had to suffer was their bad smell.

On the fourth day of his journey he crossed another beaten track, a foot-way, known as Ortesweg, at the place where a little stream, the Giesel, joins the Fulda, only a few kilometres from the place he was seeking. Here he met with a man leading a horse, who knew the district well. The part of the forest in which they met was the Eichlohe, or the oak-wood. The stranger guided him through this to the point at which the Fulda breaks its way through a rocky gorge, and it was no use going further. Sturmi returned with the man, and the next day they parted. Something made Sturmi go up the Fulda once more; and then, probably because he was not occupied in talking to a companion, he saw that he had twice passed without noticing it the ideal spot. The site of Fulda was found.

Sturmi went with great joy to tell Boniface of his success. He found the saint at Seleheim. The saint sent him and his companions back to the place, and himself went to Carloman to beg for a grant of the territory, a fairly level space some four miles in diameter, with the river running through the middle of it. Carloman made the grant, and sent commissioners to request neighbouring proprietors to add yet further territory, which they did.

Armed with the grant, Sturmi and seven other monks entered upon the work of clearing the forest on the 12th of January, 744. Two months later Boniface came with an army of workers, and began to build a church of stone, which he dedicated to the Saviour. He himself retired to a hill which commands the valley, where he spent a week in retreat; and to this little hermitage, on the hill called from him Bischofsberg, he used to come every year to recover from the fatigues of his life. He sent Sturmi to study the monastic rule at Rome and at Monte Cassino, and after two years Sturmi came back prepared to raise the tone of the monks to the highest pitch of the regular life. This he effected, and before his death the community consisted of no less than four hundred monks. Of these something will be said later on (Chapter XIX).

It will have been noticed that the river-systems had much influence in determining both routes and sites of monasteries. The importance of the river-systems of these particular parts is emphasized by a striking monumental fountain in Cassel, known as the Löwen monument. Four female figures surround the fountain, symbolizing the four principal rivers which form the Weser. Cassel itself is on the Fulda; the Werra joins the Fulda at Münden, and from that point the river is called Weser. The four rivers symbolized are the Edder, the figure holding a vase; the Werra, the figure holding a net and taking a good fish out of it; the Fulda, the figure holding an ancient oar; and the Lahn, a vase.

It was not till very late in his life that Boniface applied to the Pope for a formal confirmation of his monastery of Fulda. We have the terms of his application,[1] and the terms of the Pope's reply, both dated in 751.

"To the most reverend father, most loved lord,

[1] Ep. 86; A D. 751.

master to be venerated with fear and honour, endowed with the privilege of apostolic honour, exalted by the insignia of the pontificate of the apostolic see, to Zacharias, Boniface the humble, your servant though unworthy and last of all, yet Germanic legate most devoted, the welfare desirable of love that cannot decay.

" With suppliant prayers I beseech the sanctity of your fatherly piety, that you will with ready mind kindly receive this presbyter of mine, the bearer of my letter, whose name is Lul. For he has some secrets of mine which he should deliver only to your piety, some things to say to you by word of mouth, some things to show to you noted by letter, some needs of mine to ask about; and then to bring back to me the answer and counsel of your fatherliness from the authority of holy Peter, prince of the Apostles, for the solace of my old age; so that when all which I send has been heard and considered, if anything which I have done be pleasing to you I may improve upon it, but if, as is to be feared, there be anything which is displeasing, by the precept of your holy apostolate I may deserve indulgence or perform the penance due.

" For the predecessor of your predecessor, Gregory of memory to be venerated, when he ordained me unworthy and sent me to preach the word of faith to the German nations, bound me by an oath that I should become an aider and helper to canonical and just bishops and priests, in word, in deed, in feeling; this I have endeavoured by divine grace to fulfil; but false priests, hypocrites, seducers of the people, I should either bring by correction to the way of salvation or should decline and abstain from their

communion; this in part I observed, in part I have
been unable to keep and fulfil. In the spirit
I have fulfilled my oath, for my soul has not come
into their fellowship and counsel. In the body
I have not been able entirely to keep myself clear
of them when I have come to the Frank prince under
pressure of ecclesiastical business;[1] I have found there
such as I have been unwilling to find. Still, I have
not communicated with them in the holy Communion
of the Body of Christ.

"The apostolic pontiff aforesaid further charged
me that I should report to the pontiff of the apostolic
see the life and manners of the peoples whom I had
visited. This I trust in God that I have done.

"With regard to the information which in accordance with the promises of the Franks I gave to your
holiness some time ago about the archbishops and
their seeking the pallium from the Roman Church,
I beg the indulgence of the apostolic see. For they
have delayed to fulfil their promises, and the matter
is still put off and being discussed, and it is not known
what they are prepared to perform thereupon. But
according to my will my promise would have been
fulfilled.

"Further, there is a woodland spot in a desert of
the vastest solitude in the midst of the nations to
whom we have preached. Here we have built a
monastery and appointed monks to live under the
Rule of the holy father Benedict, men of strict
abstinence, without wine or stronger drink or flesh,
without servants, content with their own labour of
their own hands. This spot I have with lawful
labour acquired by means of men religious and God-

---

[1] See more on this point in another of Boniface's letters, p. 178.

fearing, especially Carlman, formerly prince of the Franks, and have dedicated it in honour of the Holy Saviour.[1] In this place I propose, with the consent of your piety, to restore my body wearied with old age by resting for a short time or for a few days, and after death to lie. For four peoples to whom by the grace of God we have spoken the word of Christ are severally known to dwell around this place, to whom so long as I live and have my faculties I can with your intercession be useful. For I desire by the help of your prayers, with the grace of God accompanying, to persevere in the friendship of the Roman Church and in your service among the Germanic races to whom I have been sent, and to obey your precept, as it is written[2]: 'Hear the judgement of your father, children beloved, and do thereafter, that ye may be safe'; and elsewhere— 'He that honoureth his father liveth a longer life'; and again—'Honour thy father, that a blessing may come upon thee from the Lord; for the blessing of the father establisheth the houses of sons.'"

The remainder of this letter is lost; and it has long been lost, for in the Carlsruhe MS. of Boniface's letters the page following these last words is left blank, as though the copyist hoped to find somewhere

---

[1] All churches were dedicated to the Saviour. Partly to distinguish one church from another, and chiefly to indicate the affection of benefactors for various saints, the names of saints were associated with the name of the Saviour and the churches were called by their names. St. Peter and St. Paul was the favourite dedication in the earliest Anglo-Saxon times, as in later Anglo-Saxon times was All Saints. To the Saviour the mother church of Rome was dedicated, the Lateran, as was the mother church of England (as contrasted with Britain) at Canterbury.

[2] Ecclus. iii. 1, 6, 8, 9.

the concluding parts. If after Dümmler's exhaustive
inquiries it is allowable to make a suggestion, it
seems not at all unlikely that the remainder of the
letter consisted of the list of questions to be given
to the Pope which in the opening paragraph Boniface
tells the Pope he had given to Lul, the bearer of the
letter. If that suggestion is correct, the Pope's
detailed answers in his next letter show us what
the questions were. In this connexion it must be
noted that the Pope answers Boniface's letter paragraph by paragraph, and passes immediately from
his reply about Fulda to answer the written questions
which Lul had brought. The answer about Fulda
was as follows [1]:—

"You have asked that the venerable monastery
should by privilege of the apostolic see be confirmed to you, which you have founded and built
in a most vast solitude, in the midst of the peoples
to whom you preach, and have dedicated in honour
of our Saviour God. This, in agreement with your
wishes, we have arranged. For it is a congruous
thing that a preacher of the divine ministry [2], and
an excellent minister, should attain to his desires
and carry on the good work begun even unto the
end, as it is written in the Lord's precept : ' He that
continueth to the end, the same shall be saved,' and
' Blessed is that servant whom his lord when he cometh
shall find so doing. Of a truth I say unto you, that
he will make him ruler over all that he hath.' "

Fortunately we possess a fragment of the Pope's document of confirmation ; indeed, there are two copies
of the fragment, with some slight discrepancies.

[1] Ep. 87 ; Nov. 4, 751.
[2] *Ministeru*, possibly for *mysterii*.

Each copy gives the important parts of the document. If the name Bochonia or Boconia or Bothonia still exists, it has escaped the notice of a recent inquirer; the probabilities are evidently in favour of the *c* as against the *t* in the various readings[1]:—

"Whereas thou hast asked of us that a monastery of the Saviour, constructed by thee, situated in the place called Bochonia, near the bank of the river Fulda,[2] should receive the honour of a privilege from the apostolic see, so that, being under the jurisdiction of our holy Church, whose servant by God's guidance we are, it be subject to the jurisdictions of no other church; therefore we, favouring thy pious desires, carry into effect what thou hast asked. By our authority we prohibit every bishop of what church soever other than the apostolic see from having any authority in the said monastery. No one shall presume to celebrate masses there except on the invitation of the Abbat. It shall remain undisturbed, under apostolic privilege. Whosoever, prelate of a church or what dignity soever, shall violate this decree, let him be anathema."

Fulda is now the seat of a bishopric and the Abbey Church is the Cathedral Church. The old church was properly orientated, lying at the east side of the monastic enclosure, the body of the church extending westwards within the enclosure. At the east side of the monastery was a large open space. When the church became a Cathedral Church, a large nave was built out into this open space, with the great west door, as one would naturally call it, at the extreme

---

[1] Ep. 89; Nov. 4, 751.
[2] The other copy has Vultaha, which looks more like the primitive name.

east. The old east end of the Abbey Church, with
its *confessio* and the altar and tomb of St. Boniface,
was preserved and left as it was, an external wall
being built so near to the altar and tomb that only as
it were a small Jesus Chapel is now left behind the
high altar of the new church, which is at the west
end, not the east end, of the present Cathedral Church.

The visitor to the shrine loses sight of this when he
comes into the presence of the tomb. He faces east
to examine it, and he faces west to examine the really
fine design and colouring of the three modern windows
in the containing wall to the west. These windows
are in the form of a large Romanesque arch in the
centre and a smaller similar arch on each side of the
central arch. The central window has a remarkable
representation of the shrine with the saint's body
being carried on its last journey from Mainz to Fulda,
preceded by Archbishop Lul in fullest canonicals, a
rich crimson chasuble and low crimson mitre with
jewelled circle and cross. On the window to the right
hand is shown St. Leoba dying, an aged archbishop
reading from a richly bound book, a monk with a rich
censer, and two nuns completing the scene. In the
account of the Life of St. Leoba, at page 170, the reason
of this scene being depicted will be apparent. On the
other side is the death of Sturmi, the saint holding
a golden cross and being attended by six monks.

The relics are in the treasury, set in magnificent
receptacles of silver richly gilt. Fig. 10 shows near
the bottom the top of the skull of the saint, and the
pastoral staff of ivory, about 5 ft. 10 inches long.
Up the middle of fig. 11 is the blade of the fatal
sword, fitted a hundred years ago with an ivory handle
and a guard, with the inscription " Mucro quo occisus

FIG. 10.   THE SKULL AND STAFF.

Fig. 11. The Sword.

·

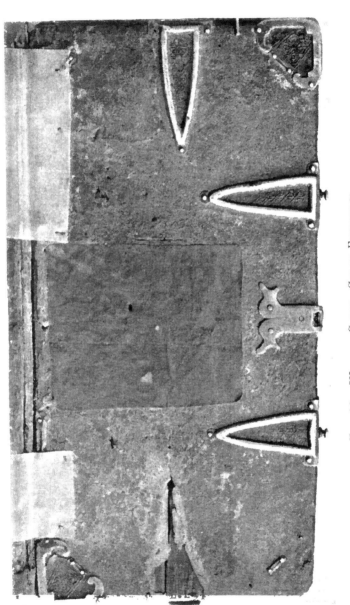

est a Frisiis anno DCCLV Bonifacius Archiepiscopus
et Martyr Patronus[1] Fuldensis. Ornatus 1791."
In a corresponding receptacle there are relics of
Leoba and other saints. There is also a reliquary
of Leoba showing her full face with large eye-holes
and a tidy nose-hole, presumably of wax, with a
beautiful open crown of gold and at top a cross of
brilliant diamonds. Among many other treasures is
a life-size silver statue of Boniface, which is carried,
along with these relics, in the great annual pageant
procession.

The Bonifatian manuscripts are in the Landes-
bibliothek, at a little distance on the north (apparent
south) side of the Abbey Church. As we shall see
when we come to the martyrdom of the saint, they
were brought from the site of his death. One of
them claims to have been in his hands when he received
his death-stroke, the sword cutting deep into the 140
leaves of parchment. A writer of about the year 800,
a presbyter of St. Martin's, Utrecht, which was closely
connected with Boniface, tells us that he inquired on
the spot, and found a very decrepit old woman who
said on oath that she saw Boniface killed, and that
when he was about to receive on his head the death-
stroke he interposed the book he was reading. Stains
on the parchment are said to be human blood.

The most interesting of these manuscripts is the
Codex Fuldensis, an early authority for the text of
the Latin New Testament. Fig. 12 shows the thick
wooden binding with plaques of silver and a silver
clasp. These are all of them real Anglo-Saxon work.

---

[1] The patron of the town or city of Fulda is St Sulpicius,
an archaic figure of whom is seen in descending to the tomb
of Boniface from the apparent south.

The plaques are filled with very pretty Anglo-Saxon interlacing work; the clasp is two dragons' heads back to back. The MS. has a large number of marginal notes on the Epistle of St. James, all written in an early Anglo-Saxon hand, Anglian runes being used instead of the usual marks of reference from text to notes.

Ernst Ranke published his book on the Codex Fuldensis in 1868 (British Museum 3021 c. 6). He takes the view that the book is of the sixth century, of the date of Victor, Bishop of Capua. He finds in it the three contemporary hands of Victor, his scribe, and the corrector, all having worked at the codex at its origin; the corrector was probably Victor himself. Some two centuries later he believes it fell into Anglo-Saxon hands, about the middle of the eighth century, when the Anglo-Saxon glosses on St. James were introduced. Later again, in the ninth century, he thinks that yet another Anglo-Saxon hand worked at it. From curious samenesses in small errors Ranke associates the text closely with Amiatinus, believing that at least they had a common origin.

The earlier part of the book is the Harmony of the Four Evangelists. Its opening sentence is "In nomine Patris et filii et spiritus sancti. Incipit prae-fatio Victoris Episcopi Capuae." The later part con-tains Epistles, the Epistle of St. James being headed in the unmistakable rough capitals, "Seq epist sci Iacobi ad dispersos."

It is clear that if Boniface copied his quotations of scripture direct from a manuscript, he used another manuscript than this. For example, in 1 Pet. iv. 8, where the codex has the ordinary Vulgate reading, "Ante omnia autem mutuam in vobismetipsis cari-

FIG. 13. PAGE OF CODEX FULDENSIS.

tatem continuam habentes," Boniface writes, "Ante omnia mutuam in invicem caritatem habete." In 1 Cor. vi. 19, the codex has with one exception the ordinary Vulgate reading, "An nescitis quoniam membra vestra templum est [v. sunt] spiritus sancti," but Boniface writes, "An nescitis quia corpora vestra templa sunt spiritus sancti." In other cases, the codex has, "Quae praeparavit Deus his qui diligunt illum," Boniface writes, "Quod praeparavit Deus diligentibus se"; the codex "non sublime sapere", Boniface "non superbe sapere"; and so on. The text used by Boniface, other than the codex, Ranke was prepared to prove to have been independent of Jerome's recension. One very curious case he discovered in the Bonifatian epistle last quoted. Boniface quotes a Petrine saying, "Sobrii estote et vigilate et excitamini." This is not in Amiatinus, nor in the collection of old texts, nor in the Sixtine-Clementine edition, nor in the original text of the codex; but it is in the margin of the codex in the *second* Anglo-Saxon hand. The guess may be hazarded that the ninth-century Anglo-Saxon hand copied it into the margin from Boniface's own letter, a copy of which had by that time reached Fulda.

In fig. 13 one of the pages of St. James is shown. The runes will be seen on this page, used as references to the marginal notes. Some details in connexion with these runes will be found on pages 157, 158.

The text contains verses 18 to 26 of the first chapter of St. James, beginning with the closing words of verse 18, "initium aliquod creaturae eius," "a kind of first-fruits of his creatures," and ending with the first half of verse 26, "si quis autem putat se religiosum esse," "if any man among you seem to be religious"

A.V., "thinketh himself to be" R.V. The page was
selected for being photographed on account of the
large number of runic letters used in it. It has, however, one marked reading, "in lege perfecta," to har-
monize with *in speculo,* in place of "in legem perfectam". A glance at the MS. shows that this is not a
case of the usual omission of a final *m* ; the final *m* is
clearly given elsewhere on this page, and the MS. is
almost entirely free from contractions. *In lege perfecta
libertatis* is no doubt the real Vulgate reading. *In
legem perfectam* would seem more natural, "looketh into
the perfect law," and it is the exact translation of the
Greek ; but while that reading does occur, it has not
reliable authority in ancient texts. Bede in his com-
mentary on St. James reads *in lege perfectae libertatis,*
and bases his comment on that reading ; it is liberty,
he says, that is in itself perfect, the law not making
anything perfect. Bede's reading has a certain amount
of authority, and it was the reading of the Sixtine
Vulgate.

Boniface did not quote from St. James till after the
year 742. In the next year or two he quoted three
times from his Epistle. This fairly points to the
Codex Fuldensis having been taken to Germany in
its English binding, by one of the English party who
went out to help him. The binding makes it
probable, the runic notation makes it practically
certain, that the precious manuscript came from
Northumbria. If it is the fact that Lul studied at
Jarrow under Bede, it may be that Fulda possesses
a treasure which Bede and Lul handled and studied
together, and it is quite conceivable that in the notes,
that is, in those by the first hand, we have the writing
of Bede himself. Taking the note in the middle of

the top of the page in fig. 13 as an example of the first hand, the writing is at least of the same school as the current script of the note attributed to Bede in the Durham MS. of Cassiodorus (Palaeographical Society, vol. ii, pl. 164). On the two hands in the note on our text much might be said. The note itself is as follows :—

"per generationem creaturae eius id est predicate euangelium omni creature id est omni creato in baptismo | nos sumus initium aliquod per passionem et resurrectionem Christi id est primi nouissimi . . ."

It has been said above that the fact of runic letters being used by the annotator may be taken as certain proof of his connexion with Northumbria. Of all the runic inscriptions in this island, only one word is found outside the Anglian parts, a name of ten letters ending in *lheard* on a stone at Dover. The tradition that Lul studied under Bede points to his connexion with the district in which runes were freely used for incision on stones, as on the memorials of the earliest Anglian nuns of Hilda's time in the cemetery at Hartlepool, on the Bewcastle Cross, &c. But we have more direct evidence of Lul's acquaintance with runes, and we cannot say the same of any other person connected with Boniface. At the end of Lul's letter to an abbess,[1] No. 98 of the collection of Bonifatian Epistles, he writes out at full length the names of all of the runic letters, in the order of the English a b c, not in the order of the runic futhork.[2] Indeed he adds names of unknown runes to make complete

---

[1] The editors accept this letter as Lul's. It was certainly written by a man carefully trained in Aldhelm's marked style.

[2] So called because the first six letters are f u th o r k.

correspondence with the English a b c, ending his list
with *ian*, *zar*, evidently for *y*, *z*.

Of the ten marks of reference on the page shown
in fig. 13, all can be taken as runic letters. The
reference mark at the lowest line is *ilc*, a known rune,
having sometimes the force of *x*. The semicircle
should be two straight lines at an angle, like a V, the
original runes being used for cutting on wooden tallies,
and therefore avoiding curves. We may understand
that the second and third reference marks are Lul's
ian and *zar*, not runes of the *futhork*. · The *y* errs
against the rule stated above, and the *z* errs against
the rule that the whole runic "alphabet" does not
contain one horizontal line, the wooden tallies being
made of Baltic timber, which splinters at the ends of
incisions along the grain. The fourth rune is *k*, not
the usual Anglian form. The last but one, which
looks like the last turned upside down, is one of the
forms in which *k* appears on the earliest runic inscriptions in Northumbria. The five remaining marks are
common Anglian runes. The one next above the
angulated B is *wen*, corresponding to *qu* (*w*); Lul
gives it a highly instructive name, significative of its
origin, *quirun*.

The same epistle (ep. 98) has another curious connexion with Bede, or rather with a legend about
Bede. Lul's letter ends with a number of triplets
of initial letters, with their interpretation. The legend
seems to suggest that Bede was specially skilled in
the interpretation of the single letters in the Roman
inscriptions which in his time abounded in Northumbria, and that he had a habit of exercising his
ingenuity in that way, quite possibly a habit of
training the ingenuity of his students by setting them

problems of this character. The interesting point is
that the triplets recorded in the Bede legend appear
in Lul's letter; and while Lul has more triplets than
the legend, they all bear in the same direction as the
legend. Bede, the story goes, was in Rome, and
was found by a Roman studying certain triplets of
letters on an iron gate, P P P. S S S. R R R.
F F F. The Roman said to him, "What are you
looking at, English bull?" Bede's reply was, "I
am looking at what you should be ashamed of," and
he read off four Latin sentences, the words of which
commenced with the twelve letters on the gate. The
Romans were so much struck by Bede's readiness and
ability that they saluted him as Venerable, a title
which the Senate afterwards confirmed. The visit to
Rome was the unhistorical part of the legend. The
triplets in Lul's letter are R R R. P P P. F F F.
M M M. U U U. A A A. The extensions which
Lul gives are " rex (with a variant *regnum*) romanorum
ruit pater patriae profectus est ferro frigore fame
monitum monumentum mortuus est uictor uitalis
ueniet aurum a nobis aufert ". Curiously enough there
is in a manuscript of the eighth century at Würzburg,
containing homilies of Jerome on the Old Testament,
an entry very similar to this, as follows:—

> Venit Victor Vincens mundum
> Rumpit Regnum Romanorum
> Fert Famem Frangit Romam
> Aufert Aurum Argentumque.

Is it too bold to suggest that this manuscript in
Burchardt's own city has a tale to tell of yet another
link between the two Malmesbury students, Lul and
Burchardt? They were possibly brothers, see cp. 49.

Two or three venturesome suggestions have been made in connexion with the above description of the Codex Fuldensis. Yet one more may be hazarded. There are some points in the general style of the writing, and in the form of typical letters, which may suggest that this codex was so early an acquisition at Wearmouth and Jarrow that it played a part, as exemplar, in the formation of the local style of writing in the scriptorium of the twin monasteries. There is nothing in the date of the manuscript (sixth century) or in the place of its origin (Capua) to conflict with the idea that it may have been one of the books acquired by Benedict Biscop, the founder of the twin monasteries, on one of his visits to the continent of Europe in search of ecclesiastical treasures. At the age of twenty five he went to Rome to visit the tombs of the Apostles Peter and Paul. He was again in Rome at the time when Theodore was selected to fill the office of Archbishop of Canterbury in 668. He came to England with Theodore and for two years taught at Canterbury as Abbat of St. Augustine's. Then for a third time he went to Rome, to purchase books of sacred literature. Coming back loaded with treasures, he passed up to Northumbria, where he built the twin monasteries and endowed them with his manuscripts.

The next book to be inspected is that whose first pages are shown in fig. 14, the book of the martyrdom, with the sword-cut passing through the right arm of the ornamental cross at the top of the first page. The formation of the initial letter on the second page with three fishes naturally suggests a Lombardic origin, and this feature persists throughout the 140 pages of the MS., all of the letters of

IN·NOMI·NE
DI
SVMMI

INCP SVBS SEQVENTIBVS
LIBRO QVI NVNCVPA
TVR SYNONIMA ID EST

Multorum... ... ... ISIDORVS ...

the alphabet being found in capitals formed of fishes. This very easy and very shapely style of capital letters lasted long. In a remarkably fine Gradual once in use at St. Augustine's Abbey at Bristol, the capital letters d and q are formed each of two fishes, a tail of one forming the top of a d in one case and the bottom of a q in the other.

That the Lombardic attribution is correct may be gathered from a very interesting entry at the end of the book, " In honore Domini nostri Iesu Christi Ego Ragyndrudis ordinavi librum istum quicumque legerit coniuro per deum vivum ut pro me orare dignemini," " In honour of our Lord Jesus Christ I Ragyndrudis have arranged this book. All you who shall read it I conjure by the living God that ye deign to pray for me." Now Ratchis, King of the Lombards, who retired into a cloister, had a daughter called Radrudis ; it is certain that Ragyndrudis was in those days of clipping syllables shortened for use in some way, and Radrudis is the obvious way of shortening it. A strong argument in this direction is found in the fact that one of the preceding Lombard kings in the same century was named Raginbert, and portions of names ran in families. She followed her father's example, and, with her mother, went into cloister at St. Petronilla de Plombiariola early in 750, a place not far from Monte Cassino. Just about that time Sturmi was in Italy studying the regular life at Monte Cassino, a monastery closely connected with Boniface in more than one intimate way, as may be seen at page 146. It is completely reasonable to suppose that Radrudis sent this book to Boniface, who had himself been hospitably entertained at the Lombard Court in the time of King Liutprand.

The book contains a number of treatises, some fifteen in all. Only two need be named here, the sixth on the list, " Fides edita S. Ambrosii de Spiritu Sancto," " St. Ambrose on the Holy Ghost," and the eleventh, "S. Ambrosii de bono mortis," " St. Ambrose on the good of death." Either of these may well have been the subject of Boniface's study at the time when the murdering heathen burst upon him, the one in preparation for the Confirmation on the next day, the other because he knew that in one way or another death must come upon him soon.

There remain the interesting little Irish Gospels, two pages of which are shown in fig. 15, and another page in fig. 16. Of the Irish character of the original from which it was copied, there can evidently be no doubt, but the writing is of a poor and rather reckless type. The initial words *In principio* are copied from one of the great manuscripts of the Lindisfarne and the Kells types, and the *Imago Iohannis* is of the regular Hibernian type, with Irish-Byzantine features. The copyist has, in one curious respect, misunderstood his original. The Apostle is meant to be shown in a frame, held by some one out of sight behind, the feet of the " some one" showing below the frame, as the hands sometimes show at the sides, and the head at the top. The copyist has treated the feet as the property of St. John, large as they are.

In golden letters is written at the end of the codex, " Hoc euangelium Sanctus Bonifatius Martyr Domini Gloriosus ut nobis seniorum relatione compertum est propriis conscripsit manibus. Quod etiam venerabilis Abbas huoggi obnixis precibus a rege piissimo Arnulfo impetravit et sanctae fuldensi ecclesiae honorabiliter restituit," " This Gospel the holy Boniface, glorious

Fig. 15. The Irish Gospels

martyr of the Lord, wrote with his own hands as is known by tradition of those who came before us. The venerable Abbat Huoggi obtained it by earnest prayers from the most pious King Arnulf and honourably restored it to the holy Church of Fulda." Huoggi resigned the abbacy in 891. Arnulf was elected king in 887.

This entry gives us, no doubt, a firm tradition of the monastery; but it is in itself not at all probable, and there is in the codex a statement which directly contradicts it. On the last page of St. John there is an entry as follows: "finit amen Deo gratias uidrung scribsit." Schannat makes it *Vidrug*, but there are certainly two letters between the *r* and the *g*. In any case there is all reasonable probability in attributing the work of writing these Gospels to the priest Wintrung, the first named of the three priests who accompanied Boniface at the last and were martyred with him, the chor-episcopus Eoban being the only one of the band who had precedence of him. The book was no doubt the private property of the writer —there being no Hibernian king there to declare it the property of the owner of the original, on the ground that as the calf belongs to the cow the copy belongs to the book—and it may well have been with him when he was killed.

No other person bearing this name Wintrung or Wintrug or Wintruge is recorded among Anglo-Saxons. The existence of a priest at Fulda, fond of writing and with tastes in a decidedly Hibernian direction, may serve to account for the very curious form which the Short Annals of Fulda take. The Short Annals, omitting for our present purpose the mention of the great eclipse of May 1, 664, and the commencement of the reigns of the Emperors of the East from 669 to 704, are as follows: "Anno Incarnationis Domini 651 Aidan episcopus obiit, 658 Finan moritur, 664 Colmani obiit, 671 Egfrid regnare cepit, 704 Osraed regnavit, 720 Redhbat rex Fresonum, 735 Beda presbyter obiit, 742 Karolus rex Francorum, 754 passio beati Bonifatii martyris." This points to a close connexion on the part of the annalist with the kingdom of Northumbria and with the Scotic origin and history of the church of that kingdom. Probably the word *Colmani* was followed by some such word as *discessus*, and a later copyist has taken that to mean departure from life, not departure from Northumbria, and has ungrammatically and contrary to fact replaced it by the usual *obiit*. The omission of the reign of Aldfrith 685–705 may have been due to his being an Oswiung born out of wedlock, or it may have been due to his prosecution of Wilfrith.

In examining the exceptional readings of the two pages of St. John's and St. Mark's Gospels, shown in figs. 15 and 16, we have the immense advantage of working with the help of the present Bishop of Salisbury's great edition of the Latin Gospels, in which he was assisted by the Reverend H. J. White, now the Professor of Exegesis at King's College, Strand.

The first page only presents one point for notice, and it is a rather remarkable one. The concluding words of the sublime preface, "the darkness comprehended it not," are "tenebrae eam non comprehenderunt". Of eighteen different texts, nine have the last words spelt thus, nine have it spelt *compraehenderunt*, and among these is the Rushworth (Mac Regol) book.

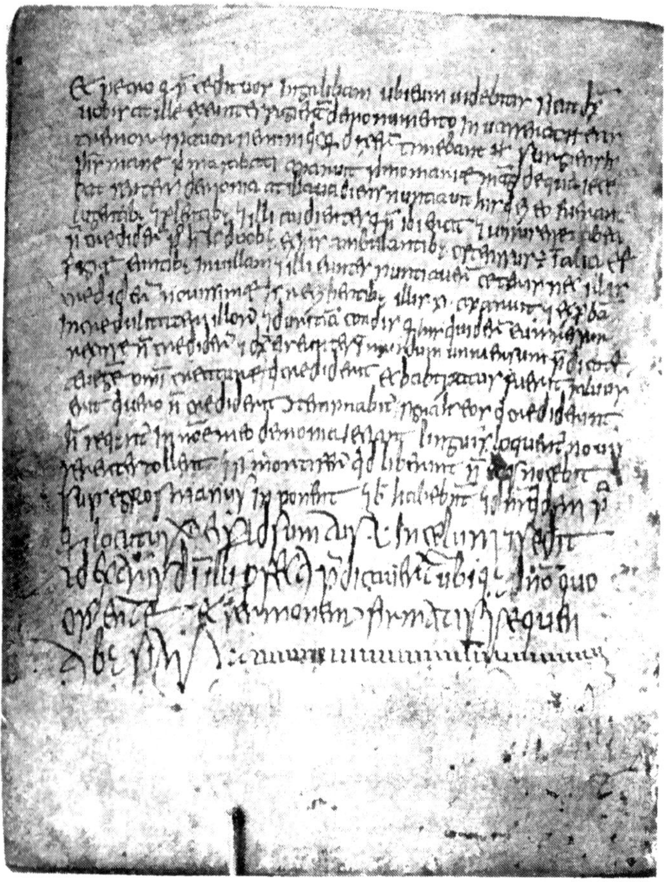

FIG. 16. THE IRISH GOSPELS.

Our friend Wintrung evidently copied a text of the Mac Regol type, but made a mistake which many since have made; he read an *e* as a *c*, and as if to emphasize his mistake he finished one line with *compra* and began the next with *chenderunt*. The line written below this is to be read as follows:—ioh[annes] gratia D[e]i [inter]p[re]tat[us].

The last page of St. Mark's Gospel, fig. 16, presents a large number of interesting points. It begins in the middle of verse 7 of the last chapter of St. Mark, "[dicite discipulis eius] et Petro quia precedit uos," &c. It may be better to give the four concluding lines in a form more legible than that which the priest Wintrung, jubilant at the completion of a second stage of his journey, thought fit to present to other eyes than his own, if indeed he did not contemplate keeping the book entirely to himself and having it buried with him when he should die a peaceful death in his cell. They represent the following words : "[et bene habebunt. et dominus quidem] postquam locutus est eis adsumtus est in celum et sedit a dextris Dei. illi profecti predicaverunt ubique domino quo-operente et sermonem confirmante [1] sequentibus signis." In verse 7, *Galiliam* is found in the Book of Armagh. Verse 8, *ille* is in the "St. Augustine's" Gospels at Oxford. Verse 9, "surgens autem *Iesus*": the best texts have not *Iesus* here, but many texts have it, including Armagh. Verse 10, "*at* illa *uadiens*": Lichfield (St. Chad) and Kells have *at*, the best texts not: *uadiens* is a mere blunder. Verse 11, *ibi erat* should be *uiueret*: the Book of Armagh has *uiuerat*, and the copyist seeing the *erat* had to give some

[1] It is certainly not *confirmante*; the *t* follows the *a* with no letter between. It appears to be *confirmatus*.

M

meaning to the preceding letters which would make sense. Verse 12, *his*, the regular reading is *eis*, Lichfield (St. Chad) has *his*. Verse 14, *autem* (the usual sign for this word) is in the Book of Armagh and other texts, not in the received text. Verse 16, *baltisatus* is in St. Chad, Mac Regol, and Lindisfarne; *condempnabitur* is in Mac Regol and others. Verse 18, *liberint* for *biberint*; Mac Regol has this blunder. Verse 19, *sedit*, many have *sedet*, but not the best. Verse 20, *quo-operente* for *co-operante*. The *e* for *a* is a blunder; the *quo* for *co* is curiously enough found only in a Spanish text much later than this.

Any one who desires to know more about the antiquities of Fulda should consult the *Fuldensium Antiquitatum libri III*, of Christophorus Browerus, British Museum Library 487 h. 18.

We must now leave the Fulda manuscripts and proceed with the history of the abbey.

There is good reason for Leoba's relics being at Fulda, and for her death being portrayed on a window in Boniface's crypt.

A *Life of Leoba*[1], *Abbess of Bischofsheim*, was written by Rudolf of Fulda. Fortunately we are able to date this Life, and the date gives it great importance. Rudolf tells us that he obtained much of his information from the presbyter Mago, "who died five

---

[1] The name is spelled Leoba throughout in the earliest known manuscript, Munich 18897, tenth century, and Lieba throughout in the next earliest manuscript, Munich 11821, eleventh century. In the most recent edition of the Letters of Boniface and Lul it is Lioba in the editor's notes and Leobgytha in the headings of the letters. In a later book of Rudolf's we find it written Leuba.

years ago." The *Annals of Fulda* give 831 as the
date of the death of Mago, so that Rudolf was writing
the Life in the year 836. It was this Rudolf who
continued the *Annals of Fulda* from the year 838.
Inasmuch as Rudolf is silent about the translation of
Leoba's remains to the church on the Petersberg [1] in
the year 837 or 838, we may take 836 as the date
of the Life. Mago had been a great friend of some
of the disciples of Leoba, and he was naturally able
to give important information. Rudolf dedicated
the Life to a religious virgin of Christ by name
Hadamot. The names of Mago's chief friends were
Agatha, Tecla, Nana, and Leoba or some modified
form of that name. We shall see at the end of the
Life what abundant reason there was that it should
be written by the chief literary member of the community of Fulda, and at the request, or by the order,
of its famous abbat, Rabanus.

At Winbrunn (Wimborne) in Britain, a place, our
author tells us, whose name of *vini fons*, fountain of
wine, came from the special excellence of its water,
there were two monasteries, one for men, the other
for women. No woman entered the one, no man
except the officiating priest the other. The women
were there for life; the mother of the community
gave her business orders to outside people through a
wicket. Tetta, the sister of King Ina of the West
Saxons, ruled both monasteries with great discretion.
That, as we know, was a characteristic of the early
women of the Anglo-Saxons; in one important case
after another they ruled with great success a double
monastery, a work to which it is not recorded that
men were put. So severe a ruler was Tetta that

[1] See p. 172.

M 2

she did not allow even bishops to enter the women's monastery. Leoba, or Leobgytha [1], or Truthgeba, was a favourite pupil of hers, and she used to tell stories of Tetta's rule. Two of these Rudolf tells.

There was a very stern sister, who was frequently appointed to the offices of provost and dean [2]. The young people hated her, and when she died and her grave was left with its usual mound of earth, they danced upon it till at last in place of a mound there was a cavity half a foot deep. Tetta summoned the culprits, made each of them promise to pray for the soul of the deceased lady, imposed a three days' fast to be spent in psalms and vigils and holy prayers. At the end of the three days the whole congregation entered the basilica singing litanies, and Tetta the abbess prostrated herself before the altar praying with tears for the soul of the deceased sister. Exactly at the moment when she finished her prayers, the earth rose in the grave and reached the level of the ground.

On another occasion, the sister who had charge of the keys locked the doors of the church at night before going to bed. The keys were very numerous, on account of the many chests in the treasury; they were of silver and brass and iron, and they were all fastened together in one bunch. She lost them all, and when the time came to get ready for the early service the church could not be opened. Tetta had the nuns called, and held the service in another oratory. When they left the oratory, they found a small dead fox with the bunch of keys in its mouth. The whole five hundred sisters thereupon entered the basilica and

---

[1] "Leobgith" in the *Annals of Fulda*, A.D 780.
[2] Praeposita, decana.

gave thanks to God. Whether the young nuns who danced on the grave of their tyrant had anything to do with this attempt to get off the midnight service, and "laid the blame on the cat", we are not told.

The daughter of two noble Angles, Dynno and his wife Aebba, the latter a relative of Boniface, was named Truthgeba or Thrudgeba, with the additional name of Leoba or Leobgytha. Her parents gave her to Tetta to be trained, and when Boniface wrote to Tetta asking that helpers might be sent, Leoba was one of the number, specially asked for by Boniface as Rudolf tells. Boniface appointed her mistress of a large number of religious women collected at Bischofsheim. This is not the best known place of that name. It is in the valley of the Tauber, and is on that account called Tauber-Bischofsheim, on the railway from Landa to Wertheim, some thirty miles from Würzburg. There she laboured long, teaching her nuns. One of the stories of wonderful works wrought by her begins thus : "On another occasion, when according to her wont she had seated herself to deliver to her disciples a reading on the divine word."

Some account of the correspondence of Leoba with Boniface is given in Chapter V. From the Life we learn some interesting facts about the relations that existed between them. When Boniface gave up his archbishopric and was going away to Frisia, he gave directions that he should be buried at Fulda. Then he sent for Leoba and bade her not desert the land of her pilgrimage. He commended her to Lul the bishop and to the seniors of the monastery, desiring them to take charge of her with honour and reverence, and declaring it to be his will that after her death her bones should be laid in the same sepulchre with his, that together they might rise at the judgement day.

She worked long after the death of her relative and nearest friend. The kings treated her with the utmost veneration, both Pepin and his sons Karl and Karlmann, especially Karl. Hiltegard also, Karl's queen, loved her as her own soul, and would have had her stay always with her, but Leoba hated the tumult of the palace like poison. The princes loved her; the chiefs supported her; bishops embraced her with exultation; she was so very learned in divine scriptures, and so wise in council, that they often conferred with her and discussed church affairs. She made a great mark by her visitation of the monasteries of nuns in her district.

One effect of Boniface's commendation was remarkable. What Abbess Tetta would have said, one ought to know a good deal of idiomatic Wessex speech of a vituperative character to say. After the death of Boniface, Leoba was wont to come to the monastery of Fulda for periods of prayer. Never before or since had this been allowed to any woman; all women were forbidden entrance. To her alone it was allowed, because of Boniface's commendation and because she was to be buried there. Still, a strict order was observed at these visits. Her disciples and her attendant women were left in a neighbouring cell, and Leoba with one attendant older than the rest entered the monastery, only in the daytime. When her prayers were ended, she went through Collation [1] with the brethren, and at night returned to the cell

---

[1] The reading of Scripture or other religious writing before or during a meal.

where she had left her disciples. When she reached
an advanced age, she settled the affairs of all the
monasteries under her charge, and by Lul's advice
went to live at Scoransheim (now Schornsheim), a
few miles from Mainz, with a company of religious
women.

When Karl was at Aachen, Hiltegard invited Leoba
to come and see her again. Unwillingly Leoba went.
She was received with the greatest affection, but
when she heard the causes of her invitation—nothing
more definite is said in the Life—she begged leave
to return. Pressed to stay a few days at least she
refused, but embracing the queen even more affec-
tionately than ever, she kissed her mouth, her forehead,
her eyes, and remaining in her arms exclaimed :
" Fare thee well to all eternity, lady and sister, most
loved. Fare thee well, thou precious portion of my
soul. May Christ our Creator and Redeemer grant
that in the day of judgement we may see without
confusion of face. But in this world we shall never
see each other again."

She returned to Schornsheim, and feeling her end
to be close at hand she received the viaticum at the
hands of a venerable English presbyter, Torahtbrat
(Torthat and Tortahat in one of Boniface's letters to
Leoba), and on the 28th day of September she died.
The death-annals of Fulda give the date as September 23, and the year as 780. There are other
differences as to the date. The monks of Fulda,
some of whom had probably taken part as younger
men in the like journey with the corpse of Boniface,
carried her body with a great following of noble
persons to Fulda. The elders remembered how that
Boniface had ordered that her bones should lie with

his; but they dared not open his tomb, so they buried her on the north side of the altar which he had dedicated to the Saviour and the twelve Apostles. Some considerable number of years later, Eigil the abbat, by permission of Haistulf the archbishop of Mainz (813–26), when a more august church was being prepared for consecration, placed the body of Leoba in the south porch near the memorial of the holy martyr Ignatius. Some small relics of Leoba are now placed in the great shrine of silver richly gilt which is the companion shrine to that in which the sword of Boniface's martyrdom is preserved.

A later book written by this same Rudolf is full of the deepest interest for all who are concerned in the affairs of Fulda. It is entitled *The miracles of the Saints whose relics have been translated to the churches of Fulda*. For the present purpose we must, unwillingly, confine ourselves to one entry.

In one of the years 836–8, evidently after Rudolf's *Life of Leoba* was written and issued, the Abbat Rabanus obtained the consecration by Reginbald the chor-episcopus of a new church which he had built. This church stood in a very prominent position on his favourite hill, the Petersberg, about a mile and a half to the east of the Abbey Church. We have in Fulda a Rhabanus street still. In this church he placed a large number of relics. On the 28th of September he added many more, and on the 29th he brought to his new church the bones of Leoba (here spelled Leuba) and placed them in a crypt behind the altar of St. Mary and the Holy Virgins in a stone chest; the chest had a wooden shell, which he ornamented with plates of metal, silver and gold. On the 29th he gathered together by the hands of the said chor-

episcopus, in the church of the holy Boniface, at the
place where first his holy body rested, the relics of
twenty-one bishops, &c. He had built up a lofty
stone pediment behind the altar, upon which he
placed, set on four columns, a wooden roof adorned
with gold and silver. Under this baldachin he placed
all these relics, in a stone chest ornamented with
gold and silver and precious stones, with metal plates
carrying in relief the figures of the several saints.
Round the chest he wrote four elegiac verses, and
round the pediment eight, four on one side and
four on the other, with eight verses in other metre
on the remaining sides. This was in the Abbey
Church. Rudolf adds a remarkable fact. Rabanus,
he tells us, during the twenty years of his rule as
abbat, constructed no less than thirty oratories for
relics, and had them dedicated by the bishops in
whose dioceses the relics had been when he acquired
them.

When Rudolf finished his account of the collection
of saints' relics at and near Fulda, Rabanus had
resigned the abbacy and had retired for philosophic
meditation to his dearly-loved Petersberg. The call
to the archbishopric of Mainz had not as yet reached
him. He held that archbishopric from 847 to 856.

CHAPTER X

Carloman asks Boniface to hold a Council of Austrasian Franks.—The Pope's advice sought.—The Pope's advice.—Unsatisfactory character of Frank ecclesiastics. — Carloman's announcement of the decrees of the Council.—Pepin's Council at Soissons.—The case of Aldebert and Clement.

THERE was much more in the letter of Boniface to Zacharias (Ep. 50) and in the answer of Zacharias to Boniface (Ep. 51) than we have as yet seen.[1]

Boniface[2] informs the Pope that Carloman, Duke of the Franks, having invited him to visit him, has asked him to call together a synod in that part of the kingdom of the Franks which is under his government (Austrasia). And he has promised that he will do something to correct and amend ecclesiastical discipline, which for not less than sixty or seventy years has been trampled on and dissipated. "If he really has this purpose, I ought to know your opinion and to have your authority, that is, the authority of the holy see. For the Franks, as we learn from old men, have for more than eighty years not held a synod, or had an archbishop, nor have they kept the ecclesiastical laws of the Church. At the present time the episcopal sees in the several cities[3] are for the most part handed over to greedy laics or adulterous clerics, to whoremongers and publicans, to enjoy as secular property. If I am by your advice to move in this matter, I should wish to have at hand the judgement

---

[1] Chapter VIII.   [2] Ep. 50, A.D. 742.   [3] *Civitates.*

and precept of the apostolic see, with the ecclesiastical canons.

"If I shall find among them those whom they call deacons, who from boyhood have passed a life of fornication, adultery, and every kind of impurity, and with such a character have come to the diaconate; and as deacons have four or five or more concubines in their bed at night, and are neither ashamed nor afraid to read the Gospel and call themselves deacons; and then in such incests come to the priesthood, and continue in the same sins and add sin to sin while exercising the office of priest, and say that they can intercede for the people and offer the sacred oblations; and lastly, worst of all, with such reputation, ascending through the various degrees are ordained and called bishops; I should have the written judgement of your authority, what you decide about such persons, that by the apostolic response the sinners may be made manifest and convicted. There are certain bishops among them, who, though they say they are not fornicators or adulterers, yet are drunkards or neglectful or given to hunting, who go armed to war and shed blood, whether of Christians or of pagans. And since I am known to be the servant and legate of the apostolic see, my voice here and yours there should be one and the same, if we should agree to send them to the judgement of the apostolic see."

In connexion with Boniface's remarks on the cessation of ecclesiastical discipline, and elsewhere on the absence of connexion with Rome, it may be mentioned that in Spain we find that fifty years before the death of Boniface the king Witiza forbade appeals to Rome and authorized the marriage of the clergy. In France, to use the general name which had a smaller

area of application then than now, there had always
been a prevailing tendency to manage at home all
home affairs, secular or ecclesiastical. There is scarcely
any trace of intercourse between the see of Rome and
the Frankish kingdoms or churches between the time
of the conversion of England and the time of Boniface.
There was a great Frankish assembly of principal
secular personages and of bishops to the number of
seventy-nine, held in 614 under Lothaire II, the
father of Dagobert, and we have the laws which they
enacted, by no means discreditable. And as late as
670, when an Anglo-Saxon lady, Bathildis, who had
been captured in war, became the queen of Clovis II
and regent of Neustria and Burgundy, there was
a certain amount of ecclesiastical order. The savage
cruelty which Ebroin, of whom we hear so much that
is bad, perpetrated upon Ledger, bishop of Autun,
the queen's principal minister in things ecclesiastical
and secular, marked the termination of ecclesiastical
order. St. Ledger was beheaded in 678, after having
lost by successive tortures, spreading over some years,
his eyes, his lips, and his tongue. It is probably to
this period that Boniface dates the cessation of ecclesiastical order in the Frank kingdoms, when he says
that there has been no synod or council for seventy
years.

Pope Zacharias replied [1] that Boniface should act as
Carloman desired, should sit with him in the Council,
and should not allow persons such as he had described
to exercise the office of priest. On receiving the order
of priesthood, the man must cease to live with even
one wife, much less may he have many wives. The
Pope's language clearly allows the deacon to have one

[1] Ep. 51 ; 1 Apr. 743.

wife.[1] With regard to other kinds of offences against
the canons, Boniface should have at hand the canons
and institutes of the Fathers, and decide as he is
instructed by them.

We have a good deal of information in Boniface's
letters about the exceedingly unsatisfactory state of
the Frankish clergy. One such letter we may go
through, on account of its intrinsic interest and
because of the person to whom it is written. It
is the only letter we possess of the many which
Boniface no doubt wrote to his former bishop in
England, Daniel of Winchester.

Boniface's letter to Daniel asks his prayers and his
consolation and advice in a great practical difficulty.

There are, he says,[2] in the land of the Franks
a great many false and hypocritical priests, who are
adversaries of God and lead astray the people by
many scandals and various errors. Some abstain
from foods, which God has created to be used; some
live on honey and milk, rejecting bread and other
kinds of food; some, and this most of all is harmful
to the people, affirm that homicides and adulterers,
persevering in their crimes, can be made priests of God.

Now when he goes to the palace of the Franks,
to seek the help of his patron the duke, he finds it
not possible to keep clear of personal contact with
such men, though he does avoid communicating with
them in the sacred mysteries of the body and blood
of the Lord. Counsel and consent with them he
shuns. His labours and strifes are with such, and

---

[1] "Apostolus dicit, ' Unius uxoris virum.' Hoc ante sus-
ceptum sacerdotium uti licitum est; nam a die suscepti
sacerdotii etiam ab ipso proprio coniugio prohibendi sunt."

[2] Ep 63 ; 742-6

with pagans, and with the mixed multitude of the
people.   Nay, when any, priest or deacon, cleric or
monk, depart from faith and truth, they join the
pagans in contumacious abuse of the sons of the
Church.   An obstacle, this, much to be dreaded, in
the way of the Gospel of the glory of Christ.

On personal contact with such priests, he eagerly
desires to hear and to follow the salutary advice of
Daniel.   Without the patronage of the Prince of the
Franks, he can neither rule the people of the Church,
nor defend the priests and the clerics, the monks and
the handmaids of God.   Without the prince's mandate,
and the fear which he inspires, he is not strong enough
to prohibit the very rites of the pagans and the sacrileges of idols in Germany.   When he visits the prince,
to obtain his help in these respects, he finds priests
of this type, and he cannot keep clear of them.   He
fears to incur grievous blame, for he remembers that
at his consecration he swore on the body of the holy
Peter that all communion with such he would decline,
if he found himself unable to convert them to better
things.[1]   But at the same time he fears more for the
teaching which he is bound to give to the people, if
he does not go to the Prince of the Franks.   Will
the bishop tell his sorrowing and doubting son what
he ought to do?   His own feeling is that he is in fact
in very great measure separate from them, if he
abstains from counsel and consent and ministry with
them, where they are uncanonical.

[1] He swore that if he knew of priests or bishops who walked
contrary to the ancient institutions of the holy Fathers, he
would with them have no communion or contact; if he could
prevent them he would; if he could not, he would immediately
report them to the apostolic lord.

The Council was held April 27, 742, nearly a year before the Pope's reply (April 1, 743) to Boniface's letter of the early part of 742. Taking it that all these dates are certain, the German editors have naturally considered the obvious question, why did the Pope so long delay his answer? They have found in the annals of Metz a statement which throws some light on a difficulty mentioned in Boniface's letter to which we have not as yet referred. Boniface had proposed to appoint a successor to himself, but he had been obliged to abandon the idea for the present. Some one concerned had assassinated an uncle of the Duke of the Franks—who the "uncle" was is not clear—and Boniface doubted whether it would be possible to carry out his purpose. The "some one" is described as *frater illius*, "his brother"; whose, is not clear. Thus the Pope was called upon to make some remark, so very early in his pontificate, on a serious political question affecting the action of Carloman or his brother. Now the annals of Metz state that Zacharias had already taken the part of Odilo [1] of Bavaria against the Frank dukes; and if that was so, we can understand his desire not to burn his fingers. But there was another reason. As we shall see, Boniface, in his letter to the Pope, brought very serious charges against the conduct allowed to Christians in Rome, and against the reported action of the Pope in his treatment of notorious offenders. Boniface's charges were definite, and it would take very considerable time for the Pope to have them looked into so fully that he could make a reply. With regard to the political reason alleged, it should be stated that Zacharias speaks of the Frank prince to Boniface as

[1] See page 103.

" our son ", " that most excellent man ", and informs
Boniface that he has written to " our son Carloman ",
begging him to hasten to do as he has promised to
Boniface, and to give him support.

This is far from being the only case in which annals
of Boniface's time differ by a year, or more. The
natural explanation is that the Council itself, and
therefore Carloman's important publication, came after
the reply to Boniface had been received. It is quite
possible that the Pope had notified his assent to the
holding of the Council in some informal manner,
which delayed his full reply to Boniface's full letter,
so that Carloman called the Council with due notice
and held it on April 21 of 742 or 743. It is more
likely that the letters are dated by the moderns on correct principles, but incorrectly, than that Carloman's
very precise date by the Christian era is wrong. The
date is given in the valuable preface of Carloman to
the decrees.[1]

" In the name of our Lord Jesus Christ. I, Karlmann, duke and prince of the Franks, in the seven
hundred and forty-second year from the Incarnation
of Christ, on the 11th of the Kalends of May, with
the advice of the servants of God and my chief men,
have assembled the bishops who are in my kingdom [2]
with the presbyters, and a Council and Synod, for
the fear of Christ, that is, Boniface the archbishop,
and Burghard and Regenfrid and Winta and Wilbald
and Dada and Edda with their presbyters, to give me
counsel how the law of God and ecclesiastical religion
may be recovered, which in the days of former princes
has fallen into decay, and how the Christian people

---

[1] Ep. 56 ; 21 Apr. 742.   [2] Regno.

can reach the salvation of their soul and perish not under the deceitfulness of false priests or bishops [1]."

The list of bishops named affords the only suggestion we have as to the name of the first Bishop of Erfurt appointed by Boniface. With one exception we know the sees of all the bishops named. The exception is Dada. The others are, in the above order, Würzburg, Cologne, Büraburg, Eichstätt, Strassburg. It is fair to suppose that Dada was Bishop of Erfurt. No list of bishops of Erfurt was found by Gams when he published his *Series Episcoporum*.

Carloman's document proceeds to give the acts and decrees advised by the Council. We may take it that one and all express the opinion of Boniface himself, and they are actually directed against definite evils of the time. They are not numbered in the original, but for convenience of reference they may be numbered here :—

" 1. By the advice of the bishops and of my chief men [2], we ordained bishops for cities and have set over them Archbishop Boniface, who is the legate [3] of St. Peter.

" 2. We have determined to gather a Council each year, that in our presence the decrees of the canons and the ecclesiastical laws may be renewed, and the Christian religion amended.

" 3. Moneys fraudulently taken from churches we restore to the churches. False presbyters and adulterous or fornicating deacons and clerics we have cut

---

[1] Per falsos sacerdotes.
[2] Per consilium episcoporum et optimatum meorum. It might be taken as " by the advice of my bishops and chief men ". King Alfred used the phrase "my archbishop".
[3] Missus.

off from the possessions of churches, have degraded, and compelled to penance.

"4. All ministers of God everywhere we have completely prohibited from carrying arms, or fighting, or going into the army or against the enemy, except only such as are specially appointed for the purpose of exercising the divine ministry, that is, performing the solemnities of masses and bearing the protection of the Saints. For this purpose, the prince should have with him one bishop, or two, with priest chaplains, and each prefect one presbyter, to hear men's confessions of sins and indicate the penance. Hunting also, and wanderings in the woods with dogs, we have forbidden to all ministers of God, and we have forbidden them to have hawks or falcons [1].

"5. We have decreed, according to the canons of holy men, that each presbyter in a diocese be subject to him in whose diocese he dwells. And always in Lent he shall make a return to the bishop showing the manner and order of his ministry, whether as regards baptism, or the catholic faith, or prayers, or the order of the Mass. And whenever in accordance with canonical law the bishop makes a circuit of his diocese, to confirm the people, the presbyter shall always be ready to receive the bishop, with a list of those who are to be confirmed [6]. And in the Supper of the Lord he must always seek new crism from the bishop.

"6. We have determined that in accordance with canonical caution we would not admit to ecclesiastical

---

[1] Walcones.

[2] Cum collectione et adiutorio populi qui ibi confirmari debet.

ministry before synodal approval unknown bishops or priests, whencesoever they come.

"7. We have decreed that according to the canons each bishop in his own diocese shall take anxious care, with the help of the count[1], who is the protector of the Church, that the people of God do not perform pagan rites, but entirely put away and spurn all heathen impurities. Sacrifices of the dead, soothsaying, divining, phylacteries, auguries, incantations, immolations which foolish men carry on with pagan rites near the churches under the name of holy martyrs or confessors, provoking to anger God and His saints, those sacrilegious fires which they call *nedfyor*, indeed all pagan observances whatever they may be, they [apparently the bishop and the count] must diligently prohibit.

"8. Again, we have determined that after this synod held on the 11th of the Kalends of May, any of the servants of God or handmaids of Christ who shall have fallen into the sin of fornication, shall do penance in prison on bread and water. And if it be an ordained priest, he shall be kept in prison two years and flogged till the blood comes. But if a clerk or a monk has fallen into this sin, he shall be flogged thrice, sent to prison, and shall there do penance for a space of one year. Veiled nuns shall be kept in like penance and shall have all the hair of their head cut off.

"9. We have declared also that presbyters and deacons shall not wear mantles like laymen, but cassocks as the servants of God : none shall permit a woman to dwell in his house. Monks and nuns

---

[1] Adiuvante graphione (the Graf).

shall study to order and govern their lives according to the Rule of the holy Benedict."

"Now in this synodal assembly held on the Kalends of March [1] at the place called Liftinas [2], all the venerable bishops, counts, and prefects have confirmed the decrees of the previous synod and have promised to observe them.

"The whole of the clergy of ecclesiastical order, bishops, priests, and deacons, with the clerks, taking the canons of the ancient Fathers, promised that they would restore ecclesiastical law by their manner of life, teaching, and ministry. Abbats and monks received the Rule of the holy Father Benedict, with a view to restoring the due form of the regular life.

"Fornicators and adulterous clerks, who have held and defiled holy places or monasteries, our precept is that they be removed thence and brought to penance. And if after this they fall into the sin of fornication or adultery, they must undergo the sentence of the former synod. And so for monks and nuns.

"We have determined with the counsel of the servants of God and Christian people, on account of impending wars and persecutions of other peoples in our neighbourhood, that under registered loan we retain by God's indulgence, for some short time, some portion of the Church's property in aid of the army, on this condition, that for each casata there be paid to the church or monastery one shilling, that is, twelve pence, and if he to whom it is on loan dies, the church is reinvested with its own property, and again, by the prince's order the property can be lent

---

[1] A.D. 743.

[2] The identification of this place has been much discussed. It is probably Estinnes in Hainault.

anew. And it is by all means to be observed that churches or monasteries whose property is on loan must not suffer penury and poverty; if poverty compel, the possession must be given back entire.[1]

"Similarly our precept is that, in accordance with the decrees of the canons, adulterous and incestuous marriages be prohibited and amended by the judgement of the bishops; and that Christian slaves be not traded to pagans.

"We have decreed also, as my father had before decreed, that whosoever performs pagan observances in any respect be mulcted in fifteen shillings."

The example of the pious Carloman was followed by his brother Pepin, who held a Council at Soissons in 744, at which the practical reforms planned by Boniface and endorsed at Carloman's two Councils were adopted. Finally, in 745, Pepin and Carloman held a joint Council of the two realms, under the ecclesiastical presidency of Boniface. Ecclesiastical discipline was set on right lines, and the change which took place between 745 and the accession of Charlemagne was very great. The Belgian historian of Boniface, Professor Kurth of Liège, an enthusiastic Roman, declares that the religious regeneration which resulted from Boniface's action throughout the realms of the two dukes is worthy of comparison with the religious regeneration of the universal Church which resulted from the Council of Trent. It is an admission of a great truth, which the modern Roman

---

[1] This clause no doubt refers to the long-standing differences between Charles Martel and the Gallican Church. He had freely seized the property and plate of the Church for the defence of the land and people against the Saracens, and there were great difficulties in the way of getting it back, so much of it as had not been made away with.

controversialist keeps in the background for English purposes ; the terrible state into which the Church of Rome had fallen at the end of the Middle Ages may well be compared with the state of things revealed to us by Boniface. As the one more than justified the Englishman's reformation, so the other more than justified the English Reformation.

In the letter from the Pope which accompanied the three palls for Neustrian metropolitans,[1] Zacharias referred to a case reported to him by Boniface in the letter which, as we have noticed, has so unfortunately been lost. It was the case of two persons not there named, false Christians rather than false prophets. Though not there named, their names are well known. Further than that, we know from the later proceedings which of the two to credit with one and the other set of enormities. It may fairly be said that Boniface had more trouble with the Christian clergy west of the Rhine than with all the pagans on the east.

These men were Aldebert and Clement. Aldebert was the worse of the two. He claimed to have the priesthood, and he was not continent in regard to his life of evil luxury. He seduced the people by preaching follies. He gave his own soul into the power of the devil, and he drowned the souls of the people in falsities, to draw them away from the Church of God and the law of Christ. He set up crosses and shrines in the fields, and drew the people away from the churches to worship there. He counted himself worthy to be called saint; he consecrated churches in his own name ; he declared that he knew the names of the angels, but the names which Boniface had reported to the Pope the Pope declared to be not

[1] Page 199.

the names of angels but the names of demons; how
the Pope knew that we do not know. Clement was
given up to luxurious living; he had a concubine,
and had two sons by her. And yet he claimed the
priesthood, and declared that he had done right in
the matter of these children, on the authority of the
Old Testament, for he had taken the widow of a
deceased brother. He maintained that when Christ
came back from the lower regions He left no one there,
but brought them all away. All these things the
Pope declared to be detestable and infamous; he
strongly approved of Boniface's action in condemning
them, committing them to custody, and describing
them as ministers and precursors of Antichrist. The
first canon of the Council of Soissons, in 744, condemned Aldebert and his heresy; the second canon
ordered the little crosses of Clement to be burned.

On the 25th of October, 745, the charges against
Aldebert and Clement came before a Roman synod,
at which the Pope, seven bishops, the Archpresbyter
of St. Susanna, and sixteen presbyters, were present,
besides a number of those of lower grade. The
culprits had evidently not made submission, and in
accordance with the injunction of Zacharias, the
complaint had been brought to Rome. We do not
find that two or three priests had come, as the Pope
had required; no one is mentioned as representing
Boniface beyond the useful Denehard, whose name
occurs in several of the letters. So much for the
account as given in Labbe, but he has mixed up two
affairs of different dates.

The document given by Dümmler does not say
anything about an injunction by Zacharias. It is
a business record of what actually took place,

evidently an extract from the official record. There were present, first of all, as President, the most holy and blessed Lord Zacharias the Pope, in the Palace Lateran, in the Basilica called Theodore's [1]; sitting with him the most holy Bishops Epiphanius Silva Candida [2], Benedict Nomentum, Venantius Penestre, Gregory of Porto, Nicetas Gabii, Theodore of Ostia, Gratiosus Velletri, and the venerable presbyter the archpresbyter John, and sixteen named presbyters. Labbe's notice of the injunction of Zacharias, and the consequential remark that the terms of the injunction were not complied with, have reference to a letter of Zacharias at a later stage, after the invocation of the intervention of the French dukes had failed of effect. · The contents of that letter (Ep. 77) will be given in the proper place.

The account opens without any preface [3] :—

The sacrosanct Gospels were placed in the midst. The deacons and all the rest of the clergy stood by. Gregory, the regionary notary and nomenclator, made the following announcement: "Denehard [*Deneardus* all through] the religious presbyter, the legate of Boniface the most holy archbishop of the province of Germany, sent to your holy apostolate,

---

[1] Later the oratory of St. Venantius. The principal basilicas of Rome, to which palaces were attached, were called *patriarchales*. Hence *patriarchium* came to mean the palace attached. The Latin here is *in patriarchio Lateranense*.

[2] It is in accordance with the common use of to-day to insert "of", but it has no representation in the Latin; the person present was Epiphanius Silva Candida, as we say John Sarum. The names being in the ablative absolute, we have *Niceta Gabiis*, and so on. In two cases the "of" is expressed in the Latin, *Gregorio Portuense*, *Theodoro Ostiense*. A curious difference occurs in the case of Gratiosus, *Gratioso Villitrias*.

[3] Ep. 59; Oct. 25, 745.

is at the curtain, and begs that he may enter.
What is your pleasure?" It is replied, "Let him
enter." When he had entered, Zacharias, the most
holy and most blessed Pope of God's holy catholic
and apostolic city of Rome, said, "A few days ago
you brought to us letters from our most reverend
and most holy brother Boniface the archbishop, in
which he related to us such things as seemed to
him opportune. For what further purpose have you
applied for admission to our private deliberations?"
Denehard the religious presbyter said: "My lord,
when in accordance with the precept of the holy
apostolate, my lord Boniface, the bishop, the servant
(*famulus*) of your piety, had summoned a synod in the
province of the Franks, and had found there false
bishops [1], heretic and schismatic, Aldebert and Clement,
he deprived them of their episcopal office, in concert
with the Frank princes, and gave them into custody.
They have not made submission, as ordered by the
synod of the Franks, but on the contrary continue to
seduce the people. Wherefore this epistle of my said
lord which I hold in my hand I offer to your holy
apostolate that ye may cause it to be read in the
presence of this sacrosanct Council." The order was
given: "Receive the letter, and let it be read in our
presence." Theophanius, the regionary notary and
treasurer, received the letter, and read it.

The letter is set out at length, but we need not
follow it in its long course. Aldebert, it states, here
called Eldebert, was a Gaul, and Clement a Scot,
that is, an Irishman. Boniface begged that they
might be put in prison till they learned not to

---

[1] *Sacerdotes.* Zacharias calls them (Ep. 77) *exepiscopi*, fifteen
months after this.

blaspheme or tear the vesture of Christ, and thus the people of the Franks and Gauls might be taught not to follow the fables and vain prodigies of heretics, and the signs of the precursor of Antichrist.

As regarded Aldebert, the people accused Boniface of having taken away from them a most holy apostle, their patron and orator, who did wonders [1] and showed signs. But under sheep's clothing he was a ravening wolf. In his early years his hypocrisy began. He declared that an angel of the Lord in the form of a man had brought to him from the ends of the earth relics of a marvellous undefined sanctity; and in their power he could obtain from God whatsoever he asked. By these claims he led captive silly women, laden with sins, and a multitude of rustics, who said that he was a man of apostolical sanctity and did many signs and prodigies. He rose to such a pitch of pride that he made himself equal to the apostles. Then he got together some ignorant bishops, who consecrated him contrary to the canons. He disdained to consecrate a church to the honour of any apostle or martyr, and asked what good it was for men to visit the thresholds of the sacred apostles. Later, he dedicated, or rather defiled, oratories in his own honour. He set up little crosses and little oratories, in the fields, and at springs, and wherever it seemed good to him, and bade men there make their public prayers, so that multitudes of the people scorned other bishops and deserted the old churches, gathering themselves together at the places which Aldebert indicated, saying, "The merits of the holy Aldebert will aid us." He gave the parings of his

---

[1] *Virtutes.*

nails, and the clippings of his hair, to be honoured
and carried about along with relics of the holy Peter,
prince of the apostles. Finally, he did the most
wicked and blasphemous thing of all. When the
people came and prostrated themselves before his feet,
and desired to confess their sins, he said to them:
"I know all your sins, for your hidden things are
open to me. You have no need to confess. Your
past sins are forgiven. Safe and absolved, return to
your homes in peace." In short, everything which
the holy Gospel says that hypocrites do, in dress,
and carriage, and manners, he copied.

The other heretic, who is called Clement, contends
against the Catholic Church, denies and refutes the
canons of the churches of Christ, refuses the tractates
and opinions of Jerome, Augustine, and Gregory.
Despising the laws of synods, he declares that he
can be a bishop of the Christian law, though he has
had two sons born to him in adultery, while called
a bishop. He introduces a Judaism, and declares
that a Christian can marry his brother's widow. He
asserts that when Christ rose again from the lower
parts of the earth, He brought with him all the spirits
that were in prison, believing and unbelieving, worshippers of God and worshippers of idols. And he
affirms many horrible things of the predestination
of God, contrary to the Catholic faith. Therefore
Boniface begs that the Pope will in the case of this
heretic also desire Carloman to keep him from mis-
chief in prison.

When this had been read, the most holy and
blessed Pope said : "Ye have heard, dearest brothers,
what has been read from this letter of those
sacrilegious men who, to their own condemnation,

have preached themselves as apostles to the people."
The most holy bishops and venerable priests made
answer : " We have heard for certain that they are in
all respects not apostles, but ministers of Satan and
forerunners of Antichrist. For who of the apostles,
or who of the saints, ever gave to the people of their
hair and nails as holy things, as that sacrilegious and
pernicious Aldebert has essayed to do. This wickedness is to be cut out by your holy apostolate, as also
that of the transgressor Clement, who despises the
sacred canons, and rejects the exposition of the holy
Fathers Ambrose and Augustine, and the sayings of
other saints." Zacharias, the most holy and blessed
Pope, said : " It is too late to-day, but at our next
meeting we will have read to us the life and prayer
which Aldebert has himself issued, and other of his
doings, and then by the help of God we can consider
what is to be done."

At the next session, still, like the last, dated on
October 25, the same ceremony of waiting behind the
curtain and being called to come in was enacted and
recorded. Then the Pope asked Denehard to tender
some further writings which he had. The same
Theophanius received and read them. The first was
an autobiography of Aldebert, which commenced
thus : " In the name of our Lord Jesus Christ. The
beginning of the Life [1] of the holy and blessed servant
of God, illustrious and all beautiful, born of the
election of God, the holy Aldebert the Bishop. He
was born of simple parents, and crowned of the
grace of God." There had been a miraculous gift

---

[1] The Latin of Aldebert is quite as bad as that of the priest
whose baptisms Boniface declared invalid (p. 104) : " Incipit
vitam sanctum et beatum Dei famulum."

of grace by an angel before he came forth from
the womb. We have no record of the rest of the
autobiography.

When it had been read to the very end, Zacharias,
the most blessed and most holy Pope, said: What do
you say to these blasphemies, most holy brothers?
Epiphanius, the most holy Bishop of the holy Church
of Silva Candida, said: "Of a certainty, apostolic lord,
the heart of your apostleship was moved by divine
inspiration to urge the said Boniface, our most holy
brother, to hold a council in those parts, so that these
schisms and blasphemies have not been concealed from
your holy apostleship."

Another of Aldebert's documents was read, namely,
a letter of our Lord Jesus Christ, which descended
from heaven, and was found in Jerusalem by the
Archangel Michael near the gate of Ephraim. By
the hands of a sacerdos named Icore it was copied,
and he sent the letter itself to the city Geremia to
another sacerdos, Talasius. The Latin of the letter,
it may be remarked, is as bad as its contents.
Talasius sent it to the city Arabia, to another sacerdos,
Leoban. Leoban sent it to the city Vetfania, where
it was received by another sacerdos, Macrius. Macrius
sent it to the Mount of the holy Archangel Michael.
Thence by the hand of an angel of God it reached
the city of Rome, and the place of sepulture of the
holy Peter, where are placed the keys of the kingdom
of heaven. And twelve papati[1] in the city of Rome
appointed three days vigil of fasting and prayer,
night and day, . . . and the rest up to the end. We
may fairly compare with this—except so far as the
insanities of all these sacerdotes, and cities, and

[1] Men of papal dignity.

archangels and angels are concerned—the letter which a Pope soon after this sent to the Franks from St. Peter, the Virgin Mary, and himself.[1]

At a third session, after the initial ceremony, Denehard was asked had he any more writings of Aldebert? Yes, he had a prayer which Aldebert had composed. The prayer was read. It began thus: "O Lord God omnipotent, Father of Christ, the Son of God our Lord Jesus Christ and Alpha and Omega, who sittest above the seventh throne, and above Cherubin and Seraphin, great piety and abundant sweetness is with Thee. O Father of holy angels, who hast made heaven and earth, and all things therein, Thee I invoke, Thee I call, Thee I summon to me most miserable, for Thou hast deigned to say, Whatsoever ye shall ask the Father in My name, I have given unto you."

In the course of the reading, they came to this passage: "I pray you, I conjure you, I supplicate you, angel Uriel, angel Raguel, angel Tubuel, angel Michael, angel Adinus, angel Tubuas, angel Sabaoc, angel Simiel."

Zacharias asked the synod what their judgement was. They declared that these writings should be burned, and the authors anathematized. They declared that the only one of these eight names which was the name of an angel was Michael, the rest must be names of demons. The holy apostleship of the Pope had taught them, and divine authority had handed it down, that only three names of angels are known, Michael, Gabriel, Raphael.

The Pope replied that the advice to burn the documents was excellent; but it would be better to

[1] See *Alcuin of York*, S.P.C.K., page 199.

keep them in his holy records for the perpetual confusion of the writer. He then anathematized Aldebert and Clement, cut them off entirely from the sacred ministry, and desired the Frankish princes to keep them in solitary confinement.

It is rather remarkable that these Roman bishops and priests should be so positive that only three names of angels were known. Uriel is known as the fourth archangel, and the three angels who made up, with the archangels, the complete number seven, were Chamuel, Jophiel, and Zadkiel. It is true, however, that these angels of the Jews have not been recognized by the Christian Churches of East or West.

Aldebert and Clement were by no means disposed of. We have a letter from Zacharias to Boniface a year and a half later, in which he tells him that Pepin, the most excellent Mayor of the Palace of the Frank race, has consulted him on several points, on which the Pope sends writings, though he is aware that Boniface knows the view of the holy see. A Council is to be called to have these writings read.

"When the Council for this purpose is assembled, Boniface is to bring before it those sacrilegious and contumacious ex-bishops Aldebert, Godalsacius,[1] and Clement, that their case may be thoroughly sifted. "If it is found that when convicted of wandering from the right way they are ready to return to the way of righteousness, dispose of them in concert with the prince of the province, in accordance with the sanctions of the sacred canons, in such way as may seem good and pleasing in your eyes. But if they persist in their pride, contumaciously proclaiming that they are not guilty, send them to us, with two or three of the

---

[1] This is the only mention of this culprit.

most approved and prudent of your priests, that their
case may receive profound investigation at the apostolic
see, and the final judgement which they prove to
deserve may be given.''   This is a useful example of
the rapid growth of the practice of summoning accused
persons to Rome for trial, as the final court of ecclesiastical appeal.

We hear no more in the Bonifatian documents of
these persons.

CHAPTER XI

It is evident that a real and great clearing out of unsatisfactory ministers of religion was effected at the Council of Soissons. This is perhaps best shown in the opening paragraph of the letter which Zacharias addressed to all who had been present or had helped to carry out the cleansing work of those who were present [1] :—

" Zacharias the Pope to all bishops, priests, deacons, abbats, and to all dukes and counts, and to all who fear God throughout the Galliae and the province of the Franks.

" Our most reverend and most holy brother Boniface the Bishop has told us that when the synod was gathered together in your province according to our monition, by the action of our sons Pepin and Carloman your princes, the aforesaid Boniface conducting it in our stead, the Lord inclined your hearts, with your princes, to his teaching, so that you obeyed all his monitions and expelled from among you both false and schismatic and homicidal and fornicating bishops

---

[1] Ep. 61 ; Oct. 31, 745.

and priests [1].   For this we give thanks to our Omnipotent God."

Curiously enough the Pope proceeds to develop the subject of the homicidal priest, and his intention seems to us better than his logic, as also better than the ill compliment he pays to the success in arms of the dukes and counts :—

"The reason why all the pagan races prevailed against you in war is that there was difference between the lay folk and the priests to whom fighting was forbidden.   For what victory is given if in one hour priests perform the Lord's mysteries and present the Lord Christ's Body for the redemption of their own souls, and afterwards, with their own sacrilegious hands, kill either Christians to whom they ought to minister the Lord's Body or pagans to whom they ought to preach Christ?"

Boniface had informed Zacharias in his first letter that among the needs of the Frank Church under Carloman was the restoration of metropolitical order; that Church had not had an archbishop for a great many years last past.

In the report of the acts and decrees of Carloman's two Austrasian Councils nothing is said about archbishops.   But the subject was dealt with at the joint Council of Austrasia and Neustria held by Pepin and Carloman some little time after, and it was agreed to appoint three metropolitans, Rouen, Reims, and Sens. The fact, and the names of the persons selected,

---

[1] One word, *sacerdotes*. To translate either only bishops or only priests seems impossible, here and in so many places. *Presbyteros* is the word used by Boniface for priests who have not been advanced to the episcopate.   *Sacerdotes* frequently has to be taken as applied to all who have received ordination to the priesthood.

Boniface reported to the Pope, but we do not possess
the letter in which he sent the information of the
accomplished fact.

Zacharias had replied on June 22, 744 [1] :—

" You have shown us how God has touched the
hearts of our most excellent sons Pepin and Carloman,
so that by divine inspiration they strive to be your
allies and aid us in your preaching.

" As regards the metropolitan bishops whom you
[' thou,' not ' ye '] have appointed for each metropolis
in the provinces, Grimo, whom we already know, Abel,
and Hartbercht [2] ; these on your testimony we confirm,
and we send palls for their most firm establishment,
for the greater glory of God, that they may go forward to better things. What the custom of the pall
is, and how they who have licence to use it are to
expound their faith, we have informed them, telling
them the use of the pall,—to preach to those who are
in their charge the way of salvation; that in their
churches the ecclesiastical discipline may be kept
unmutilated and remain unshaken ; that the priesthood that is in them may not be polluted, as formerly
it was, but be clean and accepted of God so far as
human conditions allow ; that none may be found to
deviate from the canons, and that a clean sacrifice be
by them immolated ; so that God in their gifts is
pleased, and the people of God, their minds purged
of all squalor, may be strong to show forth the sincere
duty of the Christian religion."

Four months and a half later, November 5, 744,
there came a letter showing much perturbation on the
part of the Pope.[3] It would seem that the three

[1] Ep 57.   [2] Respectively Rouen, Reims, and Sens.
[3] Ep. 58 ; Nov. 5, 744.

metropolitans had considered the position they would
be in if they accepted the pall. It must, they knew,
mean something much more than, and quite different
from, the curious statement of its use given above by
Zacharias. If that was all, every priest should have
it or every bishop and priest could do without it.

"We have received by the bearer of this present
letter the letter of your most holy brotherliness, and
on reading its contents we are plunged into wonder
and amazement, so very different is it from what you
wrote to us only last August. In that former letter
you told us that a Council had been held by the aid
of God and with the consent and assistance of Carloman; and how you had suspended from the sacred
office certain false priests who were unworthy of the
divine ministry; and you disclosed to us that you
had appointed three archbishops to be metropolitans,
Grimo in the city of Rouen, Abel in the city of Reims,
and Hartbert in the city of Sens. We learned this
also from Carloman and Pepin. You advised that
we should send three palls to the three named metropolitans, and this we granted for the unification and
reformation of the churches. But now we receive
your latest letter, and are, as we have said, astonished
that whereas you in concert with the above-named
princes of the Gallican provinces asked for three palls,
you now ask for a pall for Grimo alone. We desire
that your brotherliness will indicate to us why you
have asked at first for three and afterwards for only
one, so that we may have full knowledge and not
remain in doubt."

The natural explanation is that when Abel and
Hartbert discovered what they would be undertaking
if they accepted the pallium, they declined it, in ac-

cordance with the independence which for many centuries marked the Gallican Church.

" We have found, too, that in your letter, which has
been too disturbing to our mind, you have written of
us as though we were corrupters of the Canons and
aimed at rescinding the traditions of the Fathers, by
falling with our clerks into the heresy of simony,
which be far from us; namely, by compelling those
to whom we give palls to make presents to us, de-
manding money of them. Dearest brother, we exhort
your sanctity that you never again write to us anything of this kind, for we take it as offensive and
injurious that we should be credited with action
which we detest. Far be it from us and our clerks
that we should sell at a price the gift which we have
received by the grace of the Holy Spirit. As regards
the three palls for which, as we have said, you asked,
no one has sought any gain from them. The charters
of confirmation, too, which according to custom are
issued from our office, we have granted at our own cost,
taking nothing from them. Far be it that your
sanctity urge the charge of simony against us, for we
anathematize all who dare to sell at a price the gift of
the Holy Spirit.

" You mentioned to us also in your letter that you
had found in Bavaria a false priest who affirmed that he
had been ordained bishop by us. Your brotherliness
acted well in suspending him from the priesthood, for
a man who is false in one is false in all. By the
authority of the blessed Peter, prince of the apostles,
we enjoin upon you never by any means to allow any
one whom you find deviating from the sacred canons to
degrade the sacred ministry.

" You have asked if you are to have the right of

preaching over the province of Bavaria which was
conceded to you by our predecessor. We increase
rather than diminish that concession. And not in
Bavaria only, but in the whole of the province of the
Galliae we enjoin you that in our place you preach
with spiritual zeal the reformation of all that is
contrary to the Christian religion or the canonical
institutions."

It is very unfortunate that we have lost the letter
of Boniface in which he—as it would appear—so
frankly spoke to the Pope on the subject of the
pecuniary demands of Rome. The Pope had not at
that time become a wealthy temporal sovereign, with
money enough for his own needs and those of his
officials, and we should not have been surprised to hear
that the necessary documents cost money, as letters
patent do. It may be remarked, with regard to the
inexpensiveness of the pall, that if what the Pope
said was in accordance with the facts, a great change
came in the course of time. The chaplain of one of
our Archbishops of Canterbury who was a member of
a mendicant order, tells of the shock caused to the
archiepiscopal mendicant when the bill was presented
to him at Rome. The bill was *horribilis in aspectu et
auditu terribilis*, horrible to look at, and when read
out terrible. It is unnecessary to add that extortions
of the Court of Rome had much to do with creating
and developing the English desire to make an end
once for all.

Boniface excuses himself to the Pope in a letter [1] the
fullness and fulsomeness of the address of which con-
trasts curiously with the meagreness of the address of
his first letter to this Pope :—

[1] Ep. 86; A.D. 751.

"To the most reverend father, most loved lord, master with fear and honour to be venerated, endowed with the privilege of apostolic honour, exalted with the fillet of the pontificate of the apostolic see, Zacharias, Boniface the humble, your servant though unworthy and last of all, and yet Germanic legate most devoted, all health of unfailing love in Christ that can be wished for.

"I beg the indulgence of the apostolic see for having some time ago made known to your holiness the matter of the archbishops of the Franks and the request for palls from the Roman Church, trusting in their promises. What they promised they have delayed and not fulfilled. They are still discussing the matter, and it is not known what they will do. But so far as my will went, the promises would have been fulfilled."

Zacharias made one more answer, and the matter rested where it was [1] :—

"You have written about the Frank bishops and the palls, that the promises have not been carried out. If they still fulfil them, they will have praise; but if they do not, they shall themselves see [2]. But we, the divine grace enabling us, what we have freely received freely give. Your benign will in the matter we recognize."

The width of the commission to Boniface, that is of the area over which Boniface had developed the supremacy of the Pope, may be gathered from the list of bishops to whom on May 1, 748, he sent a letter commending to them Boniface.[3] He desires them to receive in his stead, for the strengthening

[1] Ep. 87; Nov. 4, 751.
[2] *Ipsi videbunt.* A rather inadequate threat.   [3] Ep. 82.

of their love and as a fellow labourer with them for the Gospel of Christ, "the most holy and most reverend Boniface, our brother, archbishop, legate of the holy see, our personal representative." The prelates are Reginfrid Rouen, Deodatus Beauvais, Rimberht Amiens, Heleseus Noyons, Fulcric Tongres, David Spires, Arthereus Terouane (to Boulogne, 1566), Treward Cambray, Burhard Würzburg, Genebaud Laon, Romanus Meaux, Agilolf Cologne, Hedda Strassburg. The other persons addressed are not mentioned by name; they are the most loved chorepiscopi, presbyters, deacons, and all orthodox clerics of the churches of God.

On the same day the Pope wrote another letter,[1] addressed to a large number of laymen by name, presumably covering the same wide area. The letter is interesting in itself, as it deals entirely with the duty of the lay folk :—

"To the magnificent men our sons Throand, Sandrad, Nanther, Liutfrid, Sterfrid, Gundpert, Agnus, Haald, Rantulf, Rotpert, Brunicho, Rothard, Rocgon, and all others, great and small, free born and serfs, Zacharias the Pope."

He is greatly rejoiced to hear of their faith, and good conversation, and the love they have for their spiritual mother the holy Catholic and Apostolic Church of God, and the priests thereof. He warns them against false priests and all ill-doing. He then proceeds to the special points on which he desires to instruct them :—

"I admonish you, most loved ones, fear God, honour the priests, giving to them the due of holiness; that by your aid they may remain un-

----

[1] Ep. 83.

disturbed and free from care, to preach salutary
things and keep ecclesiastical rule and vigour, all
clerics being subject to their own bishops and taught
by them the sacred Scripture   For it has been
taught us by the Lord—'Render under Caesar the
things that be Caesar's and unto God the things
that be God's.'

"An apostolic precept I give unto you, that no
secular person have in his service a cleric; a cleric
must serve in heart and mind Him whose mark
he has on his head, trained in those things which
he is taught by his own bishop.   For it is a thing
detestable and wicked that a cleric take part in
plays or spend his life with hawk and hound, and
then, harmed by such theatrical practices, become
a bishop or a priest full not of good but of evil.
For it is written, 'All ye that love the Lord abhor
that which is evil.'

"This also we exhort your Christianity, that
according to the institutes of the holy canons no
presbyter coming from elsewhere be received in
churches founded by you, unless he have been
consecrated by the bishop of your Church or have
received commendatory letters from him.   For many
false to themselves, servants usually of some one,
fugitive, inform their own lords that they have
been consecrated priests, and are ministers of the
devil, not of God; as are also they who receive
them, for it is written, 'When thou sawest a thief
thou consentedst unto him.'   Let no one of you therefore, dearest ones, put a presbyter into any church
without the assent of his own bishop, unless first his
origin and manner of life have been approved by
your own bishop.

"With regard to monasteries, also, built by you or built out of the gifts of the faithful, if a monk or a religious woman of your own kin is appointed to preside over them, the bishop of the place must consecrate them as abbat or abbess. And if there be a community there, on the death of the abbat or abbess and the election of another by the community, the consecration must be by the bishop, not by the founder. For what has once been offered to God must remain intact under the rule of the bishop. It is right, also, that one who is ordained abbat or abbess be first taught thoroughly all the divine law and sacred Scripture; that one who has learned to be in subjection may thereafter know how to rule with moderation.

"The distribution of the tithes of the faithful, which are offered in church, is not to be in the power of him that offers. The constitutions of the holy Fathers direct that they must be made by the bishop into four portions. For who, as the Lord taught, putting his hand to the plough and looking back, is fit for the kingdom of God? With regard to church money, it is ruled that it is in the hands of the bishop to be dispensed to the clergy who assist him in the churches. For it is written, 'Let him that ministereth at the altar live of the altar.' Thence also alms for the poor must be provided, funds for building churches, coverings for altars, fittings for the several churches, as means allow."

This is a very vague direction with regard to tithes.

CHAPTER XII

AMONG the almost endless interesting questions which the work of Boniface suggests, there is one which naturally stands out prominently. It is this: What kind of belief was it that the pagans to whom he preached Christ themselves held?

From Willibald's history we know that their practices were like those of our forefathers. They worshipped trees and springs, presumably as the abode or the handiwork of the powers of nature whom in accordance with a natural instinct they sought to personify. They sacrificed the flesh of various beasts; and as they are said to have sacrificed them to devils, we may understand that their sacrifices were at least in some measure intended to propitiate ill-disposed gods, though no doubt in some measure intended for the benevolent and beneficent gods of their system. These had long been the religious practices of the Teutonic races. Tacitus, in his concise way, tells us much, writing about a century after Christ. They worshipped Mercury as their chief god, and to him as such they offered on stated days human victims. To Hercules and Mars they offered animals. This means, to Teutonic gods which corresponded to these Greek and Latin gods and demigods. Some of the Suevi sacrificed to

Isis. They held sacred the thickets and the glades of woods. There was an altar consecrated to Ulysses and his father Laertes on the confines of Germany and Rhaetia, or as we should say roughly Switzerland. As in the time of Boniface so in the time of Tacitus they relied in all important matters, and also in matters of daily business, upon auguries and the casting of lots. Not otherwise was it with us Anglo-Saxons when Augustine came. He found us killing cattle in offering to devils, and eating the flesh in huts built of the boughs of trees. And through all the earlier years at least of the Anglo-Saxon Church, the Penitentiaries had to keep on forbidding us to eat horse-flesh, on account of its old sacrificial character.

But we learn much more about the religious beliefs of those to whom Boniface preached, from a letter which Daniel, his Wessex bishop, wrote to him about the year 724.[1] Daniel had evidently thought the matter out very carefully, and with full knowledge of the beliefs of the Hessians and others. We can scarcely doubt, too, that he had full knowledge of the pagan beliefs of the Anglo-Saxons still lingering, if indeed lingering is not much too weak a word. Sussex, the whole kingdom of the South Saxons, contiguous to his own diocese, had been pagan till the days of his own early youth; and the Isle of Wight, the last portion of England to persist in idolatry, had Daniel himself for its first bishop. The advice which Daniel gave to Boniface was to the following effect :—" Do not begin by denying the genealogies of their gods. Take them at their word. Ask them whether their gods, being born as they

[1] Ep. 23 ; A.D. 723-5.

say of male and female gods after the manner of
men, are not men rather than gods, and like men
came into being, not having existed before. And
as their gods had a beginning, ask them if they
think this world had a beginning, or has gone on
for ever without a beginning. If it has had a beginning, who made it ?—for before there was a world
they cannot find a place for their gods to subsist
and dwell. I speak not of this visible world only,
but of all the extent of space which the thoughts
of the pagans can conceive." That is a remarkable
phrase, for that early time. "If they should contend
that the world has always existed, without a beginning, be careful to refute that with many proofs and
arguments. Ask them who governed, who guided
the world before gods were born. How could their
gods subdue to their governance the world, which
existed before them? Ask them whence, or by
whom, or when, the first god—or it may be goddess
—was put here, or was born. Ask them if they
suppose that gods and goddesses still generate gods
and goddesses. If they do not, when or why did
they cease from generating? If they do, the number
of them must by this time be infinite. Among so
many, mortals do not know which are the more
powerful; and it is of high importance not to offend
the more powerful. Ask them whether the favour
of the gods is to be cultivated for temporal and
present happiness, or rather for future and eternal.
If for temporal happiness, ask them to tell in what
the pagans are happier than the Christians. Ask
them what gain they bestow by their sacrifices upon
the gods, to whom everything belongs. If the gods
need these things, why don't they take them? If

they do not need them, it is superfluous to imagine
that they appease the gods by them. All this should
be said not in an insulting and irritating way, but
gently and with great moderation. Then from time
to time you should suggest a comparison of their
superstitions with the Christian beliefs; but by side
touches, that the pagans, in confusion, not exaspera-
tion, may blush for their absurd opinions, and that
they may not suppose that we are ignorant of their
nefarious rites and fables. This, too, you should
point out, that if their gods are all-powerful, beneficent, and just, they should not only reward those who
worship them, they should punish those who make
naught of them. And if their gods are to do these
two things in this present temporal life, why do
they spare the Christians, who are turning almost
the whole world away from them, and throwing
down their idols? The Christians occupy fertile
lands, rich in wine and oil and abounding in re-
sources, and have left to the pagans with their gods
rough cold lands in which the gods driven out of
the rest of the world are supposed to reign. You
should often tell them of the magnitude of the
Christian world, in comparison with which very few
persevere in the ancient vanities. And lest they boast
of the rule of their gods over the heathen races as
the rule of a lawful prince, point out to them that
the whole world was formerly given over to idolatry,
until, illumined by the grace of Christ the omnipotent
builder of the world, by the knowledge of the one
God, the ruler, it was brought to life and reconciled
with God. For what else does the baptizing of the
children of Christians that is daily going on mean
than this, that each one of them is being separately

purged of the Gentile filth and guilt in which the whole world was formerly set?"

It is a very interesting argument, and goes deeper than another English argument with which we may compare it, the argument, namely, by which King Oswy succeeded in converting his guest Sigebert the Little, King of the East Saxons. Sigebert was a friend of Oswy's, and he often went up north to visit his friend. Oswy used to argue with his guest on these occasions about his idol-worship. Bede gives[1] us the substance of the argument, the main part of it evidently coming from the Old Testament Scriptures: we may date the final and successful occasion about 653. This is his summary:—

Those cannot be gods that have been made by the hands of men. A stock or a stone is not proper material for making a god, for the remains of the material are burned, or made into vessels for men's use, or cast out as refuse. God is rather to be understood as of incomprehensible majesty, and invisible to human eyes; almighty; eternal; the creator of heaven and earth and man. He governs the world, and will judge it in righteousness. His everlasting seat is in heaven, not in vile and fading matter.

The argument may not be as penetrating and thoughtful as that of Bishop Daniel three generations later; but it converted to Christianity two kings and their suites, and eventually their people.

In a book[2] published in 1908, the form in which Boniface demanded of his converts the rejection of idols and the acceptance of the faith of Christ is

[1] *H. E.* iii. 22.
[2] My *Alcuin of York*, S.P.C.K., p. 295.

given, as an example of a curious language. It must be repeated here for its own purpose. It comes so near to English and so close to modern German that its meaning is clear. It is in the form of a catechism, and is known as the *Abrenuntiatio diaboli*. A photographic facsimile which the writer was allowed to have made in the Vatican was given in the book referred to, and may properly be repeated here, fig. 17. The library mark of the MS. is " Vat. Palat. nro. 577, fol. 6, 7 ". The catechism is as follows :—

" Forsachistu diobolae ?   Ec forsacho diabolae.

" End allum diobolgelde ?   End ec forsacho allum diobolgeldae.

" End allum dioboles uuercum ?   End ec forsacho allum dioboles uuercum and [1] uuordum thunaer ende uuoden ende saxnote ende allum them unholdum the hira genotas sint."

So far the *abrenuntiatio*. Now the *fides* :—

" Gelobistu in Got alamehtigen fadaer ?   Ec gelobo in Got alamehtigen fadaer.

" Gelobistu in Crist Godes suno ?   Ec gelobo in Crist Godes suno.

"Gelobistu in halogen Gast ?   Ec gelobo in halogen Gast."

It is really unnecessary to English this, it comes so very naturally to us :—

" Dost thou forsake the devil?   I forsake the devil.

" And all the devil's wage ?   And I forsake all the devil's wage.

" And all the devil's works ?   And I forsake all

[1] Possibly *und*; but an examination of the whole fourteen lines of the facsimile shows that there is no certainty about the first letter of the word.

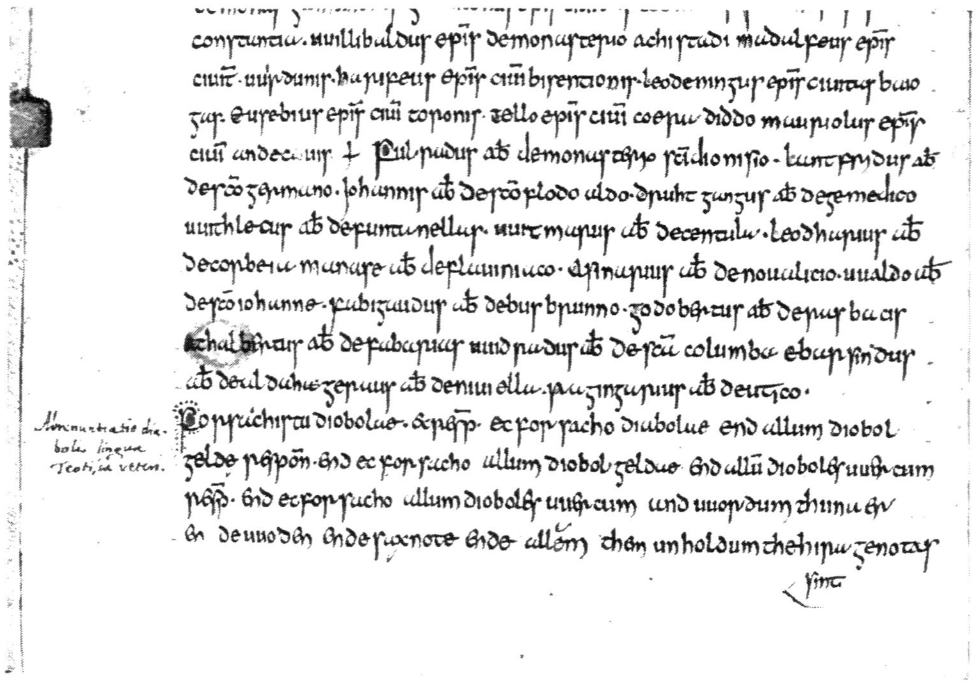

FIG. 17. ABRENUNTIATIO DIABOLI.

the devil's works and words, Thunor and Woden and
Saxnote, and all the fiends that are their companions.

" Dost thou believe in God the Father Almighty ?
I believe in God the Father Almighty.

" Dost thou believe in Christ the Son of God ?
I believe in Christ the Son of God.

" Dost thou believe in the Holy Ghost ? I believe
in the Holy Ghost."

Saxnot, or Saxneat, appears in the Saxon genealogies of the kings of the East Saxons as the son of
Woden. Saberct, the first Christian King of the East
Saxons, whose capital was London, was reputed his
grandson with seven " greats " before it. The Germans suggest that the very name Saxon comes from
him, and that as he bore the sword he corresponds to
Mars. The order of the names of the three gods,
which puts Woden, the chief god, only second, is
supposed to be the result of naming the three idols in
the order in which they stood, from dexter to sinister,
Woden being in the middle, with Thor on his right
and Saxnot on his left. In Pomerania they still
swear by "donersexen ", Thunor and Saxnot, and in
Bavaria they swear " meiner sechsen ".

It would be long and wearisome to deal in detail with
the Council at which this *abrenuntiatio* is supposed
to have been presented, namely, the Council of Liftines.
The word Liftines itself, its spelling and its locality,
has cost commentators many pages and some temper.
So much of the doings of the Council as is recorded
in the Bonifatian documents will be found at p. 184.
Elsewhere we have the bare headings of the chapters
which prohibited pagan rites.

Passing to these prohibited rites, the first prohibitions
deal with death. There were impious rites performed

P

at the grave; and impious things were done over the dead, called *dadsisas,* a word which is a trial to the Germans; they may be feasts, and they may be death-songs, called elsewhere devil-songs. A capitular of Charlemagne forbids as pagan any eating or drinking at the grave. It may be remarked that if the chapters of which we now have only the headings had been preserved, we should have had information of marvellous fullness on a large number of points on which we can now only frame carefully calculated guesses.

The next head is " of pollutions in February ". This was the time of festivals to welcome the sun on its return from winter quarters. From the Latin name *Spurcalia,* that is, pollutions, February is still called Sporkel, or Sporkelmaend, in some parts of Holland. The principal sacrifices were those of swine. The Germans think that the carnival is a survival of this paganry.

Another head is " of rites in woods, called *nimidas* ". Here again the Germans are tried. Whatever may be the derivation of the *nimidas* (not taking it to be a Latin accusative plural), no doubt sacrifices and other rites in the secret recesses of woods are meant. Sacrifices to Woden and Thunor, Mercury and Jove, are forbidden; sacrifices on sacred stones and at sacred springs; sacrifices offered outwardly to saints, but inwardly and in intention to heathen gods; phylacteries and bandages; fire produced by rubbing wood, that is, nodfyr [1], through the smoke of which persons and animals were passed; pagan processions with clothes torn and shoes cut, called Yrias; these

---

[1] " Niedfyor," in Carloman's edict. It is explained to be fire raised by rubbing two dry sticks together.

and many more were forbidden. If these things are kept in mind, Boniface's famous letter to Pope Zacharias, to which we can now turn, receives much illustration.

In connexion with Boniface's lifelong struggle against the prevalence of pagan rites, and also in connexion with his frankness of criticism when in his opinion the Pope and Rome itself deserved criticism, we may turn to one of Boniface's letters in which he had some very interesting things to say to Pope Zacharias.[1] Carnal men, he said, of the Franks, Bavarians, and Alemannians, common persons, went to Rome and saw practised there, apparently under licence and permission of the ecclesiastics, some of the very things which at home were forbidden by Boniface and his clergy. He begs that the Pope will, on all accounts, put a stop to this. He is told that every year, at the beginning of January, there may be seen, not only in the city of Rome, but close by the church of St. Peter, bands of people parading through the streets after the manner of the heathen, celebrating sacrilegious rites with songs and cries by night and day, loading their tables with feasts, refusing to lend anything out of their houses to their neighbours, no fire, or implement, or anything useful. Women, too, are to be seen, wearing phylacteries (amulets) in pagan fashion, with charms bound on their arms and legs, and publicly offering such things for sale. These things were a great impediment to those who were preaching elsewhere that pagan rites must be abandoned. The apostle—so they described St. Paul, *par excellence*—had said, " Ye observe days and seasons : I fear, lest I have laboured in vain among

[1] Ep. 50 ; A.D. 742.

you." St. Augustine of Hippo had specially preached against the retention of such rites by Christians; " Whosoever believes," he says, " in magicians and diviners and soothsayers, or in phylacteries and any other kind of auguries, though he fast, though he pray, though he perpetually run to church, though he give large alms, though he shall have tormented his body with all manner of torture, it shall profit him nothing so long as he does not relinquish those sacrilegious rites."

" If only your paternity would prohibit those paganisms in the city of Rome, it would be a gain to you, and a wonderful help to us in our church teaching.

" Further, there are married bishops and priests of the Frank race, who have been determined adulterers and fornicators, as is proved by the children born to them in their episcopacy or priesthood. They come back from Rome and tell us that the Roman pontiff has given them licence to continue in their episcopal ministry in the church. Against such we strive, for we have never heard that the apostolic see has given decisions contrary to the decrees of the canons.

" Further, I am bound to ask and seek counsel of your paternity about a certain scandal to our preaching which has lately come upon us and has greatly disturbed our mind and shamed the priests of the churches. A great personage, a layman, has come to us and declared that he received licence from Pope Gregory of saintly memory to marry the widow of his uncle. She was also the wife of his first cousin, and had separated from him in his lifetime. She is related in the third degree[1] to the man who now says

---

[1] *Genuculo.* The degree of relationship was determined by counting the two persons and the intermediates. Thus there were here (1) the man, (2) his father or mother, (3) the brother

he has licence from Rome to marry her. Further, she
took the vow of chastity and was veiled; and then,
throwing off the veil, she married. We do not
believe that he has licence from Rome, because a
synod of the Church in which I was born and
brought up, a synod namely at London in the Saxon
land beyond the sea, constituted and ordained by
disciples of the holy Gregory, Archbishops Augustine, Laurentius, Justus, Melletus, declared on the
authority of holy Scripture that such marriage was
a very great wickedness, incestuous, a horrible offence,
and a damnable crime. Pray let your paternity not
disdain to indicate to us the truth of this matter, that
scandals and schisms and new errors may not spring
up from it and spread among priests and Christian
people."

There was something very boldly Anglican in this
throwing at the Pope's head as final the decrees of
an English Council.

Finally, Boniface informs the Pope that he has
sent him a mantle of hair and a little gold and
silver.

This letter certainly deserves to be taken as an
evidence of the frankness of Boniface's criticism of
the see of Rome. He used to the fullest degree the
mysterious prestige of that see; but it seems sometimes that he is a little cautious in his recognition of
that divinely planned and appointed Vicariate of

of (2), namely the woman's husband, related in the third
degree to the man. Since marriage made both one, she, too,
was related in the third degree. She was also related to him
in the fourth degree, as the wife of his first cousin; the
relationship of first cousin having two steps between the parties,
the father or mother of the one and the father or mother of the
other, thus counted as in the fourth degree.

Christ, and, among the apostles including St. Paul, that sole headship of St. Peter over the universal Church, one or other of which the Popes of the time pressed in one letter after another, as though constant repetition of the claim was necessary to its existence.

So far, however, as any personal question is concerned, it must be remembered that this was Boniface's first letter to a new Pope, whom he had known in a less exalted station on one at least of his visits to Rome, and thus his criticisms were directed entirely to a state of things for which Zacharias was not responsible, and for which he might be respectfully asked to provide a remedy.

The answer of Pope Zacharias on these points was as follows [1] :—

"With regard to the man who has spread about the statement that he received licence from our predecessor of blessed memory to take in pernicious wedlock the widow of his own uncle, wife of his own first cousin, and a veiled sister, far be it from my predecessor to have done any such thing. From this apostolic see decisions are not issued which are contrary to the institutes of the Fathers and the canons. Admonish, exhort, chide them; cease not till they withdraw from such matrimony, that they perish not eternally. Let them remember that they were redeemed by the Blood of Christ. Let them not hand themselves over of their own accord to the power of the devil by not abstaining from this incestuous marriage, but rather to Father, Son, and Holy Ghost. We have ourselves sent a formal letter of warning to the man.

[1] Ep. 51 ; 1 Apr. 743.

"As to the Kalends of January, auguries, filacteries, incantations, and divers observances which you say are kept near St. Peter's or in the City of Rome, we judge these things to be detestable to us and to all Christians and pernicious; for God says, 'neither shall ye use enchantments nor observe times' (Lev. xix. 26), and 'surely there is no enchantment against Jacob, neither is there any divination against Israel' (Numb. xxiii. 23). So we hold it necessary for us to be careful to have nothing to do with these things, for we have been taught that they were all cut off by the Fathers. And since by the inspiration of the devil they had burst out again, from the day on which the divine clemency bade us—all unworthy as we are—to become the Vicar of the Apostle, from that day we have cut off all these things. In like manner we wish your holiness to preach to the people subject to you and to lead them to eternal life. By a constitution of our predecessor and patron of holy memory, the Lord Pope Gregory, all these things were piously and faithfully cut off, as well as many other things which by the suggestion of the devil grew in the sheepfold of Christ. For the welfare of your people we have arranged to send to you a copy of this.

"With regard to those bishops and priests [1] who hold false opinions or are proved adulterers or fornicators, and declare that they are allowed and indeed licensed by the apostolic see, your holy brotherliness must in no way believe it. As in the former case, inflict upon them canonical punishment. We wish you to do nothing but what the sacred canons teach or you learn from this apostolic see.

[1] In one word, *sacerdotibus.*

"In accordance with your holiness's petition we send letters of confirmation to the three bishops, which we wish them to receive by your hands.

"To Carloman our son we have sent other writings, that he may hasten to do what he has proposed and to give all help.

"These replies, dearest brother, we have made as God has given us on the several heads included above, for the cutting off of all scandals of the fraud of the devil. If anything else should occur, your holy brotherliness will study to amend it among the people committed to your charge as the sacred canons teach. For it becomes not us to preach anything but what we have been taught by the holy Fathers. And if anything novel should by the subtlety of the enemy arise, which your brotherliness cannot see from the institutes of the canons how to treat, do not hesitate to send it here to us, that by God's help we may without delay inform you of what may be for the amendment of a new race.

"Your holy brotherliness may be assured, dearest brother, that we have the love of thee so full in our heart that we daily desire to see thee in actual presence and thus to have thee in our company as a minister of God and a dispenser of the churches of Christ.

"For the rest, be strong in the Lord, dearest brother, be strong and labour at the work which the divine clemency hath willed thee to do. For a great hope of reward awaiteth thee, which God hath promised to them that love Him. And we, sinners as we be, cease not to implore without intermission the immeasurable clemency of God, that He who hath begun in you a good work may accomplish it even unto the end. And may the blessed Peter, prince of the apostles, co-operate with thee in all good things wherein thou desirest to be obedient unto him.

"May God keep thee safe, most reverend and most holy brother."

CHAPTER XIII

THE real nature of Boniface, the true bent of his
heart, come out in his letters to England. It is there
that we find the man; in his letters to Popes and
princes we have the missionary, the business man,
the ecclesiastical statesman. And in the letters from
England to Boniface we see the affectionate response
to the influence of a most lovable temperament. It
will be well to give here one or two examples of the
affectionateness of the response.

Of letters from England to Boniface, one of the
earliest,[1] addressed to him as abbat, before he became
bishop, and under the name Winfrid, not Boniface,
was written by a lady called Ecgburga.[2] Now that
her brother Oshere is dead, she tells him, there is
almost no one of men whom she places before him in
her regards. No day ever passes, no night will ever
pass, without thought of him. And now another
blow has fallen; her sister Wetburga is detained in
Rome, and her sorrow is greater than she can bear.
"After that Wetburga, my most dear sister (with
whom I grew up, with whom I was nursed at the
same breast, and had one mother of us both in the

---

[1] Ep. 13; 716-720.
[2] On this family see pages 238, 239.

Lord), inflicting, as it were, a wound, and renewing
my grief, vanished from my eyes and left me—I call
Jesus to witness—everywhere is sorrow, everywhere
fear, everywhere the image of death; rather would I
have died, if so it had pleased Him to whom all secrets
are known. Before that unforeseen—not bitter death
but more bitter division—separated us from one
another—her, as believe, happy from me unhappy—
knowing how much I loved, how much I cherished
her, she left me to be in servitude to this life; whom
now, as I hear, a prison confines in the Roman city;
but the love of Christ, which shone and flourished
in her heart, is mightier and stronger than all bonds,
and 'perfect love casteth out fear'." She bewails
her sins, which unfit her for her position. She longs
for the sight of him, more earnestly than the tempest-
tossed sailor longs for the harbour, the thirsting fields
for the showers, the mother on the curved shore for
the coming of her son. Her sins are such that she
must be absolved from imminent perils; she is brought
to desperation; out of the inmost recesses of her
heart she calls to him from the ends of the earth,[1]
she anxiously entreats him, most blessed lord, to raise
her onto the rock of his prayers, for he is her hope,
a tower of strength against the enemy visible and
invisible. To console her immense sorrow, to quiet
the storm of her grief, she beseeches him to strengthen
her weakness lest it utterly give way. Will he send
her some solace, it may be in holy relics, or will he
deign to send her but a very few words by letter, that
in them she may have his presence alway? These

---

[1] This and some other phrases of the letter incline some
critics to give a much later date to the letter, somewhere about
733.

things she wrote by the hand of Ealdbert, who, like St. Paul's amanuensis, sends a message of his own, reminding Winfrid that he long ago promised to remember him in his deified prayers, a further sign of not very early date.

Another very long letter from an abbess in great trouble will provide us with extracts that seem to bring the times rather clearly before us :—

"To the venerable Winfrid, named also Boniface,[1] blessed in the Lord in faith and love, endowed with the privilege of the priesthood and crowned with the flowers of virginal chastity as with garlands of lilies, and erudite in knowledge of doctrine, Eangyth, unworthy handmaid of the handmaids of God, with the undeserved title of abbess, and her only daughter Eadburga,[2] named also Bugga, eternal health in the holy Trinity."

They begin by thanking him for a letter which he had sent from across the seas, though no word of their mouth was adequate for that purpose, and then proceed as follows :—

"Most loving brother in the spirit rather than the flesh, munificently endowed with spiritual graces, we wish these pages, wetted by our tears, to make known to you alone, and God alone is our witness, that we are overwhelmed by accumulated miseries, as by a very heavy weight, by the tumults of secular affairs; as when the foaming depths of the sea dash against the rocks and the keels of the ships are turned upwards. Thus are the little ships of our souls shaken by great miseries and multifarious calamities, as it is said of the house in the Gospel, 'The rain descended, and the

---

[1] Ep. 14; 719–722.
[2] On these ladies see pages 239, 331.

floods came, and the winds blew.'[1] First of all, then, and above all that comes upon us from without, there is the memory of a chain of innumerable sins, and full and perfect trust in no good thing. And not only have we our own souls to think of, but—what is more difficult and much more burdensome—the souls of those committed to our charge, of both sexes and of various ages. We have to minister to the minds and the divers dispositions of many persons, and have to give an account hereafter before the sublime tribunal of Jesus Christ, not only for manifest sins of deed and word, but also for secret thoughts, hidden from men, witnessed by God. We have single-handed to fight a twofold foe; with ten thousand to strive against twenty thousand. Our souls are tried by the difficulties of domestic affairs and the consideration of divers discords which the hater of all good sows among all men, especially among persons of monastic life; and he knows that the powerful suffer torments powerfully." To all this is added poverty, the lack of temporal things, and the narrow dimensions of their land. Besides, the king was hostile to them, for they were accused to him by those who hated them. There was the onerous burden also of the service due to the king and the queen, the bishop and the prefect, and their attendants.[2] To come to personal sorrows, they had suffered loss of friends and neighbours, a host of connexions, a crowd of blood relations. Eangyth has neither son

---

[1] Matt. vii 25, 27. The ladies quote the passage with *impegerunt*, the ordinary Vulgate reading being *irruerunt*.

[2] No doubt in the form of expensive hospitalities when these great people, lay or clerical, used their monastery as a resting-place.

nor brother, father nor uncle, only this one daughter; she is destitute of dear ones in the world except one sister, and a mother who is very old, and the son of a brother who is in a very unhappy condition, by reason of the state of his mind and of the fact that the king greatly hates his family. They have no one else to help them, God has taken away all the rest. Some have died at home. Others have trusted themselves to the waves and have sought the thresholds of the holy Apostles Peter and Paul, and of many martyrs, virgins, and confessors, whose names God knows. . . . Much time has elapsed since Eangyth conceived the desire to visit Rome, once the mistress of the world, as so many others had done, near friends, relatives, and strangers, there to seek pardon for sin, as many had done and were still doing. She begs for an answer; commends to him her near friend Denewald; and requests him to send Denewald on to the priest and confessor Bertheri.

It would appear that Eangyth died soon after writing this letter, and that Boniface sent his reply to her daughter Bugga, who, it may be, had written another letter in the interval. Its address is in very complimentary terms [1] :—

"To the lady most beloved, and in the love of Christ to be preferred before all others of the feminine sex, our sister Bugga, abbess, Boniface the little, unworthy bishop, health in Christ.

"Be it known to thee, sister most dear, with regard to the advice you have asked for in your letter, that I neither forbid the foreign journey you propose nor confidently advise it. But I will say what I think. If you have given up the anxious

[1] Ep. 27; about 725.

charge which you had of the servants and handmaids[1] of the Lord and of the monastic life, in order
that you might in quiet contemplate God, how should
you now serve with labour and irksome care the word
and the will of secular men? It seems to me better,
if on account of secular persons you cannot at home
enjoy the freedom of a quiet mind, that you should
by travel acquire, if you will and can, liberty of
contemplation. Our sister Wetburg did so. She
has told me by letter that she has found that life
of quiet near the thresholds of the holy Peter for
which she has long yearned. But she has told me—
for I wrote to her about you—that you must wait
till the rebellions, and assaults, and the threats of
the Saracens, which have recently burst upon Rome,
have quieted down. She will send you an invitation
when that has happened. The best plan seems to me
to be, that you should be preparing the things necessary for the journey, should do as she advises, and
afterwards what God shall appoint. As to writing
something for you, pray pardon my offences, for by
reason of pressing labours and continuous travelling
I have nothing finished which I can send. When
I have finished something, I will take care to
transmit it to the presence of your dilection. For
the gifts you have sent me, the vestments namely,
I thank you, and I pray the omnipotent God that
He will give you the prize of eternal reward, with
angels and archangels, in the high summit of the
heavens. I beseech you by God, dearest sister, nay,
sweetest mother and lady, deign to pray assiduously
for me, because, for my sins, I labour under many

---

[1] The monastery over which she had ruled was evidently one
of monks and nuns.

tribulations, and am troubled much more by care and anxiety of mind than by labour of body. Know that the ancient trust between us never fails. Fare thee well in Christ."

We have seen, in connexion with the evil lives of the principal Frankish clergy, a portion of a letter from Boniface to Bishop Daniel of Wessex. The remaining portions of the letter are well worth recording here. We may take up the letter at the point where Boniface has finished his pathetic complaint about the court clerics.

He then begs the clemency of Daniel's paternity [1] to send him one solace in his pilgrimage, namely, a book of the prophets, which Abbat Winbert, formerly his master, now migrated to the Lord, had left behind him. There were six of the prophets included in this one book, and they were written in clear and separate letters. Greater solace for the old age of his life, Daniel could not send. In the land where he was, he could not procure such a book; and now that his eyes were dim, he could not read small letters run together. That was his reason for begging for this particular book, it was written in letters set out so very clearly and separately.[2]

He sends this letter by Forthere the priest, and with it a small present in token of pure affection, namely a towel, not all of silk but mixed with goat's hair, and rough for drying the feet of his dilection.

A priest who had lately come from Daniel's presence to Germany had told of the sad deprivation

---

[1] Ep. 63 ; 742-746.

[2] Anything more completely the opposite of this than the little Irish Gospels said to have been written by Boniface himself cannot be imagined (see pages 162, &c.).

which had befallen him. Daniel was now blind.[1]
Boniface quoted to him a number of texts, such as
"whom the Lord loveth He chasteneth", to console
him. He reminded him of what Antony said of
Didymus,[2] "thou *hast* eyes, with which God can be
seen, and His angels, and the glorious joys of Jerusalem that is on high." God had thus given him
the means of advancing virtue and augmenting merit,
by enabling him to see better with the spiritual eye
the things which God loves, and preventing his seeing
things which God hates. For in this perilous time,
what are bodily eyes but the windows of sin, by which
we look upon sins and sinners, and by which we draw
in to ourselves evil thoughts and desires.

Besides requests for portions of Holy Scripture we
find Boniface more than once asking for some part
of Bede's writings. Here is a letter to the Abbat
of Wearmouth and Jarrow[3] :—

"To the most beloved and most reverend Huet-
berht the abbat and to all the brethren of his holy
congregation Boniface the humble servant of the
servants of God the health of brotherly love in
Christ.

"With inmost prayers we entreat the piety of your
brotherhood to assist with your sacrosanct prayers us
labouring among the fierce and ignorant peoples of
Germany and planting the seed of the Gospel; that
the fierce power of Babylonish flame may be extin-
guished, and the few seeds may spring up from the

---

[1] The date assigned to this letter is 746, so that Daniel had
been bishop for forty-one years and must have been at least
getting on for eighty.
[2] The preceptor of Jerome.
[3] Ep. 76 ; 741-747.

Q

furrow and multiply. . . . We beg that you will deign
to have copied and transmitted to us some of the
lesser works of that most sagacious investigator of
the Scriptures, the monk Beda, who, as we have
heard, has lately shone among you as a candle of
the Church in the knowledge of Scripture. And if
it be not troublesome to you, send me one riding
cloak, a great comfort on my journeyings. As an
indication of my deep love I send you bed-spreads,[1]
as they call them here, of goats' hair. Though
they are unworthy I beg you will accept them as
a memorial."

Or again,[2] still naturally to Northumbria :—

"To a friend to be embraced with the arms of
love, a brother to be united in spiritual relationship,
Ecbercht the archbishop, adorned with the fillet of the
highest pontificate, Boniface, the humble bishop, German legate of the Catholic and Apostolic Roman
Church, health of love that decayeth not, flowering
in Christ.

"Rejoicing with thankful mind we received the
gifts and pamphlets sent to us by your sweetest
beatitude. . . . And now with deepest prayer we
entreat your clemency that your piety would pray for
us in our labours and dangers. Great necessity presses
upon us to seek the help of the just, as it is written :
'The prayer of a just man availeth much.' To narrate
all the evils that we suffer within and without, the
brevity of a letter forbids.

"And now we most earnestly beg that for the joy
of our grief you would do as you have done before,
that is, would send us some particle, some scintilla of

---

[1] Lectisternia.
[2] Ep. 91 ; 746-754.

the candle of the Church which the Holy Spirit has lighted in the regions of your province, namely some part, any part, of the tractates which the spiritual presbyter and investigator of the holy Scriptures, Beda, has by unlocking the Scriptures composed; but especially, if it may be, that which would be to us in our preaching so useful as a manual, his homilies and his work on the Proverbs of Solomon. For we have heard that he has written commentaries on these.

"By the bearer of this letter we send to thy high-ness, in place of a kiss, two wine-cups,[1] that for the love that is between us you may have a joyous day with your brethren."

This was not the only occasion on which Boniface requested Ecgbert to send him some of Bede's works. It will be remembered that, so far as we know, Bede's visit to Ecgbert at York in 734 was the only occasion on which Bede left his cloister, and that when his illness came in 735 and prevented his repeating his visit, he wrote to Ecgbert that exhaustive and painful letter on the state of Christianity in Northumbria which we value so highly now under the title of *Epistola ad Ecgbertum*. An alumnus of the School of York is bound to add that it was on Bede's visit to Ecgbert in 734 that he advised the establishment of the Cathedral School of York, which still exists under a royal name, Ecgbert's predecessor the great Wilfrith having created the School as a school for soldiers and ministers of God some sixty years before.

---

[1] "Or leave a kiss but in the cup And I'll not look for wine."
See page 312.

In the letter which enclosed Boniface's famous letter to Aethelbald of Mercia,[1] he writes [2] :—

" Further, I beg that you will deign to have copied and sent to me some tractates from the lesser works of Bede the Reader, whom, as we have heard, the divine grace has gifted with spiritual intelligence and allowed to shine in your province, so that we too may enjoy the candle which the Lord has given you.

"As an evidence of my love, I send you copies of letters of the holy Gregory which I have received from the chancery of the Roman Church : I did not suppose they had come to Britain. If you desire it, I will send more, for I received many from Rome. I also send a corporal pall, and one rough towel for drying the feet of the servants of God, when you wash them."

[3] " To the most reverend and most beloved sister, Eadburga, Abbess [of Thanet], Boniface the humble, servant of the servants of God, wishes all desirable health of dearness in Christ.

" I pray the omnipotent God, the retributor and rewarder of all good works, that He return to thee, in celestial mansions and eternal habitations, and in the supreme court of the blessed angels, an everlasting reward for all thy kindnesses to me ; for often, whether by the solace of books or by the comfort of clothing, thy piety has given me consolation. And now I pray that thou wouldst do still more for me, that is, write for me with gold the epistles of my lord, St. Peter the Apostle, to the honour and reverence of the holy Scriptures to carnal eyes when I am preaching, and because I very greatly desire to have always present

---

[1] See page 242.   [2] Ep. 75 ; 744-747.
[3] Ep. 35 ; A.D. 785.

with me the words of him who has directed me to this journey. I write this request by Eoba the presbyter. Do, then, dearest sister, by this our petition as thy benignity has been wont to do by all my prayers, that here also thy works may shine in letters of gold to the glory of the heavenly Father.

"Fare thee well, and with all powers press on to rise to better things."

Here is a long letter from a king :—

[1] " To the most blessed lord and archbishop worthily adorned with the pontifical fillet, Wynfrith, surnamed Boniface, Aethelbert [2] King of Kent wishes health in the Lord of Lords.

"A few years ago the venerable Abbess Bugga— after her visit to the most sacred places of Rome for the purpose of prayer and her return to her own land and to the monastery of holy women which she governed under ecclesiastical rule—when at her request I went to confer with her, among other desirable things was at pains to press this especially on our attention, that you had given her leave to speak freely to your affable and amiable holiness on matters of importance to her, since you and she were at Rome together and together frequently visited the thresholds of the blessed apostles. [3]

" She proceeded to tell me that suppliantly with earnest prayers she addressed you on my behalf, urging the nearness of our blood relationship, that as she, present with you, was held worthy to be imbued with your salutary precepts and confirmed by the benediction of

[1] Ep. 105.
[2] This was Ethelbert II. His reign commenced in 748, and he was still reigning when Boniface died.
[3] " Apostolorum."

your prayers, so I also, though absent and in bodily
presence unknown, yet as present in spirit, might by
thy wonted beneficence receive the same gift, to me
so necessary. And when she said that you had
promised this in undoubted faith, I truly confess that
I cannot easily set forth in words what great joy and
what great consolation it gave me. And, as is natural,
I was the more joyful because she suddenly proffered
a gift so unexpected and beyond my hopes.

" It seems in all ways useful to me and convenient
that I should as fully as possible communicate with
your splendid beatitude by means of friendly letters
or conversation with friendly messengers. Never
can I better and more effectively do this than now,
when there are present here religious men of yours,
sent by you to Britain as prudent and faithful repre-
sentatives, and now desirous of returning by the help
of God as soon as possible to the sight of thy placid
presence. It has seemed to me best to send to you
the present bearer of this letter, by name Ethelhun,
a monk in the garb of religion, along with your
aforesaid men, as the safer course, and through him
to deliver to your charity these writings of salutation
and prayer. In them I declare first of all that we
all in common return more abundant thanks to God
Omnipotent, who has conferred on you such grace of
His mercy that through the word and labour of your
preaching He has turned to the measure of the Christian faith such an innumerable multitude of gentiles
miserably deceived in the most ancient error of idolatry; whence we hope and desire that by the aid of
God very much is still to come, being certain that He
who has begun to work through you does not cease
to accomplish greater things from day to day.

"Further, by the bearer of these letters my devotion has with great affection directed to your reverence some small gifts, a silver bowl gilt within, weighing three pounds and a half, and two cloaks. These gifts we have sent to you not with any intention or suggestion of receiving from you in return any earthly gain at all or any temporal return for them. But, for it is much more necessary, I entreat on my knees with all the bowels of my mind, that since the days are evil, and various and unexpected disturbances are multiplied in this age full of scandals, you will deign to aid us by many and frequent suffrages of your prayers. And I pray that the venerable love of thy authority may ever remember to provoke to do the same thing for us all whom thou canst order or advise so to do, both so long as thou hearest that I still live, and also after my death if I am favoured by having thee as my survivor.

"This having been briefly and summarily stated, there is one thing more which I desire you to do for me. From information received, I do not at all think it will be a matter of much difficulty for you. It is, to send me a pair of falcons, whose bold nature it is to be keen to catch and strike herons and bring them to the ground. The reason for my asking you to obtain and send me these birds is, that very few hawks are found in Kent which breed such good birds, active, and fierce, that can be tamed and trained and taught for the above-mentioned purpose.

"In conclusion I beg that thou wilt write to me who write to thee, and wilt deign to inform me that what I have sent to thee is safely received. May the divine pity grant long life to thy beatitude, praying for us."

A digression into earlier times may perhaps be allowed here, with a view to identifying some of the religious ladies who wrote to Boniface from England. The following letter,[1] sufficiently interesting in itself to find a place here, is naturally included by Dümmler in his letters of the Bonifatian period, though he does not see the connexion which we shall suggest. The letter was probably written about the time of Boniface's ordination as priest.

"To the holy lady, honourable of God, the Abbess Adolana, Aelffled, handmaid of the family of the Church, greeting of everlasting safety in the Lord.

"From the time when the report of your holiness reached me from persons coming from your parts I have been moved with heartfelt love for you, even as the Lord said, 'This is My command, that ye love one another.' Earnestly we pray you to defend us before Almighty God with your sacrosanct and flame-bearing prayers. Our humbleness will not weary to render to you in return.

"We commend to your exalted sanctity and wonted piety *N.*, a devout handmaid of God, a religious abbess, a most dear and most faithful daughter of ours from her early youth. She desires, for the love of Christ and in honour of the holy apostles, Peter, that is, and Paul, to visit their holy thresholds, but we have until now kept her here, for the need and advantage of souls committed to her charge. . . . Wherefore we beg you again and again to send her on to Rome with your commendations and attendants, with the aid of the holy prince of the apostles and standard-bearer Peter, and that you

[1] Ep. 8; before 713

will provide her with anything she may ask for when she reaches you."

Evidently this lady, whose name the transcriber did not care to copy, merely marking it as *N.* (*nomen*, name), had been abbess of some cell dependent upon Whitby. There are reasons for believing that this was Hackness, and that we know a good deal more about the matter than is contained in the letter of Aelffled. Of this great lady, Aelffled, we must say sufficient to connect her with Hackness and its most interesting monument of the times of which we are writing.

First, a word as to Adolana and her monastery described as *Palatiolensis,* as it were the Little Palace. Its German name of to-day has the same meaning, Pfalzel, near Trèves. It is mentioned in connexion with Boniface in the early life of Abbat Gregory of Utrecht,—" Boniface arrived (about 722) at the Palatiol monastery of virgins on the bank of the Moselle, at that time presided over by an abbess named Addula, a very religious and God-fearing lady." This is, no doubt, the Adolana of Aelffled's letter. English ladies of the highest rank were accustomed to go in those times for higher education to French nunneries, the chief of which were Chelles and Faramoustier. There is a charter of doubtful genuineness in which this lady, named there Adela, calls herself daughter of King Dagobert II; the rôle of abbess specially suited royal princesses in those days. Of this Aelffled herself is a striking example.

She was a daughter of King Oswy of Northumbria, by Eanflaed, daughter of Edwin the first Christian king. Eanflaed was the little child whose birth was the occasion of the conversion of her father, and she

was the first of her nation to receive Christian baptism, on the Whit Sunday next following the conversion. Aelffled was placed in charge of her relative
Hilda when only a year old. Eanflaed, her mother,
entered the monastery in 670, the year of her widow-
hood. On Hilda's death Aelffled succeeded to the
government of the important monastery, and as she
was still very young, her mother the widowed queen
helped her in the management. From Bede we learn
much that is highly interesting of this powerful lady,
of whom the contemporary Life of Wilfrith speaks as
"always the comforter and best adviser of the whole
province". It is not till the year 705 that we find the
connexion we want. In that year she was called to
declare the last will of her half-brother King Aldfrith,
lately dead. She was with him at Driffield when he
died, and her declaration of his last words to her, his
last will as we now call the document which declares
it, was accepted by the synod of the province and was
carried out. On her way to Driffield she had called
for and taken with her another abbess, Oedilburga.
Hackness was on her way from Whitby to Driffield,
and the very early monument there, certainly of
a date as early as that of which we are writing, has
as its earliest Latin inscription "Oedilburga beata ad
semper te recolant amantes pie deposcant requiem
vernantem sempiternam sanctorum pia mater apos-
tolica," "Blessed Oedilburga, may they that love thee
ever remember thee, pray piously for the saints' rest of
everlasting spring, pious mother, apostolic." The next
inscription is: "—etb—ga semper te ament memores
domus tuae te mater amantissima," "Huaetburga,
may those mindful of thy house always love thee,
most loving mother." And on another part of the

same monument is *Bugga Virgo*. This last lady is not the well-known Bugga,[1] prominent in connexion with Aldhelm and Boniface, if indeed there were not two ladies of the name in that connexion. This Northumbrian Bugga of Hackness we may take to be the same as the ' Heaburga, surnamed Bugga ' of whom her mother, Abbess Eangyth, wrote in Ep. 14.

In the letter of Ecgburga to Boniface, she speaks of her sister Wetburga having left her work or gone to Rome, leaving her, Ecgburga, apparently as her successor. The suggestion is that this Wetburga is the —*etb*—*ga* of the Hackness monument, and the pious lady whose charge of souls so long delayed her going to Rome as set forth in Aelflaed's letter to Adolana. Ecgburga speaks of their brother Oshere. There is only one man of that name known to history at that time, and he was a Northumbrian of very high position. He is called the Consul of the Northumbrians, and under his leadership the Northumbrian forces defeated the Pictish army in 710. The loss of so powerful a brother would naturally deprive his sisters of their best protector. On the whole, a strong case can be made out for these three ladies Oedilburga, Huaetburga, and Ecgburga, being royal ladies ; and inasmuch as a chronicle describes an Abbess Ethelburga as daughter of Aldwulf, King of the East Angles (Aldwulf was a nephew of St. Hilda by her sister Herusuith), the whole story hangs together well. This was the view of one to whom all

---

[1] It appears to have been a favourite Anglo-Saxon name, probably a term of endearment, or a short name used in place of a long one after the Anglo-Saxon fashion. It would mean *fairy*. " Any *bug* by night," in the "bug" Bible, means any apparition. A scarecrow in a field of potatoes is a *tatty-bogie* in Scotland. A *humbug* is a sham bogie.

persons interested in the earliest Yorkshire histories, and in the runic inscriptions of the county, owe a great debt of gratitude, a Roman priest of the good old type, the Reverend D. A. Haigh.   He was a man of surprising ingenuity and insight, and in honour of his memory this digression has been inserted here.

CHAPTER XIV

THERE is much to be said about Boniface's continued interest in English persons and English things;
more than our limited space will allow to be said.
He could be very tender, and he could be very
severe. Nowhere is the frankness of his faithful
severity better seen than in his famous letter to
Ethelbald, King of Mercia 716–57. We have two
letters from him to this prince, one very pleasant,
the other very much the reverse. The first is probably early, the second is later.

[1] "To the most reverent and loved Aethelbald, King
of the Mercians, Boniface the servant of the servants
of God sends greeting of intimate regard.

"We pray the clemency of your highness that
you deign to solace this my messenger, Ceola by name,
who presents this letter, and aid him in our business
and in his own purpose, and in any need that may
chance. May you have reward from God for your
dealing with our messengers of last year, to whom,
as they informed me, you afforded help in every way.
In token of our true love and devoted friendship we
send to you a hawk, two falcons, two shields, and
two lances. These small gifts we beg you to receive,
unworthy as they are. May we all equally hear the

[1] Ep. 69.

saying 'Fear God and keep His commandments'. We beg also that if written words of ours reach you by another messenger you will deign to give audience and hear them carefully. Fare well in Christ."

In 745 or 746 there came to Ethelbald the following tremendous document [1] :—

"To the lord most dear and in love to be preferred to other kings, Ethelbald the King, wielding the illustrious sceptre of the Angles, Boniface the Archbishop, German legate of the Roman Church, and Wera [2] and Burghard [3] and Werberht [4] and Abel [5] and Wilbalth [6] his fellow bishops, greeting of love perennial in Christ. [7]

"We confess before God and the holy angels that when we hear from trusted messengers of your prosperity, and faith in God, and good works in the sight of God and men, we give joyful thanks to God, praying and beseeching the Saviour of the world that He keep you long time safe, stable in faith, and upright in good works, to rule over a Christian people. And when news reaches us of any injury to your dilection regarding the state of your kingdom or the fortune of wars, it racks us with grief and sadness. We rejoice with you in your joy and are sad with you in your adversity."

[1] Ep. 73 ; A.D. 745-6.
[2] We do not know this name as that of a bishop. Dummler declines to accept the suggestion that it must mean Witta of Buraburg, who already has names enough without this.
[3] Of Würzburg.
[4] Dummler again rejects the suggestion that this must be Authbert of Sens.
[5] Of Reims, 744-51.
[6] Of Eichstatt.
[7] Dümmler is persuaded by Hahn and others that the synod which sent this letter to Ethelbald was the Frank synod of 745.

That preface being given in full, the letter is so very long that we must be satisfied with a summary of the points.

The assembled bishops had heard with pleasure that the king gave large alms; that he put down thefts, wickednesses, perjuries, and rapine; that he was a defender of the widows and the poor; that he kept peace established in the land.[1]

But with all this, one ill report about his manner of life had reached them. They wished it was not true, but many had told them of it. The king was not lawfully married. If this were for the sake of abstinence, they would rejoice; but if, as they were told, he was living in lust, in the wickedness of luxury and adultery, they were sad.

Worse still, they are told that he does not abstain from nuns in their monasteries, a twofold sin. Among the Greeks and the Romans every one before ordination is asked if he has committed this wickedness; if he has, he is prohibited from every grade of God's ministry. He may imagine, then, of what enormity it is in the sight of the Judge.

If these things be true, they entreat him by Christ the son of God, by His coming and His kingdom, to turn and amend his life.

It is not among Christians only that this is an abomination. In Old Saxony if a daughter defiles her father's house or a wife her husband's, they have two ways of dealing with her. Either they force her to hang herself and then burn her, and they

---

[1] On the face of it, we should have supposed that the bishops who could send such a letter as this must have been specially connected with England, and wrote as English men to an English king.

hang the man over her grave; or the women of the place strip her to the girdle and scourge her from village to village, pricking her with knives till she is covered with blood; other villages take up the punishment and scourge her still further; till at last they leave her dead or as good as dead. And the Wends, the foulest and worst race of men, hold marriage in such esteem that when a woman loses her husband she puts herself to death.

If in the days of his youth he fell into lustful ways, now it is high time that he should leave such ways and should cease to set to the people of his kingdom an example which must ruin those who follow it.

If the English race really has—as in the German provinces and in France and in Italy, and indeed among the pagans, is a common taunt against the English —really has deserted lawful wedlock and taken to a foul life of adultery and sins of Sodom, a degenerate and ignoble and lustful progeny must be the result. The physical and moral condition of things will go from bad to worse as generation succeeds generation. The people will become unable to keep steadfast in faith, unable to hold their own in war, without honour among men, without the love of God. The people of Spain and Provence and Burgundy have lived that evil course, and the providence of God has sent the Saracens to destroy them.

And homicide is known to be a consequent evil. The children born under such conditions, whether in monasteries or in the world, are not suffered to live; most part of them are killed.

Further, the bishops have been told that the king violates the privileges and takes the possessions of churches and monasteries. They quote against him the substance of a remark by Jerome—"He who takes the money of his neighbour does wickedness; he who takes the money of a church does sacrilege."

Yet again, the king's prefects and counts inflict greater violence and servitude on monks and priests than any Christian kings ever before had done. From Augustine's time the privileges of churches in England remained undisturbed and inviolate down to the time of Ceolred, King of the Mercians,[1] and Osred, King of the Deirans and Bernicians.[2] Each of these kings lived a life of lust and died a terrible death, and the kingdom departed from their line.'

"Begin then," they conclude, "to guide your life in better ways, to correct the youthful errors of your past, that in this world you may have praise of men and in the world to come may be glad in eternal glory."

This terrible indictment is just the kind of remonstrance and prophetic warning that Alcuin, a generation later, addressed to the Mercians and Northumbrians from his adoptive home in France. He, too, clearly saw that physical and moral and spiritual degradation must, and indeed ought to, be the result of the evil manner of life of men and women in high positions, setting to those less highly placed a fatal example of dissoluteness. Alcuin could and did write quite as strongly as Boniface, and Northumbria was quite as bad as Mercia. We hear very little in comparison—if anything—of ill deeds

---

[1] The king's immediate predecessor and second cousin.
[2] Osred was the son of Aldfrith; he succeeded his father when eight years of age, and only reigned 705-16.

of Wessex; and it is a curious and instructive fact
that the one of the kingdoms of the Triarchy which
was not the subject of these threats and did not receive
warnings that when the time came the decadent race
would not be able to withstand attack, was the one
kingdom that survived. The house of Cerdic, reigning then in Wessex, the house a hundred years later
of Alfred the Great, is the one of the seven original
royal houses that sits now, in the person of a lineal
descendant, on the throne of the whole land, Heptarchy
and Triarchy all one, as the National Church taught
them to be.

Far from being satisfied with advising England in
secular matters, divided as it was into petty kingdoms,
Boniface was keenly anxious that the national Church
of England, one, not three or seven, should be brought
into closer ecclesiastical relations and order. He could
not see any effective way of bringing this to pass,
other than the way by which he had himself travelled
on his successful course through paganism and dissolute
Christianity to the vast spread of the Gospel and the
reformation of morals. That way was the way that
led men to far-off Rome, and brought from far-off
Rome a mysterious spiritual influence to bear upon
local problems with the force which mystery, protected
by distance, gave then, and even now can give—
though the protection of distance has long since ceased
and the veil has been raised or torn down.

Boniface was, and might well be, a devoted ad-
herent of the papacy and its authority. He was not
satisfied to give his own allegiance to the Roman
Pontiff, he wished to induce the English Church to
do the same. The conditions were entirely different,
and what was quite seemly and right in the one case

would have been out of place in the other. There was no national Church of Germany. There was a national Church of England.

The question arose in this way. Archbishop Cuthbert held a synod[1] at Clovesho in September, 747, at which two letters were read from Pope Zacharias. In these letters he warned the English to live more carefully, and threatened to excommunicate those who disregarded the warning. Thus the synod had very fully before it the claim of the Pope to intervene to so grave an extent in English affairs. That being so, it is sufficiently remarkable that no reference is made to Zacharias in any part of the rules' drawn up by the Council. The summary given of these two letters of Zacharias, which have not been preserved, is interesting in its tone. They were read, we are told, with great care and clearly, as the Pope by his authority enjoined, and they were explained in the English tongue. In them the illustrious pontiff warned in a friendly manner all the inhabitants of Britain who were of the English race; addressed them in words of truth; and finally prayed them lovingly. With regard to such as should persist in wickedness, he declared that he would without doubt pass sentence of anathema. Thereupon the prelates exhorted one another to due care in themselves and in their office. They then passed a number of canons for the regulation of the Church and the reform of abuses and neglect. If this were the place for it, an analysis of these canons would be interesting. There

---

[1] Haddan and Stubbs, iii. 360-401. William of Malmesbury (*Gesta Pont.* i. 4) declares that it was called on the admonition of Boniface, by the assistance of Ethelbald, King of the Mercians.

was nothing at all about the Pope or his anathema or his intervention or his authority.

The one canon which is of special importance for our present subject is the twenty-fifth. It is as follows :—"When bishops come away from synod, they shall hold a conference in their own diocese with the presbyters, abbats, and provosts, and setting before them the decisions of the synod, shall instruct them to keep them. And each of the bishops, if he is unable to correct and amend anything in his own diocese, shall bring it in synod before the archbishop in presence of all to be corrected." The important point is that there the canon stops. The archbishop in synod is the final appeal of the English Church. No subtlety can get over that. And we must have full in mind the fact that it was passed in presence of letters from the Pope asserting a right of anathema.

There is a long letter from Boniface to Cuthbert,[1] in which he relates the substance of canons passed at a Council he had held in Germany. These canons are so evidently correspondent to Cuthbert's canons that they must either have had a common source, or have come one from the other. It is not mere sameness of substance, it is sameness of words. If they came one from the other, the question of the relative dates of the two Councils is of much importance. The opinion used to be held that Boniface's letter was the cause of the canons being passed in the English Council. There are great difficulties of date in the way of this view. There are also great difficulties of date in the other view, that Boniface's letter was caused by the receipt of the English canons. Without definitely deciding that point, to which

[1] Ep. 78; A D 747.

attention will be called later on, we may be satisfied with contrasting the tone of the Bonifatian canons with those of Cuthbert, so far as Roman supremacy is concerned.

We have seen that at the English Council Zacharias and the Papacy itself are mentioned in the preamble only, and in courteous and full terms of recognition. There is nothing in the least corresponding to the language of the canons which Boniface tells Cuthbert his synod has passed. The précis given in his letter is as follows for Canons 1, 2, 5, 13 :—(1) To the end of our lives we will keep the Catholic faith and unity and subjection to the Roman Church. (2) We will, be subject to St. Peter and his Vicar. (5) We desire canonically to follow in all things the precepts of St. Peter, that we may be numbered among the sheep commended to him. (13) Here we come into direct comparison with Canon 25 of the Synod of Clovesho, the latter part of which may here be repeated : "Each of the bishops, if he is unable to correct and amend anything in his own diocese, shall bring it in synod before the archbishop, in presence of all to be corrected." Boniface's letter is as follows, word for word the same in the Latin as Cuthbert's canon, so far as it goes[1] : "Each of the bishops, if

---

[1] "Unusquisque Episcopus [Episcoporum, Clovesho], si quid in sua diocesi corrigere et emendare nequiverit, id [not in Clovesho] item in synodo coram Archiepiscopo et palam omnibus ad corrigendum insinuet." The Bonifatian canon then proceeds to its end as follows :—"Eodem modo quo Romana aecclesia nos ordinatos cum sacramento constrinxit, ut, si sacerdotes vel plebes a lege Dei deviasse viderim et corrigere non potuerim, fideliter semper sedi apostolicae et vicario sancti Petri ad emendandum indicaverim. Sic enim, nisi fallor, omnes episcopi debent metropolitano et ipse Romano pontifici, si quid de

he is unable to correct and amend anything in his
own diocese, shall bring it in synod before the archbishop, in presence of all to be corrected." Then came
the addition, "under the same condition to which the
Roman Church bound me by an oath when I was
consecrated, that if I saw priests or people deviating
from the law of God and was unable to correct them,
I should always send the matter to the apostolic see
and the Vicar of Saint Peter for emendation. For
thus, if I am not mistaken, all bishops ought to bring
cases where they are unable to apply correction to the
notice of the metropolitan, and the· metropolitan to
the Roman pontiff, that they may be clear of the blood
of lost souls."

William of Malmesbury confuses the matter by
stating that Cuthbert sent an account of the proceedings
of the Council to Boniface, and that Boniface replied in
a grateful letter, which William says he gives in his
Gesta Regum. He does not give any such letter there,
nor is any letter from Cuthbert to Boniface included
among the Bonifatian letters. The only letter of his
which appears there is his letter to Lul on Boniface's
death.

It is evidently impossible that the identity of these
two canons, so far as they coincide, is accidental.
And although the old view that Boniface's canon
was the earlier of the two, the canon of Clovesho
deliberately striking out all reference to the Roman
Church, gave great emphasis to the national sufficiency and independence of the Church of the English, our sufficiency and independence are abundantly
shown by the absence of any alteration of the practice

corrigendis populis apud eos impossibile est, notum facere ; et
sic alieni fiunt a sanguine animarum perditarum."

of the English Church, even if the old view of the date
of Boniface's letter be unsound.   We can point to
the anger of Pope Pascal nearly five hundred years
later, when he protested so vehemently and unsuccessfully against our sturdy independence of Rome,
reserving no obedience to the papal see, independence
maintained through Anglo-Saxon into Norman times
by the Church of England; and threatened to shake
off the dust of his feet against us.   Or, at the most
critical point in the early history of the relations of
England with Rome, we could point to the anger of
Pope Alexander against Lanfranc, the Norman archbishop of the Norman William, when he refused to
go to Rome when called to do so : " I will entirely
depose you from the episcopal office."   In neither case
did the Church of England give any heed or the Pope
take the threatened action.

It may be added that we have no record of any
such synod as that at which Boniface tells Cuthbert that
these canons of his were passed.   The only record anything like it which we possess is of a German Council
under Carloman and Boniface.   They, it is true,
did hold a Council in April, 742, five years before
the Synod of Clovesho ; but though there is a natural
resemblance between the canons passed at this Council
and the canons of which Boniface wrote to Cuthbert,
they are certainly not the same, not nearly the same,
on the point of special importance with which we
have been dealing.   The enactments of the Council
of 742 and of one that followed are given in full
on pages 181–5.   There are two points at which something of the kind which we are discussing might well
have been introduced.   At the beginning : " We have
determined to call a synod each year, that in our

presence the decrees of the canons and the Church's laws may be restored to force, and the Christian religion may be amended." Near the end : " Incorrect principles and practice of marriage are to be prohibited, and emendation is to be applied by the bishop."

So far as date is concerned, it is not easy to place the Council whose decrees Boniface communicated to Cuthbert otherwise than before Cuthbert's Council ; and it is difficult to suppose that Boniface would have passed over the vitally important difference between his canons and Cuthbert's, if he was acknowledging Cuthbert's letter containing the English canons. It is much easier, as a matter of interpretation, to treat Cuthbert's letter as an answer to Boniface than Boniface's letter as an answer to Cuthbert. One suggestion we can probably clear out of the way, the suggestion, namely, that Boniface was reporting the Acts of the Council held some years before, in 742. Professor G. Kurth, a Roman of the Romans, in his delightful little book, *Saint Boniface* (Paris, Victor Lecoffre, Rue Bonaparte 90, 3rd ed., 1902), maintains that the Council of Clovesho was held after Boniface's letter to Cuthbert, and that the canons of the Council followed closely—in some cases exactly—the pattern which Boniface sent. He remarks,[1] on the date assigned by Jaffé to Boniface's letter, that he " cannot understand how Jaffé could date Boniface's letter 748, when it is clear that it is anterior to the Council of Clovesho, which was held in September, 747.

[1] Page 102, note 1 : "On ne comprend pas comment Jaffé peut dater cette lettre de 748, alors qu'il est évident qu'elle est antérieure au concile de Cliff, qui fut tenu en septembre 747. Aussi Dummler, dans son édition de la correspondance de saint Boniface, est-il revenu à la date de 747."

Dümmler," he adds, "in his edition of the correspondence of Boniface, has gone back to 747." Of the letter itself and of the English decrees Professor Kurth says that on "patriotic and religious grounds Boniface communicated to Cuthbert, Archbishop of Canterbury, the resolutions of the Frank episcopate, and invited him to enter upon the same course. He wrote strongly against abuses which dishonoured the religious life of England, and begged him to apply a remedy. Pressed also by two letters from Pope Zacharias, the primate of England obeyed, and the Council of Cliff, convoked by him in the course of the same year, was like a far-off echo of the great synods of the Continent. The influence of Boniface is evident in the canons of the Anglo-Saxon Council, which enforced, sometimes in the same terms, the reforms which the legate of the Pope had passed in the ecclesiastical legislation of the Franks.[1] Thus the solicitude of the great reformer embraced both continent and island, and his apostolic zeal spread itself over both his countries." So far Professor Kurth. He does not appear to have noticed the essential difference between the two Councils in regard to reference of difficult matters to the Pope, and thus he was free to form his opinion of the precedence of Boniface's letter on abstract grounds, apart from controversial questions. The balance of fact and argument, a fine balance, no doubt, is with this Roman writer.

Before leaving this remarkable letter of Boniface, we may note five abuses, specially affecting the

---

[1] Kurth in a note specifies Canons 3 (against pagan observances) and 25 of Clovesho (on the duties of bishops) as reproducing literally the terms of Boniface's letter, and Canon 21 (against drunkenness) as "manifestly inspired" by that letter.

English Church, to which the great missionary calls the attention of the Archbishop of Canterbury.

First, he urges that the English synod and princes should prevent nuns and other women from going and coming between England and Rome. The risks of such pilgrimage were very great. A large proportion of the women fell into evil courses; few remained pure. Boniface declared, on his own experience, that there were very few towns in Lombardy, or in France, or in Gaul—he said nothing here of Rome, but we know what his opinion of the city of Rome was—there were very few towns in which there was not an English woman who had formed an adulterous connexion—that is, we suppose, had married a priest—or was living a life of promiscuous immorality. It was a scandal and disgrace to the whole English Church. It may be noticed that Boniface addresses the English Church as a National Church, with individual responsibilities, not as a dependence of or on the Roman Church.

Secondly—and this is in remarkable accordance with the well-known letter of Bede[1] to the Archbishop of York, published a few years before—some powerful layman, imperator or king or prefect or count, would seize by violence a monastery, taking it out of the possession of bishop or abbat or abbess, and would begin to rule it himself, to have monks under him, and to hold the money which had been purchased by the blood of Christ. Such a man must be condemned by the strictest bond of anathema before the judgement seat of Christ. Such a man is as a heathen man and a publican; with him, alive or dead, the Church of God has no communion.

[1] See my *Alcuin of York*, S.P.C.K., chapter iii.

Thirdly, the Church of England should with the greatest energy prohibit gay dress, a vain thing hated of God. These ornamental garments, as they call them, though others call them disgraceful, with very broad stripes of silk at the edges, come from Antichrist and are the precursors of his arrival. It is his craft to introduce into the cloisters of monasteries,[1] by his ministers, the immorality of gaily dressed youths, and foul consortings, and neglect of reading and prayer, and perdition of souls. These clothes, indicative of the nakedness of the soul, are the outward signs of arrogance and pride and luxury and vanity, of which Wisdom speaks, "Pride, and arrogancy, and the evil way, and the mouth with double tongue, I hate."[2]

Fourthly, it is reported that in their dioceses the evil of drunkenness is common, and that not only do some of the bishops drink so much that they are intoxicated, but by pressing upon others deep drinking they make them drunk too. Without doubt that is a wicked thing for any servant of God to do or have done. The ancient canons order that a drunken bishop or priest must amend or be degraded. This evil is a special mark of the pagans and of our race. This neither Franks nor Gauls nor Lombards nor Romans nor Greeks do. This wickedness we must restrain, if we can, by synodal decrees and the interdict of the Scriptures. If we fail, we must avoid and cut off such, to free our own souls of the blood of the lost.[3]

Lastly, in the whole Christian world such a thing

---

[1] See my *Aldhelm*, S.P.C.K. 1903, pages 318, 322-4.

[2] Prov. viii 13.

[3] In this respect also Alcuin's letters are similar in tone

is never heard of, except among the English, as the forced labour of monks in royal works and buildings. The ministers of God must not be silent or consentient in this. It is an evil not heard of in former times.[1]

---

[1] The Bonifatian letters and documents show that this invasion of clerical immunities was not quite unheard of even in the lands in which he laboured.

CHAPTER XV

WE have reached the time when Boniface passed out
of the state of regionary Archbishop and became Archbishop of Mainz and Metropolitan. The most natural
arrangement would have been that he should succeed
to the archbishopric of Cologne, for there was the seat
of the Austrasian government. And, indeed, it had
been so arranged. The Frank princes in the Council
held at Soissons had nominated Boniface to the archbishopric of Cologne. This had been communicated
to the Pope, and in very brief terms he gave his
consent [1] :—

"As regards the city up to recent times called
Agrippina and now called Cologne, in accordance
with the petition of the Franks by the precept of
our authority we have confirmed to you as metropolis, and we send to your holiness for the information of times to come, the establishment of the said
metropolitical church."

But it was not to be. The Frankish dealings in
the matter of archbishoprics were unfortunately
unstable. Boniface was made Bishop of Mainz,
and the Pope created it a metropolitical see under
Boniface as archbishop. The story is a curious and

---

[1] Ep. 60; A.D. 745.

interesting one, full of illustration of the manners of the time.

The Saxons had invaded Thuringia, and the people sent to Carloman to beg him to protect them from the devastations of the invaders. Carloman sent an army, and with it went Gerold, the then Bishop of Mainz. When it came to actual fighting, Gerold and many more were killed. Gerold had a son Gewilieb, Gervilio in the Latin, a layman in the service of the palace. He became a cleric, to soothe his grief at the loss of his father, and succeeded him as bishop.

Carloman raised another army, led it himself against the Saxons, and took Gewilieb with him. The two armies faced each other, one on each side of the river Weser. Gewilieb sent his servant across the river, to find out who it was that had killed his father Gerold. The slayer was near at hand, and the man invited him to a colloquy with the bishop. They met on horseback in the middle of the stream and entered into conversation. Gewilieb had a sword concealed on his person, and drawing it he stabbed the other, exclaiming in hexameter verse in Latin, " Take that, in revenge for my father's death ! " He fell from his horse and perished in the water. This was the signal for a general fight, in which the Saxons were beaten, and Carloman went back with his bishop, of whom no one thought the worse for what he had done; it was not put down as unjustifiable homicide. Gewilieb resumed his episcopal duties.

At the synod above mentioned, Boniface enacted that no one who had killed a man could perform the priestly office. He further objected against Gewilieb that he hunted with hawk and hound. Gewilieb saw that it was useless to kick against the prick of secular power or of canonical authority, and he was deposed. Carloman and Pepin appointed Boniface to succeed him, and in order to make the position more important they determined to make Mainz the metropolis of all Germany, and obtained the sanction of the Pope for that step. The Pope had, in fact, at the request of the Franks, confirmed to Boniface the see of Cologne as his metropolis, in the same letter in which he approved the condemnation of Aldebert and Clement. In a long letter addressed to Boniface by Pope Zacharias, the Pope replies to a letter in which Boniface had told him of this change. The Franks, the Pope says, have not kept the word they promised, and have placed Boniface not at Agrippina (Cologne) but at Mainz. The see of Mainz he is never to relinquish; but he may, as he has requested on the ground of old age and infirmity of body, if he can find a suitable man, appoint him his successor.

The see of Cologne was not filled up till 750, when Hildegar succeeded to the bishopric as a suffragan of Mainz.

The views of Pope Zacharias on this complicated matter of Boniface's metropolitical see should be set out here.

The Pope's approval of the choice of Cologne by the Frank princes as Boniface's metropolitical see had not been confined to the concluding paragraph of his his letter of 31 Oct., 745, quoted above. In an earlier paragraph of the letter he had written as follows :—

" You tell us that all [1] the princes of the Franks

[1] This would appear to bring in Gripho.

have selected a city adjoining the territories of the pagans and of the German races, where you formerly preached, that you may have it for ever as your metropolitan see and from it may instruct the bishops in the right way, and your successors may hold it in perpetual right. This which they have decreed we accept with joyful mind, as done by the inspiration of God. And if any false and schismatic bishops or priests attempt to hinder this, God will shatter their vain attempt, and that which is in agreement with the statutes of the holy Fathers will remain stablished. And inasmuch as in this also the princes of the Franks have stood out as your aiders, may the Omnipotent God reward them with the eternal prize and grant them innumerable good things."

After a delay of some two years or more, the Pope wrote[1] again on the subject, as follows : —

"Your letter mentions—as indeed a former letter on the subject of Agrippina[2] did—that the Franks have not kept the promise which they made,[3] and that your brotherliness still remains in Mainz. You have begged that with our consent, by reason of old age coming upon you, and the full span of days, and weakness of body, you may place some other in•the see over which you preside, if you can find a suitable man, while thou, dearest one, remainest legate and missus of the apostolic see. Now we, with God's help, tender this advice to thy reverend holiness, that for the salvation of rational souls, God helping you, you by no means leave the see which you hold, the holy Church of Mainz, that in thee may be fulfilled

---

[1] Ep. 80, A.D. 748.
[2] Cologne.
[3] To give him the archbishopric of Cologne.

the Lord's precept, He that endureth to the end, the same shall be saved.[1] But if, according to your petition, the Lord shall have given a perfect man, able for the charge and cure of souls, ordain him bishop for thee, and he shall be in the gospel committed to thee and in bearing the ministry of Christ, seeking out and strengthening in every place the Church of God. We pray our Lord and Redeemer, that by the sacred intervention of His holy mother Mary ever-virgin, our Lady, and of the blessed princes of the Apostles Peter and Paul, He will deign to preserve, safe and sound, thee praying for us."

The Pope eventually made the best of a matter rather awkward for his prestige. It clearly could not be left as the matter of the palls was left. As though his letter of 745[2] had not been written, or the document testifying to future times the establishing of the metropolitical see of Cologne, to neither of which he makes any reference, the following letter was sent to Boniface, correctly described in the address as Bishop of Mainz[3]:—

"Zacharias the Pope to Boniface, Bishop of the holy Church of Mainz, and through him to the said venerable Church, perpetual health.

"Whereas your brotherly holiness was sent to preach in the province of Germany by our predecessor of holy memory, the lord Gregory the Pope, and after the work had been begun and the spiritual edifice in some part built you returned to Rome and were by him ordained bishop and again sent to preach there, and have since attaining to the episcopate laboured, God going before, for twenty-five years in

[1] Matt. xxiv. 13. [2] Ep. 60.
[3] Ep. 88 ; 4 Nov. 751.

S

that work of preaching : And whereas in the province of the Franks you have in our stead held a Council, and in accordance with the institutes of the canons, God approving them, all have been bent to obedience : And whereas your holy brotherliness, occupied in these pious works, has not obtained a Cathedral See : And whereas God has given increase to your preaching, we ought to obtain for thee a Cathedral Church and confirm it to thy successors, according to the petition of the same Frankish sons of ours : Therefore by the authority of the blessed Peter the Apostle we decree that the aforesaid Church of Mainz now and for ever to thee and thy successors be confirmed as a metropolis, having under it these five sees—Tongres, Cologne, Worms, Speyer, and Utrecht—and all the German peoples to whom your brotherliness has by preaching made known the light of Christ. These things having been settled by us, we command that the sheet of this our confirmation shall be for ever kept in your church as evidence of the same."

Mainz long continued to be a metropolitical see. Before 1680 it had thirteen suffragan sees, namely, Worms, Speyer, Strassburg, Basel, Constanz, Chur, Augsburg, Eichstätt, Würzburg, Paderborn (originally Büraburg, then Fritzlar), Halberstadt, Hildesheim, Verden. Cologne became an archbishopric in 785 ; but Gams, in recording that fact, expresses the opinion, shared by others, that it was an archbishopric in the sixth century. Its suffragan sees before 1680 were Lüttich, Utrecht, Minden, Münster, Osnabrück. The other sees of the early time with which we are dealing were up to 1680 in the archbishopric of Salzburg, namely Freising, Regensburg, and Passau. The other sees of that archbishopric were at that

time Brixen, Trient, Seckau, Gurk, Lavant, Chiemsee; these, with the exception of Chiemsee which is
in Bavarian territory and is no longer a bishopric,
constituted in 1860–70 the archbishopric of Salzburg,
now held by a Cardinal Archbishop.

When Gams published his *Series Episcoporum* in
1860–70, the archbishopric of Cologne had three
suffragan sees, Trier, Münster, Paderborn; the archbishopric of Freiburg four, Mainz, Fulda, Rotten-
burg, Limburg; the archbishopric of Bamberg three,
Würzburg, Eichstätt, Speyer; the archbishopric of
München-Freising three, Augsburg, Regensburg,
Passau. None of the sees in which the life of
Boniface interests us remained in the archbishopric
of Salzburg.

Mainz (Mayence) was in no sense unworthy of
its position as the metropolitical see of the parts to
the east of the Rhine. From the time of Drusus,
the son-in-law of the Emperor Augustus, its great
importance as a strategic centre was fully recognized.
Domitian, who extended the power of the Roman
arms to the right bank of the Rhine, is understood
to have constructed a bridge across the river from
Mainz, for military purposes, and to have built the
Castellum Mattiacorum, the present Cassel or Castel,
to protect it. St. Martin had a church there in 316,
and a church of some importance is mentioned in 406.
Sidonius, a sixth-century bishop of Mainz, built a
church and baptistery, which probably existed still
in Boniface's time. Cologne had a higher prestige.
Agrippina, the daughter of Germanicus and mother
of Nero, founded here her colony of Roman veterans,
Colonia Claudia Agrippina, in the year 51; Constantine the Great built a bridge across the river.

Cologne was the central place of government under
the kings and dukes of the Austrasian Franks, and
was the chief royal place of residence at the time
when Boniface was promised the bishopric. Charlemagne completed the proposed transaction by creating
it into an archbishopric under his chaplain Hildebold,
whose library of manuscripts is still in existence, and
has for some forty years past been housed again in
the Cathedral Library, after a sojourn in Darmstadt.

Pepin succeeded to the double rule when his brother
Carloman retired from the Mayoralty of Austrasia.
After a time he put an end to the fiction so long
maintained, and was crowned king. He became
very careful in religious duties, restored in Neustria
synodal action, and continued the canonical institutions to which Boniface had successfully urged
Carloman. He raised Boniface to even higher
honour, and paid respect to his instructions in the
Lord. Boniface was now too old to move about
and preside at the synodal gatherings of Councils;
and with the king's[1] consent he put this part of his
work into the hands of Lul, his own able pupil,
whom he consecrated bishop and indicated as his
successor. What part, if any, Boniface took in the
dynastic change which set Pepin on the royal throne
it is very difficult to say. We do not find direct
evidence either way in the letters. See Appendix D.

Very near the end of his life, Boniface wrote
a letter of earnest entreaty to Pepin, now king, on
behalf of the many English men and women who
were working as his coadjutors and looked to him
for everything. His death would leave them help-
less. He addressed the letter to Fulred of St. Denys,

[1] Pepin was created king in 752.

but it was evidently intended to be read to Pepin himself [1] :—

"Boniface, servant of the servants of God, by the grace of Christ bishop, to his dearest fellow-priest the presbyter Fulred, perennial health of love in Christ.

"For the spiritual friendship of your brotherly love, which for the sake of God you have often shown to me in my necessities, I cannot express the thanks which you deserve. But I pray that God Almighty will give you the prize of eternal reward in the height of heaven, in the joy of angels. And now in Christ's name I pray that what you have begun with so good a beginning you with the good hand of God complete in the end; that is, that in my name you will salute our glorious and lovable king, Pepin, and give him great thanks for all the works of piety he has done for me, and will lay before him what I and my friends think likely to happen. It seems to us that by reason of these infirmities of mine I must soon end this temporal life and the course of my days. Wherefore I pray our king's highness, for the name of Christ the Son of God, that he would deign to inform and command me, while I still live, about my disciples, what means of support he will after my death provide for them. For almost all of them are foreigners. Some are priests, appointed in many places to minister to church and people; some are monks in our cells, and young boys set to learn to read; and some are old and have for a long time lived with me and laboured and helped me. I am anxious about all of these, that they may not be dispersed on my

[1] Ep. 93 ; 753 754.

death, but may receive from your highness the
means of subsistence, and protection, not scattered
as sheep not having a shepherd ; and that the pagans
near the march may not lose the law of Christ. For
the same reason I earnestly in God's name pray the
clemency of your graciousness that, if God will and
it please your clemency, you would appoint my dear
son and bishop-suffragan Lul to this ministry of
peoples and churches, and make him preacher and
teacher of priests and peoples. And I hope, if
God will, that in him the presbyters will have a
master, the monks a teacher of the rule, and the
Christian people a faithful preacher and shepherd.
But this especially I beg may be assured, that my
priests near the pagan march may have some poor
livelihood. Bread to eat they can obtain, but
clothing they cannot find there and must obtain
from elsewhere by means of those able and willing
to help them to live and endure in those places for
the ministry of the people, as I have helped them.
And if the pity of Christ inspires you to do that
which I ask, deign to inform me of it by these
present messengers or by letter of your piety, that
I may the more rejoice in your support, whether
I live or die."

It seems reasonable to gather from this most
touching letter that Boniface had received his principal
supplies for the maintenance of such of the work of
his mission as was conducted in newly established
churches and monasteries from the dukes of the
Franks and for the last few years from King Pepin.
The old foundations were evidently rich. Lul's
letter [1] to Gregory, Abbat of Utrecht, on his appoint-

[1] Ep. 92 ; 752–754.

ment to the abbacy, may be taken as an example; it is full of warnings as to the perils of a position great in the eyes of the world and—as we should say—with a large income.

It is evident, also, that much as we know of a dozen or so of English men and women who worked with Boniface, there was a whole army of English people at work throughout the large area of his missionary activity, whose names have not been preserved.

King Pepin granted the request of Boniface, and we have the dear old man's grateful acknowledgement of the King's kindness [1] :—

"We give great thanks to the clemency of your highness, and we pray our Lord Jesus Christ that He will give you eternal reward in the kingdom of the heavens, because you have deigned kindly to hear our petitions and have comforted my old age and infirmity. We beg you to inform us if we are to come to your court that we may fulfil your will. A certain slave of our church, and a very mendacious one, Ansfrid by name, who craftily escaped, has come to us with your notification, asking that we should do him justice. We have sent him to you with the letters themselves by our messenger, that you may learn how he has lied to you, begging that you will defend us against such falsifiers and not believe their lies."

In the last year of Boniface's life he had to write to yet another new Pope, Stephen III. He did not write immediately on hearing of his accession, being specially pressed at the time, as his letter explains. But if the accepted dates are correct, his delay extended to an inexcusable length [2] :—

---

[1] Ep. 107 ; 753–754. [2] Ep. 108 ; 754–755.

"With inmost prayers I earnestly entreat the clemency of your holiness that I may ask and receive from the clemency of your kindness intimacy and unity with the holy apostolic see, and as the disciple of your piety, serving the apostolic see, I may be able to remain your faithful and devoted servant, as under three of your predecessors I served the apostolic see, the two Gregorys and Zacharias, who ever fortified and helped me by the exhortation and authority of their letters. I pray your piety to do the like, that I may be the better able to accomplish and fulfil the precept of your paternity. If in this my Roman legation which I have held for thirty-six years[1] I have done anything useful for the said see, I desire to complete and increase it. But if I have done anything unskilfully or improperly in word or deed by the judgement of the Roman see, I promise voluntary and humble amendment.

"I pray that the piety of my lord be not displeased with me for having so long delayed to send a messenger and a letter to your presence. This has occurred by reason of my being preoccupied with the restoration of churches which the pagans have burned. They have devastated and burned thirty churches of presbyters and cells. This has been the cause of the lateness of my letter and address to your paternity, not any careless neglect."

This devastation was due, as we know from another source, to an invasion of the Saxons. We can well understand the overwhelming cruelty of this blow,

---

[1] Boniface left Rome with the commendation of Gregory II in 719. If he is correct in his arithmetic, this present letter was written in 755, the year of his death.

falling as it did upon a man always sensitive to sorrows and now old and enfeebled.

Yet another controversy was forced upon Boniface, just when he was bent upon retiring from the cares of the archbishopric to end his days as a simple missionary. The matter was stated to the Pope in the following letter,[1] an excellent example of the clearness of narrative style to which he had trained himself. There is no trace left of the stilts on which the pen of the previous generation, and his own pen in his youth, had stalked stiffly across the page.

"To the Lord, to be venerated and loved, endowed with the privilege of the Apostolate, Stephen the Pope, the humble Boniface, the German Legate or Missus of the Catholic and Apostolic Roman Church, all health of charity that can be desired in Christ.

"In the time of Sergius,[2] pontiff of the apostolic see, there came to the thresholds of the holy apostles [3] a certain presbyter of marvellous abstinence and sanctity, of the race of the Saxons,[4] by name Wilbrord, called also Clement. Him the aforesaid Pope ordained bishop [5] and sent to preach to the pagan race of the Fresians on the shores of the western sea. Preaching throughout fifty years, he converted the most part of the said race of the Fresians to the faith of Christ, he destroyed their shrines and temples and built churches, and set his episcopal seat and his church dedicated in honour of the Holy Saviour in the place and castle called Trecht.[6] And in that see and church of the Holy Saviour which he built, he remained preaching

---

[1] Ep. 109 ; A.D. 755. [2] Sergius I, 687–701.
[3] Apostolorum.
[4] He was of the race of the Angles, a Yorkshireman.
[5] Nov. 22, 696. [6] Utrecht.

up to feeble old age. He appointed an assistant bishop
to carry out the ministerial duties, and when the days
of his long life were done, he passed in peace to the
Lord. Carlmann, prince of the Franks, commended
that see to me, to appoint and ordain a bishop. Which
I did.

"But now the Bishop of Cologne usurps to himself
that see of the said Bishop Clement ordained by Pope
Sergius, and says that it belongs to him on account
of the foundations of a certain little church destroyed
by the pagans, which Wilbrord found razed to the
ground in the castle of Trecht; he built it anew
from the foundations, now consecrating it in honour
of St. Martin.[1] The Bishop asserts that by a king
of the Franks, Dagobert, the castle of Trecht with
the ruined church was added to the diocese [2] of Cologne
with this condition, that the Bishop of Cologne (for the
time being) should convert the race of the Fresians
to Christ and be their preacher. Which he has not
done. He has not preached, he has not converted the
Fresians to the faith of Christ. The race remained
heathen until the venerable pontiff of the Roman see,
Sergius, sent Wilbrord as bishop to preach to the said
race; he, as I have said, converted the race to the
faith of Christ. And now the Bishop of Cologne
wishes to absorb the see of the said preacher Wilbrord,
so that it shall no longer be a see subject to the
Roman pontiff, for preaching to the Fresian race.
I replied to him according to my belief, that by the
precept of the apostolic see, and the ordination by
Pope Sergius, and the mission of the venerable preacher

---

[1] This would be in 697, exactly a hundred years after
St. Augustine restored the Church of St. Martin at Canterbury.
[2] Parrochiam

Wilbrord, it became an episcopal see, subject to the Roman pontiff, for preaching to the Fresian race, a great part of whom are still pagan; and that this should be esteemed a greater and a stronger thing than the ruined foundations of a little church trampled under-foot by pagans, and by the negligence of the bishops left derelict. But he does not agree.

"Would your paternity now intimate to me your judgement. If this answer which I have given to that Bishop of Cologne is just and is agreeable to you, confirm it by your authority, that the precept of Pope Sergius, and that see, remain stable. You can, if it please you, give help by ordering and sending to me a copy from the records of your church of what the holy Sergius enjoined and wrote to the said Bishop Wilbrord, so that by the authority of your sanctity I may be able to convince and overcome those who oppose. But if any other course appears to your sanctity to be more just, deign to suggest [1] to me the counsel of your paternity, that I may follow it."

It is not necessary to point out how greatly it tended to build up the power of Rome that the records of the doings of the Popes were kept so carefully. Here we have Boniface assuming as a matter of course that a letter written by a Pope nearly sixty years before was recorded in the chancery. When the time of the forged decretals came, unscrupulous officials could easily falsify the records when it served their purpose to do so.

This is the last extant letter from Boniface to a Pope. We have not the reply.

---

[1] Insinuare.

CHAPTER XVI

IT is now time to proceed to the final scenes of the
life on earth of Boniface. There was, of course, much
to be set in order, but he left that to Lul, who had
entered upon the work as his successor at Mainz, and
determined to go back to his old love, Frisia, which
he had long ago left in body but not in mind.

With perfect clearness of presage he confided to
Lul the time and manner of the death he was to
meet in Frisia. "From my longed-for journey," he
told him, "I shall not return. The day of my departure is at hand, the time of my death draws near.
I shall lay down this workhouse of my body, and pass
[*revertar*] to the prize of eternal retribution. But
thou, my dearest son, must carry out to a perfect
end the building of churches in Thuringia which
I have begun. Thou must incessantly call the people
back from the wilderness of error. Thou must complete the building of the basilica which I have begun
at Fulda, and thither bring my body aged with many
circles of years." After adding much of like kind,
Willibald tells us that the archbishop finished with
this injunction: "My son, get ready everything you
can think of for my use on this journey, and in my

chest of books place the linen shroud in which my decrepit corpse shall be rolled."

After a few days the saint took ship with his companions and voyaged down the Rhine, stopping at one harbour and another for the night. In the course of time he reached the great lake of Elmere, and passed in safety to the further side, where he found himself in the heart of the Frisian land. This lake has been extended by various great storms and inundations since those times, and is now the great expanse of water known as the Zuyder Zee.

Willibald tells us that the whole land was divided by water into separate districts, each called by its own separate name ; but the people all claimed to be of one race. This is a fair account, fully justified by the later history of the Confederated Netherlanders.

Boniface appears to have spent two years in visiting the various peoples, cut off from one another by the superabundant waters. He took great pains in building churches, not allowing them to be called temples as the heathen shrines were. With the help of his fellow bishop Eoban [1] he baptized thousands of men and women and little children. This Eoban was appointed at Utrecht to act as his suffragan for the work among the Frisians, and with him priests and deacons, whose names Willibald gives. The priests [2] were Wintrung, Walteri, and Ethelheri ; the deacons, Hamunt, Scirbald, and Bosa ; the monks, Waccar and Gundwaccar, Illesehere and Bathonulf.[3] Their

---

[1] Coebaneus in Willibald, Eoban in Othlon. Othlon has chorepiscopus in place of co-episcopus.

[2] Willibald makes "sacerdotali officio praediti" correspond to *presbyteri*, and "Levitarum obsequio deputati" to *diaconi*.

[3] The corresponding names in Othlon are Wintrung, Wal-

names are given here because eventually all of them perished with their leader.

After much detailed work in the several districts, the missionary band returned from all parts to the place where Boniface was. The occasion of their rejoining him was the proposed Confirmation of the newly baptized, who were summoned to meet him about Whitsuntide at a place not named by Willibald or Othlon, but described by them as on the river which separated the Eastern Frisians from the Western—the Oster from the Wester, as the one puts it; the Oster-riche from the Wester-riche, the other. A letter of intermediate date names Dockum [1] as the actual place. Here Boniface set up his tents and awaited the arrival of the candidates for Confirmation.

theri, Adalheri, Hamunt, Skirbalt, Derso, Vaccar, Kundekar, Williheri, Hadolf.

[1] A church was soon afterwards built at Dockum, and, as the custom was, a small monastery was added. These small monasteries were certainly in many cases only what we should call parsonage houses. Indeed, the word *monasterium* is used in a mediaeval charter (Nero C. IX, Ashley, Cambs.) to describe the direction of a road where there never was anything like a monastery but there was a parsonage. These buildings were set on a mound, on account, Willibald tells us, of the frequent floods. Murray's *Guide Book to Holland* makes the remark that "all the *old* churches" in this district "are built on mounds". The church was dedicated to St. Paul and St. Boniface; and our English Alcuin, who at the time of Boniface's death was about twenty years old, is credited with a set of thirteen Latin hexameters on this church and its dedication, apparently placed as an inscription on the building. The opening and closing lines are as follows :—

> " Hic pater egregius meritis Bonifacius almis
> Cum sociis pariter fundebat sanguinis undam.
>
> .   .   .   .   .
>
> Adiuuet hinc Paulus, doctor Bonifacius inde,
> Haec illis quoniam constat simul aula dicata."

When the appointed day came,[1] June 4 or 5, in the year 755, there appeared in the early morning a large band of pagans, with shields and spears, who rushed upon the little band of Christians, some fifty in all, brandishing their weapons. The attendants of the saint's party sprang out of the enclosure with arms in their hands and threw themselves into the attitude of defence, to guard their precious charge from the pagan host. The saint heard the sudden uproar, called the band of clergy about him, took the relics of the saints which he invariably had with him, and proceeded forth from his tent. Chiding his followers, he forbad their fighting. " Cease, my children, from conflict ; lay down your purpose of battle, for by testimony of the Scriptures we are bidden not evil for evil but good for evil to return. For now is the appointed day, now is the voluntary day of our departure at hand. Be strong therefore in the Lord, suffer willingly that which He permits, hope in Him, and He will deliver your souls." To the priests and deacons and those of inferior order vowed to the service of God he said in a fatherly voice, " Brothers, be of brave mind. Fear not these that kill the body but cannot kill the soul that has an endless life. Rejoice in the Lord and fix in Him the anchor of your hope. He will forthwith give to you for ever your reward, will grant to you a seat in the hall of heaven with the angelic citizens on high Receive with constancy this momentary blow of death, that ye may live and reign with Christ for ever." Thus with words of kindness he urged them to the martyr's crown, and the pagan fury put them all to the sword.

---

[1] Willibald gives the day as the Nones of June, that is, the fifth.

The pagans then ransacked the little camp for booty. They carried off the chests in which there were a number of rolls of books, and the cases of relics, supposing that they contained quantities of gold and silver. They then went to the boats and seized the rations prepared for the day and a small quantity of wine in flasks. Having eaten and drunk greedily they began to discuss the division of the spoil, particularly the gold and silver in the chests and cases. They fell out over the discussion, divided into two bands, and fought an internecine fight for the rich booty. When the fight was over, the few survivors seized the treasure for which they had fought and tore open the coverings. Their disappointment was great. Some of the codices they scattered over the plain, some they tossed into the reeds, some they hid in one place and another. These were found a long time after, and were sent back to Fulda by their several finders, where they were collected in Willibald's time. It has already been said (p. 160) that one of these books, stained with the blood of the martyr and slashed as with a sword-cut, contains a miscellaneous collection. There is a letter of Pope Leo to Bishop Theodore, a sermon of St. Ambrose on the Holy Ghost and his tractate on the good of death, a tractate of St. Faustus, a letter of Agnellus to Arminius, a list of the countries and cities where the bodies of Apostles rest, with other documents of that character. Attention has been called to the interesting coincidence that the stain of blood should be found on this book, containing as it does the two works of St. Ambrose which the archbishop was probably reading at the very time, the one in preparation for the Confirmation, the other for his always-expected death. Three days after the martyrdom, the pagans, who had returned home, were overwhelmed by a catastrophe which destroyed their property and put an end to their lives. This punishment was inflicted upon them, Willibald tells us, by a large band of armed Christians, who pursued and put to death the murderers, carrying off their wives and children and menservants and maidservants, who eventually accepted the Christian faith.

We learn from Willibald that the body of the saint was buried for a time at Utrecht. The recovery of the body, and the acute contentions as to the place of its final sepulture, are described in a later document, the Life of Lul.

This Life of Lul was written between the years 1063 and 1074 by a monk of Hersfeld, the monastery in the neighbourhood of Fulda which Lul founded. At that time the celebrated historiographer Lambert was living at Hersfeld. The style of the Life is so like the style of Lambert's Annals and History of Hersfeld that the Life was probably written by him. We naturally cannot expect to find in this Life any account of Lul's education at Malmesbury or of his study under Bede at Jarrow. The author does tell us that Lul came from the same part of Britain as Boniface, and that he was some sort of relation to him. It tells us also of his relationship to Chunihilt and her daughter Berathgit.

The most important parts of the Life deal with the difficult question of the translation of the body of Boniface to Fulda, and the dissensions at Fulda caused by certain actions of Lul.

Lul was on one occasion, the Life tells us, spending some time with King Pepin at the royal court at

T

fact—that this plain speaking not only struck home, but was valued, and increased the respect in which he was held. The "papal arrogance" of which some later ages had to speak did not appear in the dealings of the Popes with this typical Englishman.

. A ruler of men, he was a friend of men. Stern, he was gentle and tender. Reliant on God for guidance and grace, he prized deeply, and depended greatly upon, the affectionate sympathy of men and women, whether close at hand or separated from him by continent and ocean. We cannot doubt that his missionary success was due in large part to the fact that he was so very human. The need for human sympathy and affection grew and grew upon him till it became the dominant note of his communications with friends, and indeed with strangers too.

As is the case with many men who have the opportunity of working out that on which their heart is most bent, he had to spend a great deal of time on work of a kind very different from that which his heart loved. To take the knowledge of Christ to the heathen who had it not, was much more congenial to a man of his temperament, of his gifts, than the work of dealing with the errors, the vices, of those who had the knowledge of Christ and lived worse than the heathen lived. The one was the impulse of his heart, the purpose and joy of his life ; the other was a task, a burden, imposed upon him from without. We do not find him complaining that the heathen are so obstinately opposed to his teaching, so rootedly anti-Christian. He does complain that Christians are so obstinately opposed to his discipline, so rootedly not anti-heathen. What he desires to lay down in advanced age is the rule and management of an archbishopric

of Christians, not the carrying of the appeal of Christ
to the pagan fold. The moment he can properly
escape from the ungrateful task of governing self-
willed and heathenish Christians, he goes off joyfully
to the pagan fields once more, in the work so dear to
his heart of hearts to do and to die.

Study concentrated upon Aldhelm, Bede, Boniface,
and Alcuin, has this value among others: it tells us
what were the gifts of the Anglo-Saxon race before
the several blends with Scot and Pict, with Briton
and Norman. It sets the student thinking and won-
dering whether the best of the hybrid race of to-day
is so very much better—due regard being had to the
vastness of modern opportunity and modern stimulus
—than was the best of the early Anglo-Saxon race.
The compound phrase 'Anglo-Saxon' is quite in
point here, for Bede and Alcuin were north-country
Angles, Aldhelm and Boniface were south-country
Saxons. For Bale's estimate see Appendix E.

The grandest of the modern memorials of Boniface
is of course the great basilica in the Karl-Strasse in
Munich. It was commenced by King Ludwig I of
Bavaria in 1835, on the occasion of his silver wedding,
and he and his queen Theresa are buried there. It is
professedly meant to be a close copy of a great Roman
basilica of the fifth or sixth century, and of the great
basilicas of Rome it most nearly resembles S. Paolo
fuori le Mura. But, somehow, instead of looking rich
and warm it looks thin and cold. The columnar
monoliths of grey Tyrolese marble are not bright,
and their capitals and bases of white marble do not
improve their appearance to the eye. The frescoes
are the best feature of the church, but the clerestory
windows render it difficult to examine them all

round. The subjects are taken from the real and
the legendary history of the great English missionary.
His first interview with Pope Gregory II; his consecration by the same Pope on his second visit to
Rome; the felling of the Thunderer's Oak; the
foundation of the Bavarian [1] bishoprics, Freising,
Ratisbon, Passau, and Salzburg; the consecration
of the abbey church of Fulda; the anointing of
Pepin as King of the Franks; the martyrdom; the
burial in the church of Fulda; these are the main
scenes of the twelve large frescoes. This basilica
is entered by a door in a portico, with large statues
of St. Peter and St. Paul, his own favourite dedication, on either side the door.

While this fine basilica resembles the basilica of
S. Paolo, its actual dimensions are very different.
S. Paolo at Rome is 419 ft. long and 217 ft. wide;
St. Boniface of Munich is 284 ft. long and 113 ft.
broad. Thus the Munich basilica is very much less
wide in proportion to its length than is S. Paolo.

The handsome English Church at Frankfort on
the Main, consecrated June 7, 1907, is dedicated
to St. Boniface, and has a statue of the saint. It
is worthily planted at a central spot in the lands
covered by Boniface's mission and labours.

The new English Church at Antwerp, consecrated
April 22, 1910, one of the finest English churches
on the continent of Europe, is most fittingly dedicated to St. Boniface, who began and ended his
great labours in those parts. It is worthy of its
dedication and of its purpose. The Belgian Government, which many years ago gave so liberally towards building the English Church at Spa as the

[1] "Bavarian," as they were in Boniface's time.

best compensation for doing away with the gaming tables, the Province of Antwerp, and the City of Antwerp, all three have generously helped the British community by giving large donations towards the construction; and the parsonage adjoining has been built by the City of Antwerp for the use of the Chaplain. The statue of the saint in this church is very fine.

CHAPTER XVII.

Feeling in England on Boniface's martyrdom.—Letters from
Cuthbert of Canterbury, Cineheard, and Milret.—Lul's task
in his archbishopric.—His letters to and from England.—
His death.

Soon after the death of Boniface, a synod of the
English Church was held under Archbishop Cuthbert,
probably in the autumn of 755. The decisions of
the synod on certain points were communicated by the
archbishop to Boniface's successor, Lul of Malmesbury.[1] The English Church determined to keep
always a solemn yearly commemoration of the day
on which Boniface and his companions were martyred,
namely, June 5. Further, the Church resolved that
it desired to have Boniface, along with Gregory and
Augustine, as its patron at the throne of Christ. Thus
Boniface became one of the three patron saints of the
English Church, a noble example of the honour paid
by the Church at home to her sons who labour and
die in distant parts of the world. Our archbishops
of to-day, thank God for it, are very close in spirit to
Archbishop Cuthbert of eleven hundred and fifteen
years ago.

The archbishop's letter to Lul is full of sympathy
and of interest. It testifies to the joy which the
English Church had felt in the successes of its kinsmen in Germany; and to the sorrow with which it
had followed the accounts of the afflictions that had

[1] Ep. 111.

fallen upon Lul and his companions in their work, a work so full of danger and violence from pagan persecution and heretical and schismatic opposition. Notwithstanding this sorrow, they could not but feel thankful that the English race had sent out so remarkable a man, and with him so many disciples, well brought up and excellently instructed, to carry their influence far and wide among the very fiercest nations, to bring them from the way of perdition to the way of life by exhortation and example. They had even penetrated to places where before them no evangelist had ever attempted to go.

The synod had determined that it was necessary to continue the arrangement for mutual prayer which had been made in the time of Boniface, that intercessory prayers and the remedy of masses be offered to God by each for the other, both for the living and for the dead.

This was the more necessary because of the very disturbed state of ecclesiastical affairs. Cuthbert said that he did not refer to the severe but ordinary trials of Lul and others from persecutions, violence, hatred, scandals, and the like. He spoke of special difficulties, which beset the Christian Church in very many quarters; almost everywhere, indeed, at home and abroad. There were many who neglected and rejected the decrees of the early Fathers and the laws of the Church, and after their own inventions held and declared and did things evil and harmful to the salvation of very many; as, Cuthbert says, a certain man in high authority had in the year last past said and done. The industrious Germans carefully avoid a note on this cryptic reference, and I am not prepared with a suggestion as to who the high

personage was. If it had been a secular offence,
a suggestion might have been made.

There is in this letter a very valuable incidental
evidence of the independent national character of
the Church of England. It is to us of supreme
importance that we should be well informed on this
fundamental point. Archbishop Cuthbert is en-
couraging Lul to keep his people firm in doctrine
and ecclesiastical discipline. If the people will so
remain, they will have, he says, the powerful intercession of the departed saint. It is useless, we may
remark, for any one to shut his eyes to the fact that
our early English ancestors fully believed in the
intercession of departed saints. And besides that
intercession of the martyred Boniface, Cuthbert proceeds, speaking of the German flock of Lul, they
will have the help of the prayers of the Roman
Church, whose legate Boniface was; and, equally,
of the English Church. The exact words, so far as
they relate to the German Christians under Lul's
charge, are these: "All who follow the rule of
Boniface's sacred institution and doctrine, may know
for certain that they have—whether living or dying
—the perpetual communion in prayer and the celebration of masses, both of the Roman Apostolic Church
by which he was sent to you as legate, and next,
equally with it, that same communion of all of us."
I have not seen attention called to this remarkably
clear declaration of the English position, as that of
a Church in communion with but quite other than
that of Rome, so far as any bond implying supremacy or subordination was concerned. We must
return to that point shortly.

Cineheard, Bishop of Winchester (754–80), was

one of those to whom Lul communicated the death of
Boniface, asking for a continuance of the arrangement for mutual prayer. So much is evident from
Cineheard's answer,[1] Lul's letter not having been
preserved.

Cineheard assured Lul that the arrangement made
by Boniface with Daniel (705–46) and Hunfrith
(746–54), his predecessors at Winchester, should be
most carefully maintained; and added that if in any
way they in Wessex could help Lul in any secular
matters or supplies, they would do all they could.

He begged that in return Lul and his people would
allow them to participate in anything which they
had and Wessex had not. He specially mentioned
books of secular science, particularly on medicine.
They had a supply of such books in Wessex, but the
foreign ingredients spoken of in them were unknown
in England and would be difficult to procure. If in
any other way they could help, would they deign to
do so? as indeed Lul had done by sending a rough
towel.

He had sent to the monasteries and churches in his
diocese the list of Lul's priests, deacons, monks, nuns,
and others, that prayers and masses should be offered
for them. He begged a like favour for those whose
names he had to send, specially noting those who had
been friends or dependents of himself and of his
church; or prelates. Of his poor wardrobe he sent a
woollen tunic and one of linen " such as we wear
here," shoes and other little things, a handkerchief, an
Irish cloak, and a gown " made up after our fashion ".

Another most interesting letter to Lul from England must here be given :—

[1] Ep. 114; 755-6.

"To the most loving lord, in Christ most dear, to Lulla the bishop, Milret servant of the servants of God.[1]

"It was with sadness that whether I would or no I had to leave your presence and no longer see the most holy prelate and most blessed father Boniface. By the help of your kind prayers I reached my native shores after various chances and many risks. And now, before a single year has passed, the sad news has reached us that the blessed father has passed from the labours of the flesh to the heights above. If, indeed, it is right to call it sad, when we have sent before us to the kingdom of heaven so powerful a patron, by whose sacred intercessions we confidently trust that we shall always be supported. We mourn, with many and bitter tears, that we have lost a solace in this life; but he, who by the shedding of his blood is consecrated a martyr to Christ, the glory and crown of all whom our fatherland has produced, his most blessed warfare accomplished, his most glorious end achieved, softens our grief, and soothes with joy our sorrowing breasts. We bewail our lot, abiding in a vale of tears in this life full of temptations. He, the labours of his pilgrimage ended, has attained a most glorious death, a martyr of Christ; and now, a faithful intercessor for us and our faults, he rests joyful in the realms above, with Christ in the heavenly Jerusalem, united in most blessed lot with its holy citizens. So much on the most loving father, of whose venerable life and glorious end I beg with all my force that you will send me an account.

"Another thing I desire to say, on the strength of our fraternal good-fellowship. I beseech your most

[1] Ep. 112; A.D. 755.

sweet charity with all my heart, and humbly implore
as though I were prostrate before your bodily presence,
let the bond of brotherly love which our common
father Boniface, of blessed recollection and holy
memory, with sacred words formed between us, be in
your heart permanent, not transitory. For I know
that it will be greatly profitable to me and to you
that we should endeavour absolutely to fulfil the
injunctions of so illustrious a master. Let it not be
burdensome to thee to instruct with brotherly love
me the least of all your brothers, to fortify me with
sacred precepts, to support me with kind prayers. I
promise faithfully to follow gladly in all things, to
the full of my ability, your most sincere injunctions;
in union with thee I desire to serve Christ with all
my power; that so of us it may be true, " they had all
things in common." I send you some small gifts;
accept them in the loving spirit in which they are
given.

"The purple book of metre I do not send because
Bishop Cuthbert has not returned it to me."

"Metre" was liturgically the parts of the services
which the choir took up when the chanter had pre-
cented his part. But in Epistle 116 (Cuthbert of
Monkwearmouth and Jarrow to Lul, see p. 298) it is
used in the ordinary sense as contrasted with "prose".
Cuthbert sent to Lul the Life of his namesake St.
Cuthbert written in verse and in prose, the two Lives
as we have them still.

The "purple" book consisted of leaves of parchment stained purple in accordance with the splendid
taste of the time.

This mention of the "purple" book of services may
serve to show us that Milret and Lul, and we may

presume Boniface also, had discussions on liturgical
matters, as indeed we should have expected. And
we must suppose, from what we know, that questions
of verbal and literal accuracy were in those tentative
days of great importance. They had not their texts
and their services and their expositions of the faith all
cut and dried as we have them. It was a formative
period among young churches. Having this in mind,
there is a very curious, if very minute, coincidence to
be noted in connexion with this visit of Milred of
Worcester to Boniface and Lul in 754. He died in
775, and his second successor, Denebert, became bishop
in 798. We have the profession of faith of Denebert,
which follows closely the lines of the so-called Athanasian Creed. In this profession there is one minute
variant, against every known manuscript but one.
This occurs in clause 5, " alia enim est," for the in-
variable (with one exception) " alia est enim ". This
one exception is in a MS. in the Royal Library at
Munich, Lat. 6298 (Fris. 98), which, as its class-mark
indicates, certainly came from Freising, the seat of
one of Boniface's Bavarian bishoprics. A modern
note ascribes this MS. to Corbinian, the " regionary
bishop " who died in 730, in Boniface's time; but
beyond the date and the provenance there is no special
ground for the ascription. Whether it is a mere
accident that Denebert produced the same variant
that is found in a very important document coming
from the school of Boniface whom Denebert's predecessor Milred visited, is a question less easy to
answer than the reader not seriously familiar with
the precision of early scribes can imagine.

The Munich MS., by the way, is more important
on another account. It is a transcript of a collection

of sermons made by Caesarius of Arles. A preface by Caesarius comes first; then immediately follows the *Quicunque vult*; and then come the sermons. Those who attribute the *Quicunque vult* to Caesarius find here an argument in favour of their view. The ordinary visitor to Munich can see this or any others of the manuscript treasures of the Royal Library; indeed English people with any sort of literary or historical antecedents are treated as welcome guests by the staff.

When Lul succeeded an old archbishop of seventy-five years of age, it is only in accordance with nature that there was a good deal to be set straight. The few men in any ordinary diocese who desire to act irregularly are rather inclined to take advantage of a bishop being old and distant. The bishop himself is less keen to have his eye everywhere, his hand on everything and every one. For the great bulk of the work of a diocese it may be well that a man advanced in years, if of suitable character and record, should retain his episcopal seat. But for any faults which there may be that need a closely inquiring eye, the grasp of a firm hand, the rule of a will stronger than local self-will, the activity of a younger man is sorely needed. One of our church papers remarked some time ago, not at all in an uncharitable or unkindly spirit, when some additional work was given to the bishop of a diocese, that the clergy of the diocese would probably be glad that they would not see quite so much of their bishop. The remark has two sides, points to two motive-sources. The Civil Service retires men on pension at sixty, with permissible prolongation in special cases to sixty-five. A bishop, who at the time of writing is turned seventy-six, may perhaps be

pardoned for saying that bishops should be retired at
seventy-five as a maximum, and that financial arrangements should be made in connexion with their stipend
which would provide a pension without mulcting the
successor bishop.   Retired bishops might still attend
the ordinary meetings of bishops.

The first letter of Lul's which we possess on the business of his archdiocese gives an almost unbelievable
account of a prolonged course of evil-doing on the part
of an interloping priest, backed by one of the clergy
of the diocese.   The story itself, and Lul's treatment
of it, take us to the very foundations of diocesan rule,
principle, and practice [1] :—

" We know that for evident reasons the holy and
regular institutes, confirmed by canonical authority,
both of our venerable bishops and also of our lord
King Pippin and his councillors, must be kept. Wherefore we do not dare to abstain from reporting to your[2]
charity that there has been brought into this diocese,
contrary to canonical law, by the presbyter Willefrith,
a certain presbyter ordained in another diocese, without the consent of the holy Boniface my predecessor
or of me his successor.   This presbyter despises the
decrees of your institution, and, settled in our diocese,
has scorned our rule.   For you have decreed,[3] under
the recognized authority of canons, that 'all presbyters

---

[1] Ep. 110 ; 755-756.

[2] The letter does not show to whom it was addressed.
Dümmler says to the bishops of the Franks or to the presbyter
Fulrad.   Fulrad was an important person, the Abbat of
St. Denys.

[3] The words appear to be quoted from the decrees of a
Council, Vernon, held in July 755.   A modern ecclesiastical
lawyer would argue that so recent a decree first had not been
made known to Willefrith and his friend, and next did not
apply to the friend's entry into the diocese long before.

who are in a diocese should be under the power of the bishop, and that none of them presume to baptize in his diocese or celebrate masses without the bishop's order, and that all presbyters attend the bishop's council '. 'All this the said presbyter, by name Enraed, has scorned to do, and therefore in accordance with your decree he has received from me a sentence of censure. But since even thus corrected he would not repent of the past, he has finally, in accordance with your canonical institution, been excommunicated by me. And thereafter he was received and defended by the above-mentioned Willefrith. Now let your charity judge of these affairs what is right and just; and not only of these affairs but of all the things which by his evil life he has perversely done, things which you will find set forth in this letter.

" He took away slaves, both purchased and native, from churches entrusted to him, Faegenolf our slave and his two sons Raegenolf and Amanolf, and his wife Leobthrute and his daughter Amalthruthae; he traded them into Saxony for one horse, to a man named Huelp, who had conducted them into Saxony. Willefrith, the son of the above-mentioned Raegenolf, he sent across the sea with Aenred, who gave him to his mother as a slave. A man and woman, slaves whom Aohtrich gave to our above-mentioned churches for the soul of his son, Willefrith took away and carried off secretly; the name of the slave Theodo and the name of his wife Aotlind. Our slave Liudo the presbyter Aenred traded to a servant of Aldbercht (abbat) of Aefternac, named Upbit, for one horse. Also, Erpwine our slave, whom Hredun gave to our church, he took secretly by night, unknown to the rest, with ninety-four pigs. Another time he

U

took our two slaves Zeizolf and Zeizhelm. On three occasions Willefrith took, the first time four of our oxen, the next time three, and the last time eight cows and seven oxen and seven of the best pack mares, four-year-olds, which Wenilo gave to the afore-mentioned churches, besides a large number of other horses which he drove to Hamulanburg.[1] Of gold and silver which Raegenthryth the daughter of Athuolf gave to our churches, Enraed took away from the said churches two golden bracelets and five golden brooches worth three hundred shillings, and the gifts of other faithful men and women, not in gold and silver only, but also in clothes and arms and horses."

While there was great violence on the Continent, and cruel making of slaves, England was not the home of peace in this respect when Winfrid came to man's estate and was preparing to leave his native land. Witness this contemporary letter [2] :—

"To his most reverend and most holy fellow-bishop Forthere, Berhtwald the servant of the servants of God sends greeting.

"Whereas my petition, in which I prayed before thee of the venerable Abbat Beorwald concerning the redemption of a captive girl who has been proved to have relatives with us, has contrary to my expectation proved to be in vain, and I am again disturbed by their prayers, I have thought it best to send this letter to thee by the hands of a cousin of the girl, by name Eppa. I beseech you that you yourself will obtain of the aforesaid abbat that he will accept three hundred shillings at the hands of the bearer of this letter and will hand her over to him to be brought

---

[1] Hamelburg on the Saale, to the north of Würzburg.
[2] Ep. 7 ; 709-713.

here, that she may pass the rest of her life with her
blood relations, not in the sadness of servitude but in
the joy of freedom. If your benevolence can bring
this matter to its desired end, you will receive of God
your reward and from me thanks. And our brother
Beorwald loses, according to my calculation, nothing
which in justice he owns in her. I ought earlier to
have begged that while you make mention of yourself
in frequent prayers, you will deign to remember me
also in your prayers."

This is a curious letter for an archbishop of Canterbury to have to write to a bishop of Sherborne, the
immediate successor of St. Aldhelm. It would appear
that Beornwald, Abbat of Glastonbury, kept as one of
his maid-servants a Kentish girl of a well-to-do family,
taken captive in a hostile raid by those who sold her
to him, and he declined to restore her to her relations.
The archbishop, a business man, put the market value
of such lawful ownership as the abbat had in her at
three hundred shillings, and that sum Eppa was prepared to give.

We have a hint of the difficulties of slaves in
a letter of thoughtful kindness from Boniface to
Denehard, his much-trusted presbyter [1] :—

" As regards this present young man Athalhere,
I beg you, dearest one, if difficulties arise in his case,
be at pains to help him as being a freed man, and
give assurances to his friends as for a freed man, not
for a slave. My reason for making him a freed man
is that he proposes to marry a wife, and need not
fear because he is a slave."

There is an interesting remark by Lul on the
subject of freeing slaves in the letter written by him

[1] Ep. 99

U 2

in the name of this same Denehard, Burchardt, and himself, given at page 82.

Lul set himself very vigorously to get things into order and to make his hand felt. Here is a letter which from its mention of the death of Romanus must have been written very soon after Boniface's death [1] :—

"To our dearest sons Denehard, Eanberht, Winbert, Sigehere, Sigewald, Lul the prelate, greeting in the Lord.

"We admonish you that you request all who serve God, religious men and women, and all the people in the province of Thyringia, that with one accord they pray the mercy of God that we may be freed from the present plague of rains. They are to abstain for one week from flesh, and from any drink with honey in it, and on Monday, Wednesday, and Friday, fast till vesper. Each servant of God and each nun is to chant fifty psalms each day of that week. You who are priests remember to celebrate the wonted masses for times of tempest.

"We send you the name of Bishop Romanus,[2] for whom each of you must sing thirty masses and the psalms, and fast according to our constitution. Similarly for two laics, Megenfrith and Hraban, each must sing ten masses."

It is evident that Lul was anxious to keep up his connexion with England, and valued highly, as his master had valued, the letters of his English cor-

[1] Ep. 113; 755-6.

[2] He was Bishop of Meaux, and as such he was addressed by Pope Zacharias (see p. 204) in May, 748, in company with Burchardt and many others. There is great uncertainty about the bishops of Meaux before his time; he counts in the vague lists as the 30th bishop.

respondents. The tone of warm affection that is observable in the Bonifatian letters is found in the letters from and to Lul.

There is a pretty letter from Cyneard, one of whose letters is given above, with simple touches of modesty which lead us to form a very pleasant idea of that prelate. The " as I fear " in the address is a charming personal touch [1] : —

" To the lord greatly to be loved and to us most dear of all who labour abroad for love of Christ, the prelate Lul, Cyneard bishop, unworthy as I fear, greeting in Christ.

" Gladly do we receive the brother sent by you to us with the sweetness of your gifts. We give thanks to God and to you that you have deigned to make memorial of us from such remote parts of the earth. As we find is your wish, we are always— so far as by the Lord's help we are permitted— mindful of you in our prayers, that what you undertook with a faithful and most firm mind, you may continue to the end, though many tribulations beat upon you. Almost all holy men have to suffer that at the hands of the world, but Christ working with them and confirming their constancy, they fail not. Some small and poor little part of a modest gift, only incited by love, we send to you, namely, a garment such as we wear, as my predecessors used to send to yours. We earnestly pray you in your humility and kindness to deign to accept it and to use it."

Cuthbert, Abbat of Wearmouth and Jarrow, wrote an affectionate and interesting letter to Lul [2] nine years after the death of Boniface :—

" To his most desired and sweetest friend in the

[1] Ep. 123.   [2] Ep. 116; A.D. 764.

love of Christ and of all prelates most dear, Lul the bishop, Guthberct the disciple of Beda, greeting.

" I have thankfully received the gifts of your dearness, and the more thankfully because I know that you send them with inmost affection of devotion. You send a vestment of whole silk for the remains of Beda, our master of blessed memory, in remembrance and veneration of him.   And indeed it seems to me right that the whole race of the English, in all provinces, wherever they are found, should give thanks to God that He has given to them in their own nation so marvellous a man, endowed with divers gifts, so studious in the exercise of those gifts, and living so good a life.   I learned this by experience, brought up at his feet.   And for myself you have sent a coloured wrap, to cover my body against the cold.   This I have with great joy given to Almighty God and the blessed Paul the Apostle, for clothing the altar consecrated to God in his [1] church,[2] for I have lived under his [1] protection in this monastery for forty-six years.

" And now, since you have asked for something of the works of the blessed father, I have prepared with our young men as well as I could, and sent at your will, his little [3] books on the man of God, Cudberct, composed in verse and in prose.   If I had been able to do more, I would willingly have done it.   But this past winter has long and horribly tried this island of our race with cold and frost and storms of wind and

[1] In each case St. Paul.

[2] The church of St. Paul was in the monastery of Jarrow. The church of the twin monastery of Wearmouth, which was built first, was dedicated to St. Peter.   Jarrow was Bede's monastery.

[3] Neither the prose Life of St. Cuthbert nor the Life in verse at all deserves to be called little.

rain, and so the hand of the writer was slow and could not produce any more books.

" Six years ago I sent to your brotherliness, by Hunvini my presbyter,[1] going hence to your parts and desiring to see Rome, a small present, namely twenty knives and a gown [2] made of otters' skins. That presbyter, Hunvini, reached the city called Beneventum and there migrated from this light. Neither from him nor from any of your people has any answer ever reached me as to whether you received them. I now send to your fatherliness two palls of most subtle work, one white, one coloured, with the little books; also a cloak, such as I had at hand.

"I pray you not to spurn my prayer and my need. If there is any man in your diocese who can make glass vases well, when opportunity comes, deign to send him to me. Or if by chance there is one in the power of some one else outside your diocese, I beg your brotherliness to persuade him to come to us. For we are ignorant of that art and are ill supplied. If it happens that by your intervention a glass-maker is sent to us, as long as life lasts I will treat him with kind consideration. It would delight me also to have a harper, who can play on the harp which we call rotta [3]; for I have a harp but I have not a harper;

---

[1] Cuthbert appears as Cuthbercht dia' in the *Liber Vitae* of Durham, third in the list of Nomina Abbatum Gradus diaconatus, the seventh in the list being Alchuini dia', both written in letters of gold in the original hand. Being only a deacon he must have a presbyter monk, whence the expression in his letter *meum presbyterum.*

[2] Gunna, a Celtic word.

[3] A long disquisition might be written on this word From one source and another we find that it was a word used by

if it be not a trouble, I pray you put one at my disposal. I beg you will not despise or laugh at my request. The lesser works of Bede of blessed memory which have not as yet been copied and sent to you, I promise to supply if we live."

We have a later letter from Lul to the abbat, and the abbat's reply. The tone of each letter suggests a late date, but the references to Bede's writings would seem to mean that the letters are in not very distant sequence with that which we have just read.

This is Lul's letter.[1] His complaints of ill health, headache, dimness of eyesight, are rather frequent :—

"Love which knows no ceasing grows not old. It has pleased our mediocrity to learn of your safety, that I may rejoice in the Lord with you, and that you might know what things are being done by the just judgement of God about my frailness. For I am driven by continual ill health to leave this fleeting light and vale of tears and go to give account to the pious and strict Judge. Wherefore I suppliantly entreat that you pray the more earnestly to the Lord for the salvation of my soul.

"We have sent to your love some small gift, a robe of whole silk.

"We pray also that not only for the comfort of our pilgrimage, but also for our feebleness, you will deign to send us those books composed by Beda of blessed memory, on the building of the Temple, or on the Song of Songs, or his epigrammata in heroic or elegiac verse ; send all if you can, but if not, the

barbarians, an instrument used by Cambrians and Angles, a triangular psaltery invented by David, and a sort of castanet rattle.

[1] Ep. 126.

three books on the building of the Temple. It may
be difficult for you; but I think nothing is difficult
to true love. May you fare well up to extreme old
age, you and all who with you serve the Lord.

"I commend to your love the names of our brothers
and friends departed this life, as follows."

Most unfortunately the list of names does not appear
in any of the copies of this letter, as is the case with
a letter written by him, apparently at the same time,
to Coena, that is, Albert, Archbishop of York. An
extract from this letter may be given. Besides illustrating the growing frequency of arrangements for
mutual prayer for dead and living, it throws an
amusing light upon Lul's determination to acquire
a library of Bede's works. In his letter to Cuthbert
he passionately desires the treatises on the Temple,
the Song of Songs, and his epigrams. Here he
appeals for a quite different set of works :—

"It behoves us in the name of Christ to glory in
the contumelies and tribulations and exaltation of His
Church, which is daily attacked, pressed, and harassed.
For modern princes make new customs and new laws
at their pleasure.

"I send to your love by the bearer of this letter
a small gift, a robe of whole silk of the best kind.

. "I beg that you will send me for the consolation of
my pilgrimage any which you can acquire of the
following books, written by Bede the presbyter of
blessed memory,—four books on the first part of
Samuel to the death of Saul, or three books on Ezra
and Nehemiah, or four books on the Gospel of Mark.
It is a heavy request, but I count nothing heavy to
true love.

"I commend to your holiness the names of our

brothers and friends who have departed this life. They are these."

We can now turn to Cuthbert's answer to Lul,[1] so far as it deals with the books and the list of names :—

"We have written the names of the brethren which you have sent us with the list of the brethren of this monastery who are fallen asleep, and I have ordered that ninety and more masses shall be said for them.

"The book which Baeda, the most illustrious master of the Church of God, wrote on the building of the Temple I have sent for the consolation of your pilgrimage."

We may add, in connexion with Lul's ill health, an affectionate letter from Abbat Wicbert to him. The date is far too late for this to be St. Wigbert, the first Abbat of Fritzlar, but in the letter of Boniface to that monastery on the death of the first Wigbert, the first name mentioned is another Wigbert, and he may well have been the Wicbert who writes thus to Lul[2] :—

"On the receipt of your letter[3], all our holy congregation of monks sang each to the Lord the Psalter through for you, and the priests made each five masses, that the Lord might grant to you your former health. And I told them, as you wished and had instructed me, that you proposed to come here for a time. All with one concordant voice replied that our wish is in every way to feel with you in your

---

[1] Ep. 127.   [2] Ep. 132.

[3] The actual word is *alemonia*, evidently a form of the well-known word *alimonia*. What its precise force may be here is more or less a matter of calculated guess. We are accustomed to speak of food for the mind, spiritual food, food for thought, food for reflection.

infirmity and to attend upon you in all love as upon our own brother. Come to us, if you will and can, and be with us as in your own home; and we, to the utmost of our power, for love of old standing,[1] will in every way be with you in your weakness."

Lul, whose nature would appear to have been affectionate, leaning on the sympathy of others, is understood to have completed his studies at Wearmouth and Jarrow, some phrases in his letters pointing in that direction. He was evidently a personal friend of Cuthbert, the abbat of the twin monastery. We have evidence of his regard for the place of his earlier study, Malmesbury, and for the reputation of its great founder Aldhelm. While he was still a deacon he wrote to his former master, Dealwin, asking for his prayers, as he had done the year before, and sending some small gifts not described.[2] He asks that in the same spirit of devotion Dealwin will send to him some of the works of Bishop Aldhelm, either prose works, or metrical, or rhythmical, for the consolation of his pilgrimage, and for the sake of the memory of " that blessed prelate ".

The well-known letter from a monk of Malmesbury to Lul leaves no doubt about the existence of a warm mutual affection.[3] It was written after he became bishop; how long after we do not quite know :—

" To the most holy and venerable Bishop Lul.

" I beg thee, most loved brother, as I trust in thee, be not unmindful, but ever bring back to memory

---

[1] This suggests that Lul's residence during the long time of study and ill health of which he wrote to Boniface (Ep. 103) was in this monastery. He describes his place of abode as in "Thiringia ".

[2] Ep. 71.   [3] Ep. 135.

the ancient friendship which existed between us in the
city of Maldub, when Abbat Eaba in loving kindness
was bringing thee up. This I specially remember,
that he used to name you Lytel[1]. Abbat Hereca
sends you holy salutation."

We have the signatures of Abbat Hereca to
charters from 755 to 758.

Notwithstanding his ill health, Lul attended closely
to matters of discipline, and his judgement on difficult
affairs was sought by his suffragans. We have seen
his letter on a remarkable case of ill conduct in his
arch-diocese.[2] A very severe letter of his to an
abbess and her flock has been preserved[3] :—

"Lul, small and humble prelate, to Suitha and
those under her.

"It is an apostolic precept, O Suitha, that we keep
with anxious care the Lord's flock, that the wolf find
not any outside the fold and destroy them. I trusted
that you had done this and would do it, judging from
your intelligence, you who received the discipline of
the regular life from the most blessed Boniface, the
martyr of Christ. But sad and sorrowful I am compelled to say that you are proved to have done far
otherwise. Neglecting the souls for which Christ
died, for whose life you will have to render account
at the tribunal of Christ in the day of judgement, you
have allowed two women, invested with the sacred
veil, N. and N., contrary to the decrees of the canons
and the discipline of the holy rule, without licence or

---

[1] Little Lul. Maldubh or Maildubh was the founder of the
School of Malmesbury, whence the use of his name to denote
the place.

[2] Page 298.

[3] Ep. 128.

counsel of mine, to the injury of God and of His Mother blessed Mary ever-Virgin, whose service they ought always to show forth, to go free to a far country for the perdition of their souls, with the snare of the devil, to satisfy the pride and lust of laymen, not keeping in mind the Gospel saying, 'If the blind lead the blind, both fall into the ditch,' or this, 'The soul that sinneth, it shall die.' And lest by chance you make light of this my rebuke, I will smite thee with the word of the Apostle.[1]

"For such folly as yours, know that you are excommunicated, with all those who have consented to this neglect, until you make worthy amends for your fault. Those wandering and disobedient women aforesaid you must not receive into your cell. Let them remain outside the monastery, excommunicated from the Church of Christ, doing penance on bread and water; and you likewise by complete abstinence from flesh and from any drink sweetened with honey; knowing that if you despise this chiding you despise Him who was sent by God to save sinners, that is, Christ, who said in the Gospel, 'He that despiseth you despiseth Me, and he that despiseth Me despiseth Him that sent Me,'—that is, God the Father Almighty. Our wish in Christ is that you be turned to better things."

Lul's life was not one of undisturbed peace; much the reverse of that. We may take up the Life at the point where we left it in Chapter XVII, when Lul had successfully asserted the right of Fulda to be the burial-place of Boniface. This is what the Life tells us :—

Lul then began to pay very particular attention

[1] 1 Tim. v. 20.

to Fulda, helping the monks in every possible way, constantly visiting them, attempting to ingratiate himself with them, evidently aiming at acquiring the monastery. All turned out otherwise than as he had planned and desired. All his care won him no favour, no goodwill; on the contrary, he brought upon himself the gravest hatred of all the inhabitants. It was Abbat Sturmi that brought this about. Sturmi, the Life tells us, was a man of great ability and sanctity, but of a vehement and fierce nature. He kept assuring his monks that Lul said one thing and meant another, that he was acting on an arranged plan which would have a result far other than from his smooth words they could suppose. They got to hate him.

To make things worse, some factious men turned the face of King Pepin against Sturmi, saying that Sturmi spoke with less than due reverence of the kingly majesty. On this, the king banished Sturmi, and decreed that the monastery of Fulda must pass under the control of Lul. This caused a terrible tumult in the community. Nothing was bad enough for Lul, who was openly charged with suborning the false witnesses. To appease the tumult, Lul appointed as abbat one Mark, a man of mild manners and persuasive ways. Him they rejected. Then Lul put the election of abbat into their hands. They elected Lul's most determined opponent, Prezzoldus, who was ready to fight Lul with ferocity. Under his guidance they worried Lul atrociously for two years, he always kind, they always abusive. The king was so much moved by their conduct that he recalled Sturmi and replaced him in the abbacy. Lul was so thoroughly tired of the whole affair that he turned his attention to the site in the forest of Bochonia which had first been selected by Sturmi as the site for Boniface's monastery, afterwards settled at Fulda. Boniface, it appears, had secured this site as well as the site of Fulda, and he had given the property to Lul. Here Lul now founded a monastery, and built a church which he dedicated to the apostles Simon and Thaddeus. His position enabled him to secure for his foundation and his church immense gifts. But his greatest treasure was the body of an Englishman. The remains of Wigbert of Fritzlar had been moved about from place to place under pressure of Saxon inroads; they were now resting for a time in the little fortress of Buraburg, by no means adequately treated. Lul determined to translate them to his new church at Herollosvelt (Hersfeld). He obtained permission from King Karl, and the plan was carried out with great pomp.

The state of Leoba's health now caused him much anxiety. He felt that he must carry out Boniface's injunctions as to her burial at Fulda, but she was living inconveniently far off. Our author tells us that Lul put the matter before her and advised that she should come to live nearer Mainz, so as to be less distant from Fulda when her day should come. It was thus that, as we have seen, she went to live at Schornsheim, where she died.

Lul's friend and suffragan Albuinus, that is Witta, Bishop of Büraburg, but acting, our author tells us, as chor-episcopus, was taken in his old age by Lul to Hersfeld, and there died at the moment when he completed the celebration of Mass in Lul's presence. He was buried there with the greatest honour. Lul followed him in 786, on the 16th of October, in the thirty-second year from his ordination. Sixty years after, the brethren unearthed his sarcophagus to place his remains in a conspicuous position. They found that his countenance was as fine, his form as dignified, his sacred apparel as bright, as if he were only slumbering peacefully.

So far as the dissensions at Fulda were concerned, the death of Lul did not bring peace. Indeed it was accompanied by very drastic action. The Short Annals of Fulda have the following entry:—" Lul the bishop died. Hatrat and others were sent into exile." The excellent Abbat Ratger at the beginning of the next century brought a period of peace and harmony; the annalist notes with evident surprise, as an unwonted occurrence, that in the year 802 "Ratger was elected abbat with wonderful concord of the brethren".

CHAPTER XVIII

The practice of gifts.—Gradual growth of arrangements for mutual prayer.—The Lindisfarne *Liber Vitae.*

ALTHOUGH the point must have struck any one who has read the Bonifatian letters here given, it seems worth while to collect from the several letters some of the many evidences of a pretty custom which prevailed, that of sending presents to accompany a letter. "Parcel Post" does a good deal for us in that way in modern times, but the postal methods of the Bonifatian times did at least as much in proportion as our most advanced methods do now. The practice of private messengers for the conveyance of letters, books, and presents of all kinds, must have been very convenient. As we read through some of the longer lists of presents, and again through the descriptions of minute parcels of spices and so on, and think of the long journeys by sea and land, we realize that the people of those times, considering the endless difficulties of packing and of carriage, did their work surprisingly well.

Ecburga, in an early letter to "Wynfrith",[1] asks him to send her some holy relics or a few words of his writing. The same lady, under another name, Bugga, in a letter dating about 720-2,[2] begs "Boniface or Wynfrith" to send her, as he had promised, some gatherings of Holy Scriptures. She regrets that she had been unable to obtain the Acts of Martyrs, for which he had asked; she will send them

---

[1] Ep. 13; A.D. 716-720. [2] Ep. 15.

if and when she can.   She sends fifty shillings and
an altar pall, as she cannot get any greater gifts.
Boniface in a letter some ten years later [1] apologizes
for not having sent her any carefully written sentences in accordance with her request.   Pressing
labours and continuous journeys have prevented him.
He will write some when he can, and send them.
He thanks her for gifts and for clothing.   Leobgytha
asks him to send her as examples for the avoidance
of rusticity some words of his affability. [2]   She sends
him a little gift, not further described.   Boniface
thanks Eadburga of Thanet for sending him gifts of
portions of Holy Scripture. [3]   He sends to Pechthelm, [4]
Bishop of Whithern, a corporal pall with white stig-
mata, and a rough towel for wiping the feet of the
servants of God.   He requests Dudd, [5] a former pupil
of his, to send him some treatises on the Apostle Paul
other than the two which he already possesses, namely
on the Romans and the First of Corinthians, and
indeed anything which he can find in his treasury
which may be useful.   His early possession of a
treatise on the First of Corinthians explains the
exceedingly frequent quotations from that epistle in
his letters.   In Epistle 35 he thanks Eadburga for
the frequent solace of books and clothing sent by her,
and begs that she will write for him the Epistles of
St. Peter in letters of gold.

Torthelm, Bishop of Leicester, [6] sent a modest little
gift, not otherwise described, with his answer to a letter
from Boniface asking for his prayers.   Denehart, Lul,
and Burchardt, [7] beg the Abbess Cuniburga to give to
them, if they are her property, two young boys,

[1] Ep. 27.   [2] Ep. 29.   [3] Ep. 30.   [4] Ep. 32.
        [5] Ep. 34.   [6] Ep. 47   [7] Ep. 49.

Beiloc and Man. They send her small quantities of incense, pepper, and cinnamon, spices being usual gifts, highly valued. It will be remembered that when the Venerable Bede was dying, at about the date of this letter, he sent his attendant monk, Cuthbert, to bring the other monks that he might distribute his little property among them. Silver and gold he had none, but he had in his chest pepper, napkins, and incense, and these he divided among them. Gemmulus, the Roman deacon,[1] sends to Boniface a small quantity of coczumber, a specially fragrant kind of incense, to be used—he tells him—at Matins and Vespers and at celebrations of masses. Three years later (October, 745)[2] he sends specified amounts of four spices, namely, four ounces of cinnamon, four ounces of costum an aromatic plant, two pounds of pepper, and one pound of coczumber. Boniface had sent him a silver cup and a napkin, and he describes this collection of spices as but a poor return. To Daniel, Bishop of Winchester, Boniface sends a cape, not of whole silk but mixed with wool, and a rough towel to wipe his feet.

Along with a letter to Aethelbald,[3] King of the Mercians 716–57, Boniface sent suitable gifts— a hawk, two falcons, two shields, and two lances. Lul sent to Eadburga of Thanet[4] a silver writing-style, with some storax and cinnamon; and to Dealwin,[5] formerly his master, some worthless little gifts. He asked the latter to send him some writings of Aldhelm, as a memorial of that blessed prelate. The presbyter Ingalice has received from Lul gifts not described,[6] and sends in return some very smallest

[1] Ep. 54.   [2] Ep. 62.   [3] Ep. 69.   [4] Ep. 70.
[5] Ep. 71.   [6] Ep. 72.

gifts—four knives "made in our fashion"; and a
silver calamister, for crisping the hair. Boniface sends
to the presbyter Herefrith some incense (*timiama*) and
a napkin (*sabanum*).[1] He asks Ecgbert, Archbishop
of York, to have copied and to send to him some
treatises of Bede; and sends him some letters of
Gregory the Great, a corporal pall, and a rough towel
to wipe the feet of the servants of God when he
washes them. He asks Huetbert,[2] Abbat of Wearmouth and Jarrow, to send him some of the lesser
works of Bede and a riding-cloak (*clocca*); he sends
a bedspread of goats' hair. He thanks Cuthbert,[3]
Archbishop of Canterbury, for gifts; and asks Andhun
rather imperatively why he has not sent the Frisian
garments which he ought to have sent.[4] Theophylact,
Archdeacon of Rome, sends to Boniface[5] cinnamon,
spice (*costum*), pepper, and incense (*incensum*); and
again spice, cinnamon, and dried gum (*serostyrax*).[6]
Boniface thanks Ecgbert, Archbishop of York,[7] for gifts
and books, no doubt some of Bede's works as asked for,
and sends, in place of a kiss, two wine-cups or mea-
sures of wine. The German editor prefers the latter
meaning of *cupella*; but to an Englishman who
knows his " Leave a kiss but in the cup And I'll not
ask for wine ", the wine-cup is the better substitute
for a kiss.

Ethelbert, second King of Kent of that name, sends
to Boniface a silver cup, gilt inside, weighing three
pounds and a half, and two riding-cloaks (*repte*).[8]
Milret, Bishop of Worcester, sends to Lul small gifts;
a book of purple verse (or of words for the choir) he
does not send because Cuthbert has not as yet returned

[1] Ep. 74.   [2] Ep. 76.   [3] Ep. 78   [4] Ep. 79.
[5] Ep. 84.   [6] Ep. 85.   [7] Ep. 91.   [8] Ep. 105.

it. Cinehard, Bishop of Winchester, sends to Lul[1] a long list of things, a tunic (he writes a "tonic") of wool and another of linen, "such as we wear here," shoes and other little things, a handkerchief (it may mean almost anything), an Irish cloak, and a short gown "made up after our fashion". Two lists of gifts are sent from Cuthbert, Abbat of Monkwearmouth and Jarrow, to Lul,[2] the one of gifts received from Lul, the other of gifts sent to him. Cuthbert acknowledges the receipt of a pall of whole silk to clothe the relics of Baeda of blessed memory, and a coverlet for Cuthbert's own use because of the chilliness of his body. This latter Cuthbert preferred to use as a covering for the altar of St. Paul, at Jarrow. Cuthbert sent in return two books on his namesake saint, one in prose and one in verse, being no doubt the prose Life and the metrical Life of the saint which we possess. Six years before, he had sent to Lul twenty knives and a gown of otters' skins, which had not reached their destination (see p. 299). He now sends two palls of most subtle work, the one white, the other dyed; also some small books and a cloak which he had at hand. Breguin, Archbishop of Canterbury, sent to Lul a box made of bone for use in the priestly office.[3] Alhred and Osgeofu, King and Queen of Northumbria, send to Lul a dozen blankets and a gold ring.[4] Eardulf, Bishop of Rochester, sends him a cloak for out-of-doors (*reptem ruptilem*).[5] Cynehard, Bishop of Winchester, sends him, with thanks for gifts received, a garment from · his wardrobe, "as our predecessors were wont to send to yours."[6] Lul sends to Coena,

[1] Ep. 114. [2] Ep. 116. [3] Ep. 117. [4] Ep. 121.
[5] Ep. 122. [6] Ep. 123.

Archbishop of York, a pall of whole silk of the best kind, and asks for some of Bede's expository treatises;[1] to Cuthbert, of Monkwearmouth and Jarrow, a pall of whole silk,[2] Cuthbert later acknowledging a gift from him of a towel and a cotton cloth. Botwin, Abbat of Ripon, sends to Lul half a dozen candles.[3] Finally, Berchtgyth sends to her brother Balthard, telling him he must come and see her before she dies, "a poor little gift, to wit, one witta." What Berchtgyth meant by a *witta* Balthard learned when he opened the parcel. Du Cange cannot tell us, unless we are prepared to accept "a money penalty" as its meaning. At a guess, a knife, that is, "whittle", seemed suitable, but Dr. Skeat tells us that "the alleged Anglo-Saxon *hwitel*, a knife, is a mere myth". There is, however, an Anglo-Saxon word *hwitel*, which means a cloak or mantle, and we may take it that when Balthard opened the parcel he found a warm cloak.

In close connexion with the kindly custom of giving useful and pretty things one to another, we find abundant evidence of the custom of correspondents giving prayers to God each for other.

The early Anglo-Saxon practice of begging for prayers would appear to have come in large part from the sense of weakness in women, but it very soon became a feature in the letters of men. Ecburga, in a letter to "Wynfrith" about 716–20,[4] begs him to set her on the rock of his prayers and support her with his suffrages. Under another name, as Bugga, in a letter to "Boniface or Wynfrith" about the years 720–2,[5] she ascribes her peace of mind to

---

[1] Ep. 125.   [2] Ep. 126, 127.   [3] Ep. 131.
[4] Ep. 13.   [5] Ep. 15.

his prayers, and begs him to continue to offer prayers
to God for her. She proceeds to beg that he would
offer masses for the soul of one of her male relations
who had been specially dear to her. Daniel, Bishop
of Winchester,[1] about the same time or a year or two
later, finding himself seriously ill (he lived for twenty
years after this), begs not Boniface only, but those who
with him served Christ in the spirit, to pour forth
prayers to the Lord for him. Boniface,[2] unworthy
bishop, begs the Abbess Bugga, his dearest sister, nay
mother and lady, pray assiduously for him, tried as
he was in mind and body. Leobgytha requests
Boniface [3] to protect her against the poisoned darts
of the hidden enemy with the shield of his prayers.
Boniface begs Eadburga of Thanet to pray for him,[4]
inasmuch as by his sins he is tossed in the storms of
a dangerous sea; and uses the very same words in
another appeal of the same date to some person not
named, a common form, as it were. Writing to
Pechthelm, Bishop of Whithern, formerly the deacon
of Aldhelm, about the same date, 735,[5] he occupies
half of the letter with enforcements of his appeal for
prayers. To his former pupil Dudd [6] he writes that
though he may have been a poor teacher he does hope
that Dudd will be at pains to support him with
prayers poured forth to God.

The whole of a letter of some length from Boniface
to Abbat Aldherius,[7] a person not otherwise known,
is devoted to requests for prayers, first for himself,
next for German idolaters, and next for the souls
of those who have worked with him and are dead.
This letter, which unfortunately cannot be dated at

[1] Ep. 23.   [2] Ep. 27.   [3] Ep. 29.   [4] Ep. 30.
          [5] Ep. 32.   [6] Ep. 34.   [7] Ep. 38.

all, appears to be the first definite mention of an arrangement for prayers for the departed members of a community other than that to which the person praying belonged. The whole of another letter of Boniface,[1] of some length, addressed to all English men and women, lay, cleric, and religious, asks prayers for the pagan Saxons. Only one answer to this appeal has been preserved, that from Torthelm, Bishop of Leicester 737-64; he promises intercession both in the celebration of masses and in the daily prayers. Denehart, Lul, and Burchardt, asked Abbess Cuneburga to grant them the prayers of her sacred congregation.[2]

Gemmulus, the Roman deacon, asks the prayers of Boniface and of all the church that is with him,[3] and informs him that he makes mention of them in his prayers at the *confessio* of St. Peter and of St. Paul. In Epistle 55 the congregation of three monasteries enters into a bond with two abbats and a presbyter for mutual prayer for their departed members. Gemmulus, named above, again three years later (Oct. 745)[4] assures Boniface of his prayers, and begs for prayers in return. Daniel of Winchester proposed the arrangement of mutual prayer.[5] Boniface, who knew how to harrow the ladies of his correspondence with accounts of his labours and trials, wrote at length to Eadburga of Thanet,[6] as in Epistle 30, on the need for her prayers which his sufferings created; and begged her to pray for the pagans committed to his charge. His demands for prayers became more pressing as time went on, and these demands began to appear at the beginning instead

---

[1] Ep. 46. [2] Ep. 49. [3] Ep. 54. [4] Ep. 62.
  [5] Ep. 64. [6] Ep. 65.

of at the end of his letters. It is so with Epistles 66
and 67, the former to a man not named, the latter
to Leobgytha, Tecla, Cynehild, and the sisters
with them. Lul, of the next generation, asked for .
prayers at the beginning of his letters to Eadburga
and Dealwin.[1] Presbyter Ingalice thanks Lul for his
prayers,[2] and informs him that " our whole congregation " prays for the welfare of Lul and his. Boniface
asks the presbyter Herefrith for the prayers of the
fraternity,[3] the earliest use in these letters of the name
which became the title of the books in which the
names of those engaged in bonds of mutual prayer
were inscribed, Fraternity-book, *Verbrüderungsbuch.*
Writing to Ecgbert,[4] formerly bishop but by this
time Archbishop of York, he makes formal request
for a formal binding together of the two fraternities
for mutual counsel and help. To Andhun he writes,
" Pray for us, and we for you."[5] Pope Zacharias
writes that he prays for Boniface, Boniface praying
for him.[6] Boniface proposes to Elfwald, King of
East Anglia, that they shall send, each to other, the
names of departed friends, for mutual prayer. Passing
over many other such notices, including a request
from Ethelbert, King of Kent, for Boniface's prayers
for him in life and after death, we may refer to a
very full statement of the practice of mutual prayer
contained in the letter from Cuthbert, Archbishop of
Canterbury, to Lul,[7] on Boniface's death. In this
letter the archbishop desires to renew with Lul and
his companions the close arrangement for mutual
prayer, which had existed between Canterbury and
Boniface. Milret, Bishop of Worcester, wrote in

---

[1] Ep. 70, 71.   [2] Ep. 72.   [3] Ep. 74   [4] Ep. 75.
   [5] Ep. 79.   [6] Ep. 80.   [7] Ep. 111.

the same sense to Lul;[1] and Cinchard, Bishop of
Winchester, with fuller details than are found in any
other letter. From that time forward the practice
was thoroughly established and understood. Breguin,[2]
the next Archbishop of Canterbury, renewed with Lul
the arrangement for mutual prayer which had stood
unshaken in Boniface's time. Eardulf,[3] Bishop of
Rochester, sends the names of three of his relations,
all virgins vowed to God, to be mentioned in masses
and prayers. Lul sends to the Archbishop of York
a list of "our brothers and friends departed this
life";[4] but in the most tantalizing way the earliest
copyist omitted the names, breaking off short with
Haec sunt, "these are the names." The same thing
occurred at the end of his letter to Cuthbert of
Monkwearmouth and Jarrow.[5] Cuthbert replies[6] that
the names thus sent had been entered along with
the list of those of their own community which had
passed away; this has an interesting bearing on the
compilation of the fraternity-books by the addition
of whole groups of names of persons not members of
the community. The list of Lul's defunct companions may not improbably be still contained in
the *Liber Vitae* of Lindisfarne. It would indeed
have been delightful to recognize their names there
as well as read them in Lul's letter, a unique delight.

It has been mentioned cursorily a few lines above,
that Breguin, Archbishop of Canterbury, wrote in
this sense to Lul. He reminded him of their having
met and formed a friendship in Rome long before,
and begged that the arrangement for mutual prayer
and mutual masses, made with Boniface, might be

[1] Ep. 112.   [2] Ep. 117.   [3] Ep. 122.   [4] Ep. 125.
      [5] Ep. 126.   [6] Ep. 127.

continued between the archbishop and his priests and monks on the one side and Lul and his priests and monastic institutions on the other. The letter concludes with a very interesting mention of the death of Abbess Bugga, Boniface's correspondent and friend [1] :—

"We are keeping the day of the burial of the religious servant of Christ, Bugga, who was an honoured abbess. The day of her deposition was December 27. She specially begged me, while she still lived, to transmit this to your beatitude. Be careful to do as she hoped and trusted, for her father and patron in Christ was Boniface the bishop."

The letter from Aeardulf, Bishop of Rochester,[2] referred to above, written in his own name and in that of Aearduulf, King of Kent,[3] gives us the names sent to Lul to be inscribed on his memorial tablets. The combination of the suffragan-bishop of Rochester and the sub-king of Kent is of course an interesting example of the relations existing between Rochester and Canterbury. The bishop and the king are evidently nearly related to one another, and their names only differ by one letter. The concluding paragraph of the letter is as follows [4] :—

"We send to you the names of our relatives who have gone before, that is, Irmigi, Noththry, and Duhchae,[5] begging you to have them in your oblations

---

[1] Ep. 117; 759-65.

[2] A.D. 747-78

[3] Sub-king under his uncle Alric (760-94), during whose reign he died.

[4] Ep. 122; 760-78.

[5] Our word duck, in the sense of "darling", has nothing to do with the water-bird of the same name. It appears to be a Frisian word.

of masses and in the suffrages of your prayers. We are ready to do the same for you."

Here is a similar request from the important Burgundian monastery of Luxeuil.[1] The Latin of the copies is very bad :—

"Doto[2] and all the monks of St. Peter, the prince of the Apostles, to the holy lord . . . Lul.

"Although, father most loved, we are separated by a great extent of country, geographical distance does not divide in mind those whom divine love has joined in heart. We desire your holiness to know that in obedience to our father Abbat Dodo and for love of you we cease not in our assiduous prayers to pray for the mercy of the Lord for you and for your most devoted congregation committed by God to you. Therefore with greeting and humble prayer we beg of you that this congregation of St. Peter you will always have in commemoration, and among all your friends, bishops and their clergy, abbats and their monks, abbesses and their nuns, you will ever pray both for the living and for the dead, so that by your prayers we may attain to the wished-for home of Paradise. And we pray you to send to us by brief, by the hands of this present messenger Saganald, the names of all your friends, alive and dead, that we may pray for them as we pray for our own brethren."

A similar request came to Lul from the king and bishops of the West Saxons,[3] but in their case it was not a new proposal :—

"To the lord most blessed and with special love to

[1] Ep. 133.
[2] Doto (in the address) or Dodo (in the letter) was abbat of St. Peter, Luxeuil, in Lul's time.
[3] Ep. 139.

be venerated, to Bishop Lul, I Cyneuulf,[1] King of the West Saxons, with my bishops[2] and a large number of officers[3], eternal safety in the Lord.

"We testify to you that according to the measure of our possibility whatever your holiness shall desire or order we are ready gladly to do, as we were pledged to that most reverend and most holy man of God your predecessor Boniface, whether in prayers devoted to God or in any other matters in which human frailty under God's guidance is found to afford mutual solace. We pray you in like manner that you remember to pray the Lord for our littleness and for our congregation, with those who with you call upon the name of the Lord Jesus. The bearer of this letter, formerly sent to us by you, we commit to your kindness, for he will take care faithfully to obey us in all things."

In a letter to Optatus, Abbat of Monte Cassino, which we know to have been written very late in the life of Boniface,[4] because Optatus only succeeded to the abbacy in May, 750, and no reference is made in the letter to his election as a recent event, Boniface proposes a close and intimate spiritual union between the congregation of Monte Cassino and him and his inner body of workers. His definite proposal

---

[1] Cynewulf succeeded to the throne of Wessex in 757, his predecessor Sigebeorht having been deposed after a reign of one year. It is evident from the letter itself that Cynewulf wrote soon after his accession, Boniface's death being a recent occurrence. King Cuthred had died in 756, and the disturbed state of the succession prevented an earlier appeal.

[2] We can safely name the bishops as Cyneheard, eighth of Winchester (754–66), and Herewald, third of Sherborne (736–66). No further subdivision of the original diocese of the West Saxons had at that time taken place.

[3] Satraps.   [4] Ep. 106; 751-4.

is, first, that for the living of both congregations there shall be prayer in common, and next, that for those passing out of this world there shall be prayers in common and celebrations of the solemnities of masses, and that for this purpose the names of defunct members shall be sent by each to the other.

It may seem a far cry from Fulda to Monte Cassino; but, as we have seen in the story of the foundation of Fulda, the first abbat of Fulda, Sturmi, studied the monastic rule at Monte Cassino; and we may remind ourselves that Wunnibald and Tidbert resided for several years in that monastery. A connexion quite as strong or stronger, and much more recent, was created by the retirement of Carloman, the donor of the site of Fulda, to Monte Cassino, where he lived and died as a monk; if, indeed, Carloman did not select Monte Cassino because of the connexion of Sturmi and Boniface with it. We have a letter [1] of Pope Zacharias in 750 or 751 to Optatus the abbat and Carloman the monk of Monte Cassino, on the subject of a reconciliation between the brothers of Carloman, Pepin and Gripho.

In the Vienna codex of letters of the Bonifatian connexion we find a "common form" for arranging or continuing a system of mutual prayer.[2] It runs thus :—

"To the holy and venerable brothers, so-and-so provost, and all those under him in Christ, the brothers of such-and-such a monastery send greeting in Christ.

"We send to you the names of our brethren lately departed that you may in your holy prayers in the

---

[1] Dümmler, in a later collection of letters of the period, p 467, Ep. 18   [2] Ep. 150.

accustomed manner have them in memory and may
send the list of names to your (associated) monasteries; as we ourselves do as often as names of
departed brethren come from you or from other
monasteries. This is &c."

We may fairly take it that Boniface and his companions and immediate successors played a leading
part in the formation of confraternities, brotherhoods
binding together monasteries in various parts of
Europe in affectionate bonds for mutual prayer. The
subject is in itself so very attractive, and the
early lists of membership of confraternities are of
such exceeding interest and importance, that something more than a mere passing glance must be
bestowed upon the lists which survive. Among
these, none can exceed in interest for the English
Church the *Liber Vitae*, called 'of Durham', but in
early fact of Lindisfarne.[1]

The *Liber Vitae* would appear not to have been
originally a Confraternity Book, in the sense of a
collection of names of the brethren of monasteries
associated in a bond of mutual prayer. As in the
Salzburg book, of which we shall have to speak, the
earliest names of those for whom prayers and intercessions were to be made suggest that the compilers
had in mind St. Paul's instruction, "for kings and
for all that are in authority."

The first twenty names of the kings and dukes in
this charming little volume are written in letters of
gold; after that, all that are in the first hand are
alternately in gold and silver. The silver pigment

---

[1] The class mark of this MS. in the British Museum is
Domitian A. vii.

has turned black,[1] which greatly spoils the appearance of the pages, the gold remaining clear and bright. The blackened silver shows very strongly through the parchment. Thus the third name in fol. 1, col. 2 appears to be Eadberchtudla, the middle three letters specially blurred and the last four the wrong way round. These four are the initial letters of Alduulf on the next page, and the remaining letters *ulf* blur the *cht* of Eadbercht. Of the queens and abbesses only the first six names are gold, the others alternately silver and gold. Of the anchorites, the first twenty are in gold, the remainder (only eight) alternately silver and gold. Similarly for the priest-abbats. Of the nine deacon-abbats, evidently a disappearing class, all are in gold. Of the abbats not in holy orders, the first twenty are in gold, the others alternately in silver and gold. Under the other headings the same arrangement is observed. This enables us to picture to ourselves a skilled monk in the scriptorium of Lindisfarne, with a number of separate rolls of parchment on which names had been entered down to his time, each on its own proper list. He prepared an *Album*,[2] a collection of sheets of white parchment in quaternions, carefully spacing them out into various numbers of pages according to the probable number of names in each

[1] The editors of the second volume of the Palaeographical Society's publications (Plate 238) remark that "the silver has almost entirely disappeared, leaving bare the black ink beneath". Their judgement on any such matter is final; but on the face of it the explanation that the black ink is left bare is quite inadequate to meet the remarkable spread and blur of the black material.

[2] The *Album*, or White Book, was the customary name for the parchment lists of names kept covered on the altar and thus retaining their colour, as contrasted with parchment books much handled and carried about and exposed to weather.

class ; and in letters of gold he copied from the separate lists the names there found. In this way he appropriated two whole pages to kings and dukes, so placing the names in gold letters as to show that he intended to have three columns on each page. To queens and abbesses he appropriated four whole pages, and again so placed the early names as to show that there were to be three columns. For the anchorites he left only one page, of which in all only about a column and a half, for twenty-eight names, has been used, the order or class of anchorites having soon ceased, or else the work of the first hand having itself at that point ceased and no other having taken it up so far as the list of anchorites was concerned. For priest-abbats he left two pages ; for deacon-abbats only one page ; for abbats (not in Holy Orders) three pages, one of which is still blank. And so on for the other grades.

The practice of commemorating the dead by name in the Service of Holy Communion was of course a very early one,[1] but this is no place for a treatise on the history of the practice. So far as the English Church is concerned, we have a most interesting example in the case of Venerable Bede. He reminds Eadfrith, Bishop of Lindisfarne, in his preface to the *Life of St. Cuthbert*, that he, Eadfrith, had given orders to Gudfrid, the mansionary of the monastery, to inscribe his name, when the time should arrive, in the *Album* of the holy brotherhood. The name Beda occurs more than

---

[1] Tertullian (*de Corona militis*, c. iii) states that "oblationes pro defunctis pro natalitiis annua die facimus". Cyprian (*Ep.*1) directs that a certain name (Gemmius Victor) be no longer retained among those read by the priest at the altar, "neque enim apud altare Dei meretur nominari in sacerdotum prece qui ab altare sacerdotes et ministros voluit avocare."

once in the still extant *Liber Vitae*, as written out
fair from original rolls probably well within a century of Bede's death. There can be no doubt as to
which of the several Bedas whose names are recorded
in the Lindisfarne Book of Life (called ' of Durham ')
is our own dear Beda. It is the first of the name,
written in letters of gold on the reverse of folio 18,
the fifteenth name in the second column, each of the
three columns on each page containing twenty names.
This is the earliest of many pages full of names under
the heading *Nomina Praesbyterorum*. That Beda,
who died probably in 735, should come thirty-fifth
in the list of deceased presbyters closely connected
with the brotherhood of Lindisfarne, appears to show
that the White Book of Lindisfarne was commenced
at a very early date.

In a book printed in 1672 we find the following
statement regarding the *Liber Vitae* of Durham [1] :—

" There did lie on the High Altar an excellent fine
book, very richly covered with gold and silver, containing the names of all the benefactors towards
St. Cuthbert's Church from the very original foundation thereof, the very letters of the book being, for
the most part, all gilt, as is apparent in the said book
till this day. The laying that book on the High
Altar did shew how highly they esteemed their
founders and benefactors, and the quotidian remembrance they had of them in the time of Mass and
divine service. And this did argue not only their
gratitude, but also a most divine and charitable

---

[1] *The Ancient Rites and Monuments of the Monastical and Cathedral
Church of Durham, collected out of Ancient Manuscripts about the Time
of the Suppression.* London, printed by W. Hensman at the
King's Head in Westminster Hall, MDCLXXII.

affection to the souls of their benefactors, as well
dead as living ; which book is still extant, declaring
the said use in the inscription thereof."

Inasmuch as the first kings whose names appear
in the *Liber Vitae* are Edwin and Oswald (Edvini,
Osuald), and the first queens Raegumaeld and
Eanfled, the·two wives of Oswy (Osuio), we must
understand that the *Liber* in its earliest form lay
on the altar of Lindisfarne from the beginning to the
time of the pillage by the Northmen.

The practice had become highly systematized in
Northumbria in early times. The names would seem
to have been kept under ten different headings,
(1) kings and dukes, (2) queens and abbesses, (3) anchorites, (4) presbyter-abbats, (5) deacon-abbats, (6)
abbats, (7) presbyters, (8) deacons, (9) clerks, (10)
monks. It will be observed that there is no list
headed "bishops". There is a list of bishops, indeed,
but they are not described as bishops, and they are
entered on a page originally reserved for names of
presbyters, and are written in a hand of the thirteenth
century, some three or four hundred years after the
first six names on that page. This later list begins
with Paulinus, Aidanus, Finan, Colman, Tuda, Ceadda,
Wilfridus, Eata, Bosa, Johannes, Egbertus, Aethel-
bertus, Eanbald. How it can possibly have happened
that Aidan and Finan, Eata and Bosa, were not
entered upon the early lists, it is very difficult to say.
The mislaying of so important a list seems to be out
of the question ; as is also the explanation, not in
itself unnatural, that bishops were of comparatively
small esteem in a monastery of Irish type. Another
curious feature is found in the position of the anchorites. They have precedence over presbyter-abbats,

and they are all of them specially marked as priests; there are only twenty-eight names; Bilfrith comes last but seven, and that is an argument in favour of the early date at which this present book was written out from the earlier sheets.

It may be well to say something of the names in one or two of these classes.

The kings begin with the first Christian King of Northumbria, Edwin. The apostate pair who succeeded him are omitted, as Bede tells us was the recognized practice, and the golden list proceeds with Oswald, Oswy, Ecgfrith, Alchfrith, Aelfuin. The two last named were sub-kings, sons of Oswy, Alchfrith dying in some mysterious way in or about 664, and the other in 679. The list then leaves Northumbria and receives Anna, King of the East Angles, presumably because he was father-in-law of Ecgfrith. Oslaf, not identified, comes next, and then Ethelred of Mercia, no doubt because he was brother-in-law of Ecgfrith; probably from this connexion, which however was not the only family tie with Mercia, three successive kings of Mercia are included in the list; reigning from 715 to 729. The names of Northumbrian kings follow, with here and there names not identified, presumably those of dukes who did not make a large enough mark in history to have been elsewhere recorded; these unidentified names increase largely, in proportion, as we get further down the list. A name of much interest is that of Unust, one of several forms of the name of Angus or Ungus, King of the Picts, who died in 759 according to our Annals, 761 in the Irish Annals. He founded the monastery of St. Andrew, and was an ally of Eadberct of Northumbria, whose name follows his three places lower down. After seven other names, we come upon a group of three names, Cyniuulf, Earduulf, and Alduulf, all victims of the notorious King Ethelred of Northumbria.[1] Cyniuulf and Alduulf were two of three dukes whom Ethelred put to death in 778. Earduulf was a patrician whom Ethelred captured, sent to Ripon, and there put to death; the monks who took charge of his body restored him, and he lived to be crowned king at the great altar of St. Paul in York Minster in 790. Lówer down still we come upon very interesting names, Mægenfrith, Aelfuald, Karlus, Custantin. Karlus is King Karl, afterwards the Emperor Charlemagne. In 793 Alcuin wrote to Lindisfarne, after the Danish invasion, telling the bishop and monks that King Karl, not as yet emperor, will help them as far as he can; and in 796 Karl, still king, sent presents to the episcopal sees of Northumbria. Mægenfrith was the treasurer and chamberlain of Karl, a friend and correspondent of Alcuin; to Alcuin's influence we must attribute his presence here. Custantin is Constantine, son of Fergus, King of the Picts 790–820. Aelfuald was King of Northumbria 806–8. Inasmuch as Mægenfrith died in 800–1, and Charlemagne in 814, we see how accurately these four names are placed in the order of their death.

We must pass over other interesting names in order to come to the last two of the " nomina regum vel ducum " in the first hand. If we can identify these, they will enable us to date the work of original compilation. The names are Uoenan and Eanred. Uoenan (Hugh), or Eoghenan, was King of the Picts

[1] For this evil time in Northumbria see my *Alcuin of York*, S.P C.K. 1908.

836–9, and was killed in battle with the Danes.
Eanred was King of Northumbria 808–40. The
succession to the throne after Eanred's death was so
confused by expulsions and usurpations that we cannot
say what was the date of the next death of an actual
reigning king. Still, the fact that 840 is the latest
date of death recorded by the compiler and first-hand
scribe gives a sufficiently near approximation to the
date of compilation, which we may with some confidence place in the middle of the ninth century.

It would be quite as interesting to run through
the names of queens and abbesses; indeed, for ecclesiastical purposes much more interesting, so many
queens, ex-queens, and princesses having founded
and governed monastic institutions. They are richly
represented in this fascinating list of 196 great ladies,
covering a period of about 200 years. A mere glance
through the list focuses, to the mind of one who knows
the history of the time, the disproportionately large
share which Anglo-Saxon women had in the Christian-
ization and the civilization and the education of our
rude forefathers. Needless to say, the ecclesiastical
interest grows apace when we come to the starry
lists of male ecclesiastics of various assorted grades,
and is not diminished when we pass from the abbats
in Holy Orders to the abbats who were not in
Holy Orders, the first name naturally being that of
Biscopus, the remarkable man who stamped the mark
of his character upon the Christianity of Northumbria.

One special point in connexion with the list of
queens and abbesses may for our present purpose be
mentioned here.

It is an interesting fact, but not surprising, that
we find in the list a number of abbesses who in one

way and another are connected with Boniface and his companions. It is of course not at all certain that the name found in the list designates the particular person of that name with whose history we are familiar, but at least it is more probable in the case of women than of men, and among women, most probable in the case of abbesses. The number of ecclesiastical ladies great enough and well enough known to have a place in this list cannot have been so large that while we know of only one of a given name, and of her we know much, there were in fact other abbesses of the name, although no caution is given in our early annals in the way of any note of distinction. We certainly know the names of a large number of the early abbesses, and in the cases which we are now about to quote we do not know of duplicates.

Of Boniface's correspondents we have [13 (al. 2)[1] 20] Eangyth, and [13 (al. 2) b. 27] her daughter Heaburg. These are certainly not common names. Leoba's name does not appear; but an abbess of her mother's name does appear [13 (al. 2) 34], Aebbe, presumably the Abbess of Coldingham, who died in 683; she was a sister of King Oswy, and we know of her from Bede. We have [13 (al. 2) 6] Cuthburg and [32] Cuoenburg, who cannot but be those two sisters of Ine who founded and governed the monastery of Wimborne, where Leoba and others who appear in our story were trained. In 13 (al. 2) 25, Cyniburg, we have the Cuneburga (bearing in mind that y is modified u) to whom Lul and his companions wrote

[1] In the Surtees Society's edition of the *Liber*, the correct folios are given as marked in the volume. But the actual names of the *Liber Vitae* only begin at folio 12. Some investigators call that folio no. 12, others call it no. 1.

the letter given at p. 82.   An interesting coincidence,
if it be nothing more, is found in the fact that we
have [14 (al. 3) 41] an abbess Berhtgith and
[37 (al. 26) 23] a monk Baldhard.   This recalls the
two affectionate letters in the Bonifatian collection
(147, 148) from Berhtgith to her dearest brother
Balthard, in the latter of which she earnestly entreats
him to come to her, or that she may go to the place
where their parents lie, and ·there end her days.   It
may seem that from folio 14 (al. 3) to folio
37 (al. 26) is a very far cry.   But the fact is, that
Baldhard is at least as early in the list of monks as
Berhtgith in the list of abbesses.

The long array of the names of monks in the first
hand in the *Liber,* page after page of them, nothing
but the bare name of each, gives at first sight a sense
of absolute vagueness, of helplessness.   But a good deal
can be done by comparison of names here and there,
with the names of witnesses and other persons which
appear in the early Anglo-Saxon charters.   In this
way it can be made fairly clear that large groups of
monks' names from some associated monastery were
entered by the first hand all together, so that if we
find a name we think we can identify, and some
thirty places below another name which, if our
theory is correct, ought to be both geographically
and in date closely associated with the other, it may
well be that between the two some thirty names were
entered in a bunch by the first hand, and should be
taken as making no more separation between our two
identified names, than as if the thirty were only one.
Three examples must suffice, one of them connecting
the Northumbrian *Album* with the great monastic
school of the diocese of Bristol, Malmesbury.   Any

one who wishes to go at more detail into this most interesting investigation should consult *Die Namen der Bonifazischen Briefe im* liber vitae ecclesiae Dunelmensis, *von H. Hahn. Neues Archiv*, XII. 1. v. Hannover, 1886.

1. Folio 39 (*al.* 28), names, 15 Ethelbald, 51 Cuthlac, 57 Ecga. King Ethilbald went into exile in his youth with an attendant named Ecga. He went into retirement in the cloister at Croyland. At the time of his banishment, the hermit Guthlac was at Croyland. The fact that these three names come within a compass of forty-three names is at least curiously suggestive of a Croyland group of at least forty-three persons all entered as one.

2. Among the signatures to a deed executed in 675 by Leutherius, Bishop of Winchester, and the Presbyter Aldhelm, Abbat of Malmesbury, the following names appear :— Cuniberctus, abb. ; Haeddi, abb. ; Wymberhtus, presb. ; Hiddi, presb. ; Hedda. In the *Liber* we find, folio 15 (*al.* 4), names, 5 Aldhelm, pr. ; 15 Cynibercht, pr. ; and folio 24 (*al.* 13), still in the oldest hand, and among the earliest names of clerics, 5 Haddi, 6 Hiddi, 8 Cynibercht, and folio 25 (*al.* 14) Vinibercht. These are all contemporary, and we probably have a considerable list, under more than one head, of members of the monastery of Malmesbury in its very early times.

3. Between 29 (*al.* 18) 1 and 22 we find in the list of clerics Vynfrith, Aldmon, Beretvini, Haduberct, Heardred, Helmvald, Cynhelm, Hiuddi, Hygbert, Plaegvini. Between 34 (*al.* 23) 50 and 35. 57, we find in the list of monks Vynfrith, Aldmonn, Beretvini, Haduberct, Heardred, Helmvald, Cynhelm,

Hiuddi, Hygberct, Plegvini. It is practically impossible to avoid the conclusion that we have here two long lists sent in by one and the same monastery, the list of clerics later than the list of monks, the ten monks named above having in the interval been admitted to minor orders.

CHAPTER XIX

THE ancient Necrology or Confraternity Book
which comes nearest to the *Liber Vitae* in the principle
of its contents is found at Salzburg, in the library of
the ancient monastery of St. Peter, founded by St.
Rupert; the Cathedral Church being the representative
of the ancient monastery called of St. Rupert of
Salzburg. The present writer had the great pleasure
of studying its earliest pages with the learned Abbat
of St. Peter's, Herr Hauthaler. Besides the genial
kindness of the abbat, who had the precious manuscript brought from the library of the monastery to
one of his pleasant private rooms for the stranger to
study, there was an interesting link with England in
his Christian name, Willibald.

But there is a special connexion on the part of
England with this important document. Arno, Archbishop of Salzburg, whose name is the only name
written in the list of defunct bishops and abbats in
capital letters, was the intimate friend and close
correspondent of our Yorkshire Alcuin. Under the
name of Albinus, Alcuin appears in that list, "Albinus
abb.," seven names above that of his friend Arno,
a man much younger than himself.

Some idea of the structure of the most complete
of the Necrologies and Confraternity Books will be
conveyed by a statement of the various headings
under which the lists of names are placed in this

Salzburg book (library mark M). The book was edited in 1890 by Sigismund Herzberg-Fränkel as *Necrologia Germaniae* Tomus ii. 1, Diocesis Salisburgensis, Berlin, Weidmann. A useful companion to this fine edition will be found in the article entitled, "Ueber das älteste Verbrüderungsbuch von St. Peter in Salzburg," von S. Herzberg-Fränkel, *Neues Archiv*, XII. 1. iv.

The names are placed under the following headings :—

1. List of patriarchs and prophets of the Old Testament.

2. List of the holy apostles, martyrs, and confessors.

3. List of living bishops and abbats.

4. List of living monks.

5. Congregation of St. Amand.

6. List of canons.

7. List of living *pulsantes*.

8. List of living kings with their wives and children.

9. List of living dukes with their wives and children.

10. List of living bishops.

11. List of living abbats.

12. List of living priests, deacons, and clerics.

13. List of living nuns and religious women.

14. Common list of living religious men.

15. Order of defunct bishops and abbats.

16. List of defunct monks.

17. List of defunct *pulsantes* and religious men.

18. List of defunct kings with their wives and children.

19. List of defunct dukes with their wives and children.

20. Common list of defunct bishops and abbats.
21. List of defunct priests, deacons, and clerics. ·
22. List of defunct nuns.
23. Common list of defunct men.
24. Common list of defunct women.

This portion of the manuscript, called technically the Older Book to distinguish it from the other part of the manuscript called the Later Book, was commenced under Virgil in the year 784, and was carefully kept up by Arno and other prelates till the time of Archbishop Deotmar, after whose death in a battle with the Hungars in 907 very few names were added. The Later Book was arranged by Abbat Tito in the year 1004, and was kept up for almost two centuries.

Some idea of the care taken in the Older Book, and the pains bestowed, may be formed on the number of names found under the most comprehensive head, the " Common list of defunct men ", those who did not come under any of the other headings of dead men. The names entered in the first hand, which we may take to mean those recorded under Virgil, are 440 ; in later hands, down to the closing of this earlier record, there are more than 1,000 further names.

An entry written below the list of patriarchs and prophets is a prayer that the Lord will remember His servants and handmaids, and those who have commended themselves to the monastery by prayers and confessions, and those who have given gifts, their names being written in the book of life and placed above the holy altar.

The sovereigns living at the commencement of the work were entered as Charlus rex and Fastraat, Pippinus, Charlus, Luduib. The dukes (of Bavaria) were Tassilo and Liutpirga, and Deoto (Theoto).

The *pulsantes* were postulants for some higher order, probably religious men serving a probation for admission as monks. The description of the class comes no doubt from the Book of Revelation iii. 20, " Behold, I stand at the door and knock—*ecce sto ad ostium et pulso.*"

The most interesting lists are naturally those of the earliest bishops, abbats, and monks of Salzburg itself. The list of bishops and abbats in the first hand, that is, in Virgil's time, stands thus [1]—

> Or. Epor uel abb. defunctor.
> Hrodperhtus ep. et abb.
> Anzogolus abb.
> Uitalis ep. et abb.
> Sauolus abb.
> Izzio abb. Cundperht eps.[2]
> Flobrigis ep. et abb.
> Iohannis ep. et abb.

The first named, St. Rupert, was also Archbishop of Worms; his episcopal dates are 536-60. The names which follow are not in the historical order, and the list is not quite complete according to modern discoveries. Between the times of Rupert and John there was great obscurity. With John we are on sure ground. He is noted in the list published by Gams [3] as " first diocesan bishop ", and that no doubt is correct. He was Boniface's bishop, 739-45, and at his death Virgil, the author of the Older Book, succeeded, possibly only to the abbacy. In

---

[1] Page 18 of the published edition ; column 1, page xiv, of the manuscript.

[2] Cundperht eps. is added in a later hand which appears not to have made any other entry.

[3] *Series episcoporum*, Ratisbon, 1873.

a previous chapter, page 108, some remarks will be found on the difficulty of fixing the identity of this bishop. Gams makes his episcopacy commence in 745, but states that he was consecrated in 767.

The list of defunct monks of Salzburg has an interesting and unusual, if not unique, feature. After nineteen or twenty names have been written in the first hand, there is a marginal note—*hinc sub uirgilio*, "from this point the deaths are in Virgil's time." There follow in the same first hand eighty-five names, and then comes another marginal note—*usque hic sub uirgilio*, "down to this point in Virgil's time." This would give us eighty-five deaths of monks between the years 745, when John died, and 784, when Virgil died, rather more than two a year. The second hand, which added *uirgilius ep.* to the list of the dead bishops and abbats, made no other entry. A next hand completed the entry of Virgil by adding *et abb.*, and then another hand wrote immediately below Virgil's name *Albinus abb.* Arn, or Arno, the intimate friend of our English Alcuin, Abbat of St. Martin's, Tours, better known among his continental friends as Albinus, succeeded to the charge of this book in 785, when he became bishop (archbishop, 798), and died in 821. Thus it so happened that the first name he had to direct the entry of in this column was that of his dearest friend, in 804, who knew as a Yorkshire man that Arn meant an eagle, and regularly addressed the archbishop as Aquila, with many playful references to his wings.[1]

Arno is the only prelate whose name is written in capital letters in the list of deceased bishops in the Salzburg manuscript, where he appears as ARN ·

[1] *Alcuin of York*, ch. xvi.

ARChieps.   Gams inserts two early bishops, Erchan-
fried and Otakar, in his list of bishops of Salzburg,
and he includes in his list Anzologus and Savolus,
who are marked only as abbats in the manuscript.
The list in the manuscript does not profess to be a list
of Salzburg dignitaries only; between Virgilius and
Arno it has a patriarch and five bishops not of Salzburg.   It may be added that Arn appears also on
page vii of the manuscript as *Arnus episcopus* at the
head of the "Ordo monachorum vivorum.   Congre-
gatio S. Amandi."

There is considerable difficulty about this monastery of St. Amandus; no one who has not a certain
amount of spare time should enter upon the inquiry.

The Abbat of St. Peter in Salzburg, Herr Willibald
Hauthaler, who is recognized in the *Necrologia* and
in the *Neues Archiv* as thoroughly acquainted with
the manuscript and its connexions, assured the
English stranger to whom he was so kind that
St. Amand is Bec in Normandy, and that the whole
congregation of Bec, with the bishops Arno and
Siccharius at their head, had entered into a brotherhood bond with Salzburg in the time of Virgilius;
that it was through the geographical nearness of Bec
to Tours that Alcuin and Arno became close friends;
and that through that friendship Karl, not yet
emperor, having learned the value of Arno, had him
sent to Salzburg, raised to an archbishopric for him
after he had been there some years.   Herr Hauthaler
read out a portion of an article on Arno in the most
recent German Church Dictionary in evidence of
this.   No other evidence appears to point this way.
St. Amandus was specially honoured at Salzburg, and
his name may well have been given to a community

there named from him. The best-known monastery of St. Amand, much more likely than Bec to have introduced Arno to Karl, was in the Low Countries, and was long since ruined, *monasterium Elnonense*.

There is a great deal of Bavarian history in this Necrology. Take, for example, page 26 of the published Salzburg edition, page xx of the manuscript, "Ordo communis episcoporum vel abbatum defunctorum." Quaintly enough we shall find ourselves at Iona before we have done with this *Ordo*.

Haimrammus ep. is Emmeram of Regensburg, Gurbinianus ep. is Corbinian of Freising, Agnellus ep. is of Säben, Uiuolus ep. is Vivilo of Passau. That group is understood to give the name of the first bishop known of each see. Agnellus is an exception, if that really is the meaning of the group ; the well-known Bishop Ingenuin of Säben is passed over.

Ermperhtus ep. is Erenbert of Freising, Beatus ep. is of Passau, Sedolius ep. is unknown, presumably of Säben, Gannipald ep. is of Regensburg. This group is of the time of the bishops consecrated by Boniface, as is in the Salzburg list Johannes. Vivilo, having been consecrated shortly before Boniface's arrival in Bavaria, is in the first group of four ; it will be remembered that the Greek Pope spelled him Phyphyllo.

Sidonius ep. is of Passau, Joseph ep. is of Freising, Sigirih is of Regensburg. In Salzburg they did not know of a bishop of Säben contemporary with these.

By the side of these, still in the first hand, come Erhard ep. of Regensburg and Anthelmus ep. of Passau, and between them Liudinus, who must be the same as a bishop without a see, mentioned elsewhere under the name Liuti. Then follow Manno

ep. of Neuburg, Wisurih ep. of Passau, and Killach
ep. With Killach and Wisurih the first hand, the
hand of Virgilius, ends. The theory about Killach
is that he was a bishop from the monastery of Hy
(Iona, Ioua Insula, the Island of I or Y or Hy), from
which cloister Virgilius himself came. This theory
is strongly supported by the fact that in the accompanying list of abbats, abbats of Hy are found.
That list is a very remarkable one to be found in
the Necrology of St. Peter of Salzburg. There are
nineteen Irish names in Virgil's hand. The first
name, Patricius ep., is only placed there on the general
principle of the lists, which was to give the earliest
name that could be found; all Irish lists must begin
with St. Patrick. The rest of the list in its turn
begins with the earliest local name: Columbe abb.,
Barthani abb., Lassarani, Firenoi, Seiani, Sufnei,
Commeni, Sailfei, Adomnani, Kerani, Columbani,
Konomblo, Tunochodo, Dorbeni, Feilgon, Killeni,
Killeni, Zslibdeni. The last name is a Bavarian way
of representing the Irish Slebhine; his date was
752–67. After a gap left for names of other Irish
abbats who should die, the hand of Virgilius entered
" Item Eparsuindus abb., Ernust abb., Scaftuni abb.,
Taato abb., Oportunus abb.," the first of Niederal-
taich, the last of Mondsee. The most correct spelling
of the names of the first nine abbats of Hy may
be given here for comparison with the Salzburg
spelling: Columba, Baithene, Laisren, Fergna, Seg-
hine, Suibhne, Cuimine, Failbhe, Adamnan.

In the list of defunct bishops, the first hand ending
as we have seen with Killach and Wisurih, the next
hand entered a parcel of names, some of which are
well known to us : Uuillipald ep., Arpio ep., Lul ep.,

Albuin ep., presumably in the order in which they died, though that is not sure.

It may be added that the bishops of Saben or Seben (*de Sabiona*) were originally bishops of Brixen, beginning with St. Cassian, to whom (with St. Stephen) the Cathedral Church is dedicated. To St. Cassian succeeded St. Ingenuin, with a suggested date 591–605. They appear to have become bishops of Seben in the person of Alim, whose first subscription is found in 770. Arbeo or Arpio, who appears in the Salzburg list, is dated about 828–42, but that does not at all suit the order which places the death of Arpio before that of Lul. In 976 St. Albuin succeeded to the bishopric, and he transferred the see to Brixen again about 992. He and St. Ingenuin are patrons of the see. From that time the bishops have resided at Brixen.

From the death of Ingenuin, about 605, to the succession of Alim in 770, there is a confused list of supposed or actual bishops, among whom Agnellus, named above, is found.

THREE SWISS CONFRATERNITY BOOKS.

We may now turn to a series of Necrologies which are more strictly of the character of Confraternity Books than the *Liber Vitae* of Lindisfarne or the Verbruderungsbuch of St. Peter of Salzburg. And again we find a special connexion with the story of Boniface's work.

It·has been said at p. 146 that at the death of Sturmi there were four hundred brethren at Fulda. In a place which might be described as on the face of it unlikely, we find set out the names of about 365 monks at Fulda as living, and close upon 100

z 2

as dead, apparently at the time of the death of
Sturmi the first abbat.   Much more than twice as
many more are recorded as living, and more than
as many more as dead, but all in later hands.   The
465 names spoken of are all written in one hand,
copied evidently from a roll or rolls sent from Fulda
to a monastery with which it was united in a bond
of mutual prayer.   The earliest hand gives only the
names of those who had died down to the year 782,
the year of Sturmi's death.   An indication of the
early date of the roll may be found in the heading—
"Nomina fratrum de congregatione Sancti Bonifacii
de monasterio quod Fulta nominatur," where the
spelling Fulta goes back to the earliest form of the
name of the river, Vultaha.[1]

The manuscript in which these names are set out
is in the Cantonal Library at Zurich, "Hist. 27."
It has been published by Paul Piper in the *Monu-
menta Germaniae Historica*, with two similar documents, in the volume entitled *Libri Confraternitatum
Sancti Galli Augiensis Fabariensis*, Berlin, Weidmann,
1884, the Confraternity Books of St. Gall, Augia,
and Pfäfers.

"Augiensis" is a description dear to the heart of
a German editor.   It is capable of application to
Augia Brigantina (Bregenz), Augia Dei (Gottesau),
Augia Dives (Reichenau), Augia Major (Rheinau),
Augia Minor (Weissenau), Augia Sanctae Mariae
(Marienau), Augia Virginum (Magdenau).   For our
present purpose its application is confined to Augia
Dives, that is, Reichenau, and Augia Major, Rheinau.
But here again comes in a delightful opportunity for
editorial disquisition.   "Augiensis" is continually

---

[1] See page 151.

used as descriptive of chronicles, annals, and so on, of Reichenau. Their full description is Rinaugiensis. The full description of anything taking its name from Rheinau is Rhinaugiensis; but even this is not certain. Reichenau is of course the well-known island below Constance, and Rheinau is the island below Schaffhausen, so that geographical neighbourhood and insular position on the Rhine add to the complications. The library of the monastery of Richenau (founded 728, secularized 1799) was one of the greatest in Europe; it was divided after the secularization and was housed at various centres. The library of Rheinau (a monastery founded by Duke Wolfhart of Alemannia in 778, secularized in 1862), though very much less famous, was in itself remarkable; there still are several interesting MSS. at Rheinau.

The manuscript itself settles the question of the original home of this treasure of archaeology and history. It has this inscription, "Necrologium Augiense sub Abbate Erlebaldo conscriptum anno circiter 830." In the list of abbats of Reichenau from St. Pirminius the first abbat, A.D. 724, the ninth in the list is Erlabald, 823–38. Thus Reichenau was the place of writing, and the first scribe copied the rolls from Fulda down to the point which they had reached in the year 782.

Quite apart from the inscription, which is not in itself of critical value, the MS. speaks clearly on this point. On p. 3 it has a list of fifty-two monasteries bound together in bonds of brotherhood, for mutual prayer. The first is *Insula Monasterium*, Reichenau itself; the second is St. Gall; the third Favaria, that is Pfäfers; the fourth Desertina, that is Disen-

tis; the tenth is Salzburc; the sixteenth is Fulda.
Across pp. 4 and 5 we have "Nomina uiuorum fratrum Insulanensium ", and the first is Erlebaldus abba,
the second being Heito eps., Erlebald's predecessor
who had been raised to the episcopate. Some idea
of the importance of the monastery may be gathered
from the fact that the names of forty-two priests
are given among the brethren themselves. On p. 6
we have the *Nomina defunctorum,* and these are
headed by the earliest abbats, beginning with St. Pirminius.

But, and here is a crowning source of ambiguity,
while the MS. itself was written at Augia Dives
(Reichenau), and so might well have acquired its
distinctive title of Augiensis, it is in fact called
Augiensis because it came from Augia Major
(Rheinau). Paul Piper, the editor of this Augiensis
manuscript, remarks in his preface that to Ferdinand
Keller of Zürich it is due that the precious book was
not sold into Italy or England or some other land.
Keller, whose home was in Zürich, knew of its existence, and noticed the fact that it was not named in
the catalogue of MSS. transferred to Zürich at the
secularization. He urged his inquiries for this
vastly important treasure so actively that at last it
was handed over from the monastery and safely
lodged in the Cantonal Library, "Hist. 27." How
it came to Rheinau from Reichenau is not known.
A piece of internal evidence as to the date of its presence at Rheinau appears to have escaped the notice
of those who have examined the book. At p. 136 of the
Augiensis codex there is an entry of the "promise
of obedience" (see p. 346) of Frater Johannes de
Landdeck to the authorities of Augia Major. It

is dated 1442. The codex was therefore in use at Rheinau as long ago as 1442.

To speak first of the names of the monks of " Fulta " as written in the first hand, they are, so far as we can test their dates by notices in the Annals of Fulda and elsewhere, so much out of chronological order, that the German editor makes a suggestion not in itself unnatural. He believes that the writer who began the now existing list had in his hands a document of more than one page, in double columns on each page, the left-hand column containing the names of monks resident at Fulda in 780, the first year of Abbat Baucolf (whose name is first in the list) the successor of Sturmi, the right-hand column containing the names of monks added under Abbat Ratger (the successor of Baucolf), whose abbacy lasted from 802 to 817. That may well have been so. He suggests, further, that the writer copied the columns on the first page (different as their dates were) in a continuous list, followed by the next page in a continuous list, and so on, so that the list which we have now may be composed of alternate portions of two lists of two different chronological periods. However that may have been, the hint is one of great value in connexion with puzzling problems of date in regard to such a document as the *Liber Vitae* of Durham.

In the earliest hand we have the name of Eigil or Egil, as a living monk, and he became the fourth abbat in 819. The name of his predecessor as abbat, Ratger (802–817), appears as that of one living, but, curiously enough, not in the first hand. It needs almost as much ingenuity to explain these and other like inconsistencies in these puzzling lists of the living and the dead as it needed to "keep up appearances", σώζειν τὰ φαινόμενα, in the case of fresh astronomical discoveries in the time of Ptolemaic astronomy. The names of all the early abbats of Fulda appear in the lists, not as abbats, but as monks living at the time of entry; they are found also, without description as abbat, in the lists of the dead. Only three persons in the whole long series of lists have a description attached to their names, and in each case the name and the description are in capital letters, the only capitals used in the lists. These three are BAUCOLF ABB. as living, STURMI ABB. as dead, and MEGINGOZ EPS. as dead.

The St. Gall Confraternity Book has a list of seventeen names with Pernoldus eps. as the first name, headed "Nomina fratrum sancti Bonifacii in Traiecto", the principal monastery in Utrecht being that of St. Martin. St. Martin's itself also had sent names of monks to St. Gall, thirty-six in number, the first name in this list also being Pernoldus eps. This dates the St. Gall list of Bonifatian monks at least two centuries and a half later than that of the earliest Fulda lists which we are considering, Bernold, or Bernulf, having been bishop or archbishop there 1028-54. The handwriting of the list agrees with this date. The list was certainly written by an eleventh-century scribe.

The oldest part of the St. Gall lists, as they now appear, consists of twelve pages written about the year 810. These pages contain first the names of monks of Weride, in Canton Solothurn, on an island called now Schönenwerth in the Aar; it is first mentioned in the will of Remigius, Bishop of Argentoratum (Strassburg), dated in 778; his death is usually put in 783. Then come the monks of Tours, a list which naturally has a direct call upon the attention and interest of English people who know anything of the remarkable history of one of the three greatest of the Anglo-Saxon learned men, Alcuin of York. This list is headed by Fridigisus abb., Alcuin's immediate successor, who ruled from 804 to 832. This list is headed "Nomina fratrum", &c., whereas the Weride list which precedes it is headed "Nomina fratrum canonicorum", &c. This distinction goes to show that at the date of writing Weride was a secular monastery and Tours was not. In 818 Fridigisus secularized his monasteries of St. Martin of Tours, St. Othmar, and St. Bertin, and it may fairly be argued—if it were not unnecessary to do so in presence of other clear evidences—that the list was entered in the Confraternity Book before 818. There are also in this first hand a series of princes and some names probably of donors.

About the year 815 another quaternion was added, which contains the first list of bishops, a list which as we have seen has no corresponding list in the *Liber Vitae* of Durham till after the Norman Conquest. We may probably assign as a reason the jealous sense or desire of independence on the part of monasteries. The names also of aulics and counts appear in this quaternion. Further additions took place in 828, 839, and 885. When the brotherhood was at its fullest dimensions, twenty-seven monasteries of men and twelve of women were in fraternity with St. Gall.

It is probable that we know the name of the original writer, for in the first row of names, which

begins with Huadalricus presul, a bishop (Luso-
nensis) whose successor came in 814, we find written
between the twenty-fourth and twenty-fifth names
Andustrius peccator, "the sinner Andustrius."

There are two lists of princes, both in the first
hand. Page 3 has a list of kings, nine of them, from
Karolus imp. Magnus to Karolus imp. Novissimus;
and a list of queens, nine in number, beginning with
Hemma regina, Hiltigart, Irmingart, Gisla. The
second list is on p. 6. It begins with Pippinus rex,
Carlomannus, Carolus imp., item Carolus, Pippinus
rex. Quite possibly the presence of this list may be
accounted for by the fact that the last of these
Pepins, the third son of Charlemagne (by Himil-
trud), called originally Carloman but renamed or
surnamed Pepin at Rome in 781, was eventually sent
into the monastery of St. Gall for plotting against
his father, dying in 811 in his father's lifetime.

A very interesting feature of the St. Gall book
is its list of "promises" from very early times. The
lists are in a separate codex, united with the Confraternity Book. The first page has twenty-seven
signatures to the promise of obedience and steadiness before God and His Saints. The first name is
that of Abbat Audomar, who governed the monastery
from the year 720. After him three presbyters sign
as *ego* so-and-so; and then, the fifth name, "ego
Petrus diac. promitto ut supra." Piper understands
this Peter to be the writer of the original list, about
720 to 737. The third page is headed *Iohannes eps.
uel abbas*; his date was 760 to 781. After fourteen
pages of signatures of promises, averaging twenty-
five names each, we come to a change of formula;
conversio morum is promised, as well as obedience

and steadiness. A little later, in 959, the chamberlain Ruom promises *conversio morum* according to the rule of the holy Abbat Benedict. The latest name but two of all the very long list can be identified and dated : he was Ymmo, provost in 962.

The Confraternity Book of Pfäfers (Favarias) is of less interest than either the St. Gall or the Reichenau book; and, though it is more completely in its early condition than the others, it is not so orderly. There is a curious entry at the beginning which appears to date the commencement of the book somewhere not long after 800. It is in simple Latin, "The mother of the lord Abbat of Pfäfers, Gebene, by name Imma, who was a lay woman but afterwards turned nun." Gebene was Abbat of Pfäfers from 814 to about 826. The names of royal people written by the first hand enable us to date the first hand about 830.

After the mention of Imma, mother of Gebene, the first list of names is that of brethren of Reichenau (*Fratrum Insulanensium*). This list begins with Liutpertus eps. This was Ludbert, Archbishop of Mainz, 863–89, whose penultimate predecessor was our Fulda abbat Hrabanus Maurus; the prince Karl, son of Pepin of Aquitaine, comes between them. The next name is Ruadho *domn. et abb.*; he was Abbat of Reichenau 871–913. Thus the first page and half of the second (they are folios 22 and 23 in the codex) are evidently very late by comparison with the date of the first hand.

Next, dealing only with the first hand, come the names of brethren of the city of Constance. Then the names of the brethren of St. Gall, beginning

with Grimaldus abb.; he was abbat 841–72, from
which we are led to suppose that the first hand made
a few rather casual entries of royal people in 830,
and some ten years after entered lists sent from other
monasteries. Then come lists of presbyters of Aviasca,
beginning with Calvio *archipresb.* Then defunct
abbats of Pfäfers, from Adalbert, about 740. Then,
brethren of the monastery of Disentis (*Desertinense*).
The deed of a formation of a Confraternity between
St. Gall and Disentis, dated 846, is extant. The
Disentis formula for entering upon such a brotherhood, drawn up apparently in 836, is also extant.
To pass from Aviasca to Desertum, that is, from
Biasca to Disentis, means to the Swiss tourist the
Lukmanier Pass (*in luco magno*, in the large wood),
the lowest pass but one between Italy and Switzer-
land. Other associated monasteries were Clavades, now
Livate, formerly Clivate; de Plano, on the level
ground near Werdenberg; Tobrasca, now Tuverasca;
Tobrense, now Tüffersthal.

It may be added that this Pfäfers book contains
full lists of treasures in relics, books, service-books,
vestments, &c., &c. Most interesting lists.

It is great good fortune that has preserved for us
these three Swiss Confraternity Books; for the monasteries at which they were kept were in confraternity
with one another. Thus in the St Gall book we have
lists of the brethren in Augia (not Rheinau, because
these are included also as the brethren in Rinoua)
and the brethren in Favaria. In the Reichenau
book we have the monastery of St. Gall and the
monastery of Favaria.

One general remark applies to these three Confraternity Books. Their lists of names are not sub-

divided as are the names in the Salzburg book and
the *Liber Vitae*. The names of members of associated monasteries were added under the head of each
monastery as they came in from time to time. They
are thus much less helpful in regard to the status
of the persons, and in other respects there is more
of vagueness about them.

APPENDIX A

PAGE 7

IN order to give some fair idea of the kind and amount of change which Othlon made in Willibald's narrative, apart from the addition of valuable information, a well-known passage descriptive of the youthful zeal of Boniface is printed here in parallel columns. It enables us to compare the Latin prose of 760–80 with that of 1100.

WILLIBALD.

Cum esset annorum circiter quatuor vel quinque, Dei servitio se subiugare studuit, multoque mentis conamine de monasteriali iugiter vita insudare, et ad eam mentis quotidie nisibus anhelare. Cum vero aliqui, sicut illis regionibus moris est, presbyteri sive clerici, populares vel laicos praedicandi causa adissent, et ad villam domumque praefati patrisfamiliae venissent : mox quantum possibilitatis eius pusillanimitas in infantia sua praevaluit, coepit cum eis de coelestibus loquendo tractare, et quid sibi suaeque infirmitati in futurum proficeret

OTHLON.

Qui nimirum, magna parentum sollicitudine nutritus, magnarum etiam virtutum per incrementa temporum amator est factus. Nam cum adhuc parvulus esset, si quem forte clericum vel laicum verbi divini notitiam deferentem audire contigisset, mox quantum aetatis suae teneritudo praevaluit, quid sibi suaeque qualitati exinde profectuosum foret tractare coepit. Cumque ita meditatione diuturna sese ad superna erigeret, patri etiam ea quae animo gerebat revelavit, et ut suae consuleret voluntati rogavit. Audiens haec autem pater eius primum obstupuit, deinde

WILLIBALD.

interrogare. Cumque ita diu de coelestibus diuturna mentis meditatione cogitaret, ac totum se in futurum extenderet, et ad superna erigeret, patri etiam demum haec quae animo gerebat revelavit, et ut suae consuleret voluntati rogavit. Quo comperto obstupefactus pater, magna cum increpationis instantia, partim minis ne se desereret prohibuit, partim etiam blandimentis ad saecularis curam instigabat negotii, ut temporaneo eum transitoriae haereditatis subiungeret lucro, et sese quandoque defuncto suae terrenae facultatis custodem imo etiam haeredem relinqueret.

OTHLON.

eum increpans, nunc minis nunc vero blandimentis, ad saecularis vitae curam impellere studuit. Ad haec etiam ut eius animum adhuc tenerum a concepti perfectione propositi facilius declinaret, promisit se post vitae suae tempora eum et praediorum et omnium rerum suarum haeredem facturum.

The palmary example of the value of the insertions which Othlon made as the result of his reading and local inquiry may also be given here.

WILLIBALD.

Sicque sanctae rumor praedicationis eius diffamatus est, in tantumque inolevit, ut per maximam iam Europae partem

OTHLON.

Praedicans ergo et baptizans sanctus praesul Bonifacius in Thuringorum et Hessorum regionibus, perspexit messem

WILLIBALD.

fama eius perstreperet; et ex Britanniae partibus servorum Dei plurima ad eum tam lectorum quam et scriptorum, aliarumque artium eruditorum virorum congregationis conveniret multitudo. Quorum quippe quamplurimi regulari se eius institutioni subdiderunt, populumque ab erraticae gentilitatis profanatione plurimis in locis evocavere: et alii quidem in provinciam Hessorum, alii etiam in Thuringiam dispersi, late per populorum pagos et vicos verbum Dei praedicabant.

OTHLON.

quidem esse multam ibi sed operarios paucos ad copiosam multitudinem credentium instruendam. Unde in provinciam patriamque suam mittens, exinde tam feminas quam viros religiosos, scientiaque varia imbutos, plures venire fecit, suique laboris onus inter eos divisit. Inter quos erant praecipui viri Burchardus et Lullus, Willibalt et Wunnibalt frater eius, Witta et Gregorius: feminae vero religiosae, matertera scilicet sancti Lulli nomine Chunihilt et filia eius Berathgit, Chunidrut et Tecla, Lioba et Waltpurgis soror Willibaldi et Wunnibaldi. Sed Chunihilt et filia eius Berathgit valde eruditae in liberali scientia in Thuringorum regione constituebantur magistrae; Chunitrud in Bagoariam destinata est ut verbi divini semina ibidem spargeret; Tecla vero iuxta fluvium Moin in locis Kihhigen et Ochsnofrutt nuncupatis collocavit; Liobam quoque ad Biscofeschein, ut illic multitudini virginum congregatae praeesset constituit.

APPENDIX B

PAGE 53

APPEAL TO ENGLISH KNOWLEDGE.

WE may take as an example at once of Boniface's thoroughness, and of his trust in the learning of the English Church, and of his very sturdy disinclination to be made to take a view merely because the Romans took it, three letters which are placed together in the collection of Bonifatian Epistles, and must be dated about 735. They are addressed respectively to Pechthelm, who was Bishop (730-5) of Candida Casa in Galloway and had been deacon of Aldhelm; to Nothelm, who had as Archpriest of London sent much valuable information to Bede and was now Archbishop of Canterbury (735-40); and to Dudd, an abbat of Glastonbury as we know from other sources. In all three he asks if anything is known about spiritual relationship through sponsorship. After telling Pechthelm[1] that he is sending a corporal pall marked with white stigmas, and a rough towel for wiping the feet of the servants of God, he puts to him the case on which he asks for an opinion. A man had acted as godfather to a boy, had raised him as the custom was from the font, and made him his adoptive son. The boy's mother became a widow, and the man who was godfather to her son married her. The priests throughout all the land of the Franks, and the Gauls, as also the Roman priests, declared that the man was guilty of a very great

---

[1] Ep. 32 ; A.D. 735.

crime. What kind of crime, if so it was, Boniface did not know. He was not aware that the Fathers had enumerated it among crimes in the ancient canons or in the decrees of the pontiffs, or the Apostles in their lists of sins. If Pechthelm can find anywhere any discussion on this point in ecclesiastical writings, he is begged to let Boniface know. We have no trace of any letter in reply, or indeed of any letter from Pechthelm.

To Nothelm the archbishop he writes [1] to beg that the prayers promised by the late archbishop may continue to be offered on his behalf. He asks for a copy of the letter in which Pope Gregory replied to the questions of Augustine, the first teacher of the English, in which instructions were given about the degrees of propinquity within which matrimony was lawful; he had applied to the record-office in Arme, and the officials asserted that there was no copy of it in their possession. We happen to know from Bede, whose death-year this was, that Nothelm had himself visited Rome and searched the archives for Gregory's letters, which he took to England with him and sent up to Jarrow for incorporation in Bede's *History,* where this particular letter is still found. [2] He then states his case, more clearly than he states it to Pechthelm, and tells Nothelm that the Romans say it is not only a sin but a capital sin, so that divorce must be made. The Romans further declare that under the Christian emperors the crime of such matrimony was punished with death or perpetual banishment. If Nothelm can find anything about it anywhere, Boniface begs he will let him know. For himself, he cannot understand why spiritual propinquity in

---

[1] Ep. 33; A.D 785.   [2] *H. E.* i. 27.

conjunction with a union of the flesh should be so great sin, when it is considered that in baptism all alike are counted as sons and daughters, brothers and sisters, of Christ and the Church. Will Nothelm tell him at the same time in what year the first preachers sent by Gregory arrived in England? Here again no letter from Nothelm to Boniface is known to be extant.

To Abbat Dudd of Glastonbury he says[1] less on this particular point. They were very old friends. Their friendship began in Dudd's boyhood, when Winfrid was his teacher and became greatly attached to him. "I was," he says, "but a poor preceptor, but you know how I tried to be most devoted to you. Mindful of that devotion, have pity on me, now an old man [he was fifty-five years old], fatigued with the tempests of this sea of Germany, tossing on all sides; and help to support me by pouring out prayers to God for me, and by sending me holy scriptures and the spiritual tractates of the holy Fathers." He asks specially for treatises on St. Paul's epistles, having himself only two of such, one on the Romans and one on the First of Corinthians. But indeed anything he finds in the sacred chest which he thinks Boniface has not got, he is to send. At the end of the letter he asks Dudd if he knows or can find anywhere anything about the sin of marrying under the circumstances already described.

[1] Ep. 34; A.D. 735.

APPENDIX C

PAGE 122

. IT cannot but be interesting to see in what language Boniface wrote his congratulations to the new Pope, Zacharias, whom he had known as a friend in Rome on his visit to Gregory III. We find it in the opening paragraph of his first letter to the Pope.[1] It will be well, for this purpose, to keep to the "we", "you", "thou", of the Latin, though for general purposes it would be perhaps pedantic to do so.

"To our dearest lord, endowed with the fillet of the highest pontificate, the apostolic man[2] Zacharias, Boniface the servant of the servants of God.

"We confess, lord father, that—after the news had come that the predecessor of your apostolate, Gregory of venerable memory, pontiff of the apostolic see, released from the labours of the body had migrated to the Lord—greater gladness and joy we have never heard, and for it we have with hands raised heavenwards given thanks to God, than that the Arbiter most high has granted[3] that your clement fatherliness should rule the canonical laws and guide the helm of the apostolic see. Therefore with bended knee and deepest prayers we earnestly implore that as we have been for the authority of the holy Peter devoted servants and submissive disciples of your predecessors, we may as we desire deserve, by keeping the Catholic faith and the unity of the Roman Church, to become obedient servants of your piety, subjects under canon law. And whomsoever God

---

[1] Ep. 50. [2] Viro apostolico.
[3] The election was Dec. 8, 741.

has given to me as hearers and disciples in this legation of mine, I cease not to invite and incline to the obedience of the holy see."

The response of the Pope to this congratulation and declaration of obedience "under canonical law" is found in the opening and closing paragraphs of the letter of reply [1] :—

" To our most reverend and most holy brother and fellow bishop Boniface, Zacharias, servant of the servants of God.

" Having received the letter of thy most holy brotherliness by Denehard your religious priest, and learned that as we always desire thou art well, we returned great thanks to our almighty and most merciful God, who deigns to prosper thee in all good things. For thou givest us great joy in our heart as often as the letters of thy holiness are sent, when we find that which relates to the saving of souls, and hear that daily in the bosom of holy mother church new peoples are by thy preaching added."

The closing paragraphs of the letter are as follows:—

" If anything new happen, by the astuteness of the enemy, which your holy brotherliness cannot deal with by help of the institutes of canons, do not hesitate to send it on to us, that by God's help we may without delay send an answer which may tend to amendment of the new races. For, dearest brother, your holy brotherliness should know that love for thee is so fixed in the recesses of our heart that we would we could see thee every day and have thee in our company as a minister of God and a dispenser of the churches of Christ."

Gregory's friend Zacharias was one of many

[1] Ep. 50

Greek Popes of Rome in those times. Muratori [1] expresses the belief that the influence of the exarchs and other imperial officers appointed from Constantinople caused the elections to the papacy to fall to ecclesiastics of their own nation. These Greeks, he continues, did no injury to the honour of the see of St. Peter, for they maintained the true faith of the Church, and were not driven out of the right way by the threats of the Greek Emperors. A main reason for there being so many Greek ecclesiastics in Rome is to be found in the widespread successes of the Mohammedans in various parts of the Greek empire, which had the effect of driving the higher classes of the inhabitants of those provinces to seek refuge westwards. For a long period of time there were more Greek than Latin Popes. [2]

APPENDIX D

PAGE 264

BONIFACE naturally kept as clear as possible of the political tension which the death of Charles Martel brought about among his sons. The chief difficulty was caused by the fact that a third son, half-brother of Pepin and Carloman, Gripho, son of a later wife, Swanahilde, had to be provided for after the original partition between Pepin and Carloman had been

---

[1] *Annali d'Italia*, A.D. 705 (Milan, 1758, vi. 58).
[2] See my *Theodore and Wilfrith*, S.P.C.K., p. 80.

arranged by their father. Gripho plays so small a part in the Bonifatian letters that it is not necessary to enter upon any consideration of his political action. We have seen, in glancing at the story of the dukes of Bavaria, that the alliance of Duke Odilo, Boniface's friend, with Gripho was very disastrous.

We have one letter from Boniface to Gripho, and it is difficult to place it accurately. It is an appeal to Gripho to assist the bishops and presbyters of Thuringia "if God shall have given thee the power". Dümmler dates the letter at the end of 741, shortly after the death of Charles Martel. But Boniface makes very distant allusion to the decease of his father, as something long past; and we do not know that Gripho had anything to do with Thuringia at that time, or indeed at any time. Others have dated it in 747, because in that year Gripho, having rebelled against Pepin, had betaken himself with his attendants into Saxony, on the confines of Thuringia. But it would have been very indiscreet on Boniface's part to write such a letter to Gripho when in the act of rebelling against his immensely powerful brother Pepin. Still, the terms of the letter distinctly point to some probable invasion of Thuringia by forces gathered from a pagan vicinity; and it is not to be forgotten that the letter tells that Gripho or Gripo had been specially committed to the care of Boniface [1]:—

"Boniface, servant of the servants of God, to Gripo son of Karl, all health in Christ.

"I beseech and adjure your piety by God the Omnipotent Father and by Jesus Christ His Son and by the Holy Ghost, by the Holy Trinity and Unity of

[1] Ep. 48; 741-7.

God, that, if God shall have given you the power,
you study to aid the servants of God, the bishops
and presbyters who are in Thyringia, and to defend
the monks and handmaids of Christ against the
malice of pagans, and to help the Christian people
that the pagans destroy them not : so that at the
tribunal of Christ you may receive everlasting
reward.   And know that the memorial of you is
with us before God, as your father when alive and
your mother some time ago [1] commended you to me.
We pray God the Saviour of the world that He may
direct your way and your life to the salvation of your
soul, that you may remain ever in the grace of God
here and in the future world.   Meanwhile remember,
my dearest sons [2], what the psalmist says, 'The days
of man are as grass, he flourishes as a flower of the
field.' . . . Act therefore, my sons [3], so that the prizes
of your reward may shine and grow in the lofty
height of the heavens."

So far as the existing letters from and to Boniface
are concerned, no trace of confirmation can be found
for the usual statement, that Boniface took an active
part in advising, or at least approving, and in carrying out, the change of dynasty from the Merovingians to the family of the dominant Mayors of the
Palace in the person of the third Pepin, the Short.
The first Pepin was of Landen, Mayor of the Palace
in Austrasia; the second, of Herstal, was grandson
both of Pepin of Landen and of Pepin's brother
Arnulf; the Pepin of our story was the son of

---

[1] *Iam olim.*

[2] Dümmler prints without comment *filii carissimi*; Migne
prints, but with more than usual ·space between the words,
filii charissimi.

[3] *Filii*, both in Dümmler and in Migne

Charles Martel [1] and through him the grandson of Pepin of Herstal. Charles Martel died in 741, leaving three sons, Carloman the oldest, who for six years ruled as Duke of the Franks in the eastern part of the Frank kingdom, Austrasia; Pepin, who for six years ruled as Duke of the Franks in the western part; and Grypho, the youngest, by another mother. Carloman became a monk in 747; Pepin from that date ruled in both parts, and became king in 752; Grypho gave trouble by his claims upon a share of the rule, and rather opportunely died in 753. Charlemagne, the son of Pepin the Short and Bertha, was born in 742, and the second Carloman, his younger brother, in 751. They were crowned at Soissons joint kings in 768. Charles Martel's great defeat of the Saracens near Tours was in 732. These dates will show what important periods and events fall within Boniface's continental life, 719–55.

The Northumbrian Willibrord's influence with Charles Martel prepared the way for the West Saxon Boniface's influence with Charles Martel's sons Pepin and Carloman; Boniface's influence with Pepin in turn prepared the way for the Northumbrian Alcuin's influence with Pepin's son Karl, afterwards Charlemagne.

---

[1] It is of course well known that Charles Martel, Carolus Martellus, was so named because he was the Hammer of the Saracens. It has long been a dream of the present writer that Martel may have been attached to his name at an earlier date, his mother having possibly been of Marteau, the village under the walls of the vast Château of Franchimont.

APPENDIX E

PAGE 281

BALE, Bishop of Ossory, perpetrated a curious travesty of Boniface's work.

John Bale had been a blatant tool of Thomas Cromwell under Henry VIII, and had fled to Basle under Queen Mary. He had much to say of Boniface in his account of the "Illustrious Writers of Greater Britain now called England and Scotland". He richly earned the sobriquet of "Bilious Bale". Never since the birth of Christ, he wrote, had there been any one who more openly played the part of the second beast in the Apocalypse (Rev. xiii. 11), that came out of the earth having two horns like a lamb and speaking as a dragon, than did Boniface. His two horns were the Benedictine monks and the canons regular. He came second to the first beast (Rev. xiii. 1), the Pope, the great Antichrist, from whom he took authority as legate to the Bavarians, Sclaves, Thuringians, Hessians, Saxons, Dacians, Frisians. He signed a hundred thousand people in Bavaria with the mark (Rev. xiii. 16) of the papacy, and compacted the kingdom of Antichrist by terror rather than by pious doctrine. He became chief of the priests in Gaul. He held synods, ordained bishops, confirmed mass-priests, built monasteries, condemned the marriage of ministers, instituted pilgrimages, taught purgatory, caused worship of images and the bones of the dead, admitted vestals to preach, against the instruction of St. Paul, made many go to Rome with oblations.

He tyrannically deposed Childeric, the lawful king
of the Franks, put in his place the traitor Pepin,
absolved the people from their allegiance to the king,
and did all this on the strength of pontifical canons.
He converted the noble kingdom of the Lombards
into the patrimony of Peter, and by a marvellously
subtle plan, which soon after took effect, transferred
the empire of Rome from the Greeks to the Gauls.
And all these things this Boniface did, that he might
make them that dwell on the earth worship the first
beast.

INDEX

A

Abrenuntiatio diaboli, 212.
Adolana, 286.
Aebbe, 80.
Aelffled, 286.
Aethelbald of Mercia, rebuke to, 242.
Alcuin, 2.
Aldebert and Clement, 186, &c.
Aldhelm, 2, 7, 21, 25.
Aldhun, 85.
Aldwulf, king, 88.
Alemannia, 97.
Alfred the Great, 17.
Amöneberg, 33.
Anglo-Saxon race at its best, 281.
Anselm, 26.
Appeal to English learning, 53, 357.
Arculfus, 111.
Austrasia, 54.

B

Bale, bilious, his estimate of the saint, 366.
Baptism, 105.
Bathouulf, martyred, 273.
Bavaria, 31, 102-4.
Bavarian bishoprics, 92.
Bede, 9, 12, 16, 17, 25, 32, 231; requests for his writings, ch. xiii.
Benedict Biscop, 160
Beorwald of Glastonbury, 8
Berathgid, 77.
Binna, 33.
Bishoprics founded, 92, 122.
Bishops, aged, 291.
Boniface (Winfrid), *see also* 'Letters'. Main dates of his life, 1, 2; Willibald's Life, 3; Othlon's, 4-6; parentage, 7; studies, 7, 8; goes to Frisia, 9; returns, 10; final departure, 10, 28; earliest letter, 22; imitation of Aldhelm, 22; letter of commendation, 27; modern memorials of, 27, 282; goes to Rome, 28; interview with Pope Gregory II, 30; letter of commendation, 30; visits Lombardy, Bavaria, Thuringia, 31; joins Willibrord in Frisia, 32; goes to Hessia, 33; reports success to the Pope, 33; summoned to Rome, 34; examined by the Pope, 35; consecrated and named Boniface, 87; oath to the Bishop of Rome, 38-40; letters of commendation, 41-46; letters of the Pope to Boniface, the Thuringians, and Charles Martel, 49-60; Charles Martel's letter, 61; the Thunderer's Oak, 63-65; foundation of Fritzlar, 65; letter to Fritzlar, 73; idols thrown down, 75; Thuringians dealt with, 75; foundation of Ohrdruf, 76; helpers come from England, 77; letter to English ladies, 78; receives the pall, 87; dedicates churches, 89; third visit to Rome, 90; founds Bavarian bishoprics, 92; difficulties with ecclesiastics, 104; his relatives, 112; founds three

WORKS ON CHURCH HISTORY

PUBLISHED BY THE

SOCIETY FOR PROMOTING CHRISTIAN KNOWLEDGE.

Alcuin of York.

By the Right Rev. G. F. BROWNE, D.D., D.C.L , Bishop of Bristol. With numerous illustrations. Small post 8vo, cloth boards. 5s.

Ancient British Church, A popular History of the.

With Special Reference to the Church in Wales. By the Rev. E J NEWELL, M A. With Map. Fcap. 8vo, cloth boards. 2s. 6d. [A lucid book on a department of History hitherto much neglected.]

Archbishops of Canterbury, Some Notable.

By the Rev. MONTAGUE FOWLER, M.A. With six coloured portraits. Crown 8vo, cloth boards 3s. [A selection of lives of the Primates of all England, showing the continuity of the Church of England.]

Art-teaching of the Primitive Church.

With an Index of Subjects, Historical and Emblematic. By the late Rev. R. ST JOHN TYRWHITT. Post 8vo, cloth boards. 3s. 6d. [Notes on Christian Art down to the period of the first Italian Renaissance: for Educated Persons.]

Attila and his Conquerors.

By the late Mrs. RUNDLE CHARLES. Crown 8vo, cloth boards. 2s. [A Story of the Days of St. Patrick and St. Leo the Great.]

Augustine and his Companions.

By the Right Rev. G. F. BROWNE, D.D., D.C.L. Sm. post 8vo, cloth boards. 2s. [This book is meant to follow " The Christian Church in these Islands before the coming of Augustine," and to show how much the Church of England owes to St. Augustine and Pope Gregory]

British Christianity during the Roman Occupation.

By the Rev. R. V. FRENCH, D.C.L., LL D., F.S.A. Sm. post
8vo, cloth. 6d. [*A scholarly and popular account of all that is
known about British Christianity in Roman Days.*]

By-Paths of English Church History.

·Home Missions in the Early Mediaeval Period. By the Rev. C.
HOLE, B.A. Post 8vo, cloth boards. 1s. 6d. [*Gives a clear view
of some of the roots of English Christianity.*]

Called to be Saints.

The Minor Festivals devotionally Studied. By the late CHRISTINA
G. ROSSETTI. Post 8vo, cloth boards. 3s. 6d. [*A deeply Spiritual
Book, and likely to be largely used by those who would learn the
Lessons taught by the Lives of immediate Followers of our Lord.
for Devotional Use.*]

Canterbury, Historic.

By the Rev. T. NORMAN ROWSELL. Small post 8vo. Cloth. 6d.
[*A monograph on Canterbury, tracing its History from the introduction of Christianity till the present day.*]

Case for "Establishment" Stated, The.

By the Rev. T. MOORE. Post 8vo, paper cover, 6d.; cloth boards,
2s. [*Meets all the arguments used by the Liberation Society.*]

Catechism on the Church of England, A.

Its Composition, Discipline, and Doctrine. By the Rev. DAWSON
F. CHAPMAN, M.A. Fcap. 8vo, paper cover, 2d.; limp cloth, 6d.
[*An exposition of the Catholic Church and of its Teaching.*]

Celtic Church in Scotland, The.

Being an Introduction to the History of the Christian Church in
Scotland down to the death of St. Margaret. By the Right Rev.
JOHN DOWDEN, D.D., Bishop of Edinburgh. Fcap. 8vo, buckram
boards. 3s. 6d. [*The writer brings a wide knowledge to bear upon
his subject, and deals with it in a bright and interesting manner.*]

Charlemagne.

By the late Rev. E. L. CUTTS, D.D. Crown 8vo, cloth boards.
2s. 6d.

Chats about the Church.

A handy Church Defence Manual for Working Men. By
FREDERICK G. BROWNE. Post 8vo, cloth. 6d. [*An able
refutation of Liberationist fallacies, in dialogue form.*]

Christian Church in these Islands (The) before the Coming of Augustine.

By the Right Rev. G. F. Browne, D.D., D.C.L., Post 8vo, cloth boards. 1s. 6d. [*A lucid and scholarly account of this obscure period of English Church History: for General Readers.*]

Christian Life and Worship, Recent Discoveries Illustrating Early.

Three Lectures delivered in the Chapter House of St. Mary's Cathedral, Edinburgh. By the Right Rev. Arthur J. Maclean, D.D. Small post 8vo, cloth boards. 2s. [*Presents, by a comparison of the earliest documents on Christian worship, the conditions of Christian life at the outset.*]

Christian Missions before the Reformation.

By the Rev. F. F. Walrond. Post 8vo, with four illustrations, cloth boards. 1s. 6d. [*For General Readers.*]

Christian Missions of the Middle Ages; or, A Thousand Years.

By the late Rev. John Wyse. Crown 8vo, with four illustrations, cloth boards. 1s. [*Principally suited for Educated Persons.*]

Christian Worship: Its Origin and Evolution.

By Monsignore Duchesne. Translated by M. L. McClure, from the Third Edition of 'Les Origines du Culte Chrétien.' Second English Edition, revised. Demy 8vo, cloth boards. 10s. [*The Third Edition of the French original was lately published in Paris. This translation represents not only that edition, but contains also additional matter just received from Monsignore Duchesne. There is also added, by request, a Translation of 'Peregrinatio' of Etheria (Silvia).*]

Church Endowments.

By Sir John Conroy, Bart. Post 8vo, paper covers. 2d. [*Disposes of the Fallacies of all Liberationists upon this Question.*]

Church History in Queen Victoria's Reign.

By the Rev. Montague Fowler, M.A. Post 8vo, cloth boards. 3s. [*This work treats in a sober and impartial manner the important ecclesiastical movements of the last fifty years and more, and ought to be specially interesting to the young.*]

Church History in England, from the Earliest Times to the Period of the Reformation.

By the Rev. A. Martineau. 12mo, cloth. 3s. [*For Reference and General Use.*]

Church in the New Testament, The.

By the Rev. W. F. SHAW, B.D. Post 8vo, limp cloth. 6*d*. [*Deals with the indirect evidence in the New Testament as to the Worship and Constitution of the Church in Apostolic Times.*]

Church in Roman Gaul, The.

By the Rev. RICHARD TRAVERS SMITH. Crown 8vo, with Map, cloth boards. 2*s*. 6*d*.

Churchman's Life of Wesley, The.

By R. DENNY URLIN, Esq, of the Middle Temple, Barrister. Crown 8vo, cloth boards   2*s*. 6*d*.

Church of England, The: its Planting, its Settlement, its Reformation, and its Renewed Life.

Four Addresses by the late Rev. EDMUND VENABLES, M.A. Post 8vo, cloth boards. 1*s*. [*A Useful Summary.*]

Church of England, The.

An Historical Sketch by the Rev. H. W. CARPENTER, Canon and Precentor of Salisbury.   Small post 8vo, cloth boards.   6*d*. [*A short sketch for the use of Sunday School Teachers and others*]

Church Progress and Church Defence.

By the Rev. HENRY LEACH, M A.   Small post 8vo, limp cloth. 6*d*. [*Reprinted with additions, from the " Quarterly Review," at the request of His Grace the Archbishop of Canterbury, and with the permission of Mr. John Murray.*]

Church Property, not National Property.

A Lecture delivered at Swindon by Sir JOHN CONROY, Bart. Post 8vo, paper covers. 2*d*. [*Discusses the contention of the Liberationists that Church Property is the Property of the Nation.*]

Colet, Fisher, and More, Lectures on.

By the Rev. CANON A. J. MASON, D.D. Small post 8vo, cloth boards. 1*s*. [*Short biographies of three representative men who reflect the spirit of their age.*]

Conquering and to Conquer: a Story of Rome in the Days of Saint Jerome.

By the late Mrs. RUNDLE CHARLES With four page illustrations. Crown 8vo, cloth boards. 2*s*. [*Presents a Fair Picture of Society in Jerome's time: for General Readers.*]

Constantine the Great.

The Union of Church and State. By the late Rev. E. L. Cutts, D.D. Crown 8vo, cloth boards 2s. 6d.

Constitutions and Canons Ecclesiastical (made in the Year 1603, and Amended in the Year 1865).

To which are added, Articles agreed upon by the Archbishops and Bishops of both Provinces, and the whole Clergy, in the Convocation holden at London in the Year 1562, for the avoiding of Diversities of Opinions, and for the Establishing of Consent touching True Religion. Post 8vo, cloth boards. 1s. [For General Use.]

Council of Trent, A Short History of the.

By the late Rev. R. F. Littledale, LL D., D.C.L. Post 8vo, cloth boards. 1s. [A short critical account of this Council, with its Historical Bearings.]

Conversion of the Heptarchy, The.

By the Right Rev. G. F. Browne, D.D., Bishop of Bristol. With several illustrations. Post 8vo, cloth boards. 3s. [This is the continuation of the Bishop of Bristol's Monographs on the Conversion of England. It is full of interesting particulars obtained from research at first hand.]

Crusades, History of the.

By the late Rev. G. G. Perry, M.A. Fcap. 8vo, with four illustrations, cloth boards. 1s. 6d. [An account of some of the most interesting episodes in the History of the Crusades]

Descriptive Lantern Lectures on English Church History.

By the Rev. C. A. Lane. Crown 8vo, cloth boards. 2s. 6d.

Dictionary of the Church of England, A.

By the late Rev. E. L. Cutts, D.D. With numerous woodcuts. Crown 8vo, cloth boards. 3s. 6d. [A Manual for the Use of Clergymen and Schools.]

Disendowment, Lectures on.

The Clergy and Party Politics, by the late Archbishop Temple; The Church in Wales and the Welsh People, by the Right Rev. the Lord Bishop of Bangor; The Continuity of Possession at the Reformation, by the Right Rev. the Lord Bishop of Bristol; How the Church received her Property, by the Ven. Archdeacon Sinclair, D.D.; Village Disendowment, by the late Rev. Prebendary Harry Jones; Why Confiscate Church Property? by the Rev. T. Moore, M.A. Small post 8vo, cloth boards. 1s. 6d. [These Lectures are meant to present briefly the Church's Claims to her Possessions and Privileges.]

Disestablishment and Disendowment, A Working Man's View of.

By HENRY J. ROBERTS, Member of the London Society of Compositors. Post 8vo, limp cloth. 6d. [*A fresh and interesting booklet on this subject.*]

Disestablishment and Disendowment: What they Mean, and What must Come of them.

An Address by the late Right Rev. W. C. MAGEE. Post 8vo, stitched. 5s per 100.

Disestablishment and Disendowment.

By HUGH SEYMOUR TREMENHEERE, C.B. Demy 8vo, paper cover. 3d. [*A résumé of arguments on this subject chiefly gleaned from Lord Selborne's Book.*]

Early Christian Missions of Ireland, Scotland, and England.

By the late Mrs RUNDLE CHARLES. Crown 8vo, cloth boards. 2s. 6d. [*Shows what we may learn in regard to Unity from the Ancient Christian Missions of these Islands.*]

Early Missions to and within the British Islands.

By the Rev. C. HOLE, B.A. Post 8vo, cloth boards. 2s [*The History of British Missions from the Introduction of Christianity till the time of Archbishop Theodore.*]

Englishman's Brief on behalf of his National Church, The.

New, revised, and enlarged edition. Post 8vo, paper covers. 8d. [*Traces the History of the Endowments and Privileges of the Church of England, and defends it—on the admissions chiefly of accredited Nonconformist Teachers—from the usual attack.*]

English Christianity in its Beginnings.

By the Rev. E. H. PEARCE. Small post 8vo, cloth boards. 1s. 6d.

English Reformation and its Consequences, The.

Four Lectures, with Notes and an Appendix By the Right Rev. W. E. COLLINS, D.D. Small post 8vo, cloth boards 4s.

First Book on the Church, A.

By the late Rev. Canon GARNIER. With Diagrams. Post 8vo, cloth boards. 1s. [*A book to be put into the hands of the Working Man or Young Churchmen generally.*]

First Church Workers, The.

Lessons from the early days of the Church in Jerusalem. By the Rev. W. E. CHADWICK. Post 8vo, cloth boards 6d. [*A short account of how the Gospel was originally spread.*]

Foundation Stones.

Fifteen lessons with story illustrations on the Founding of the Church in England. By AUSTIN CLARE. Small post 8vo, cloth boards. 2s. [*A pleasantly written and simple account of the origin of Christianity in these Islands.*]

Gallican Church, The.

Sketches of Church History in France. By the late Rev. JULIUS LLOYD, M.A. Post 8vo, cloth boards. 1s. 6d. [*A Sketch of French Church History from the Earliest Times till the Concordat*]

Handy Book of the Church of England, A.

By the late Rev. EDWARD L. CUTTS, D.D. Crown 8vo, cloth boards. 4s. [*A work which aims at meeting Inquiries upon the main points of the Church's History and present position. It covers a large area, and ought to be in the hands of all Church Workers as well as in those of General Readers.*]

Hear the Other Side.

A Word about Disestablishment and Disendowment. By the Rev. J. TRAVISS-LOCKWOOD. 8s. per 100. Paper covers. 2d. each.

Historical Church Atlas.

Illustrating the History of Eastern and Western Christendom until the Reformation, and that of the Anglican Communion until the present day. By the Rev. EDMUND McCLURE, M.A. Containing 18 coloured maps, besides some 50 sketch maps in the text. Cloth boards. 16s.

Historical and Dogmatical Position of the Church of England, Lectures on.

By the Rev. W. BAKER, D.D. Post 8vo, cloth boards. 1s. 6d. [*Supplies in short compass a clear Account of the Historical Position of the Church of England: for General Readers.*]

History of the English Church in short Biographical Sketches.

By the late Rev. JULIUS LLOYD, M.A. Post 8vo, cloth boards. 1s. 6d. [*Leads the Reader by a series of selected Lives to a general idea of the Church History of England: for Parochial Libraries, &c.*]

Illustrated Notes on English Church History.

Vol I. From the Earliest Times to the Dawn of the Reformation. Vol. II. The Reformation and Modern Church Work. By the Rev. C. A. LANE. Crown 8vo, cloth boards. 1*s.* each vol. The two parts in one volume. 2*s.* [*Deals with the Chief Events during the Period. The illustrations, amounting to about 100 in each volume, add to its popular character.*]

John Wyclif: his Life, Times, and Teaching

By the Rev. A. R PENNINGTON, M.A. Fcap. 8vo, cloth boards. 3*s.* [*This work embodies the result of recent researches: for General Reading*]

Lapsed, not Lost.

A Story of Roman Carthage. By the late Mrs. RUNDLE CHARLES. Crown 8vo, cloth boards 2*s.* [*A Story of the time of St. Cyprian.*]

Lessons from Early English Church History.

Three Lectures delivered in the Cathedral Church of St. Paul, London, by the Right Rev. G. F. BROWNE, D D., D C.L. Small post 8vo, cloth boards. 1*s.* 6*d.* [*These Lectures are true Lessons, and have much to teach the Ordinary Churchman.*]

Martyrs and Saints of the First Twelve Centuries.

Studies from the lives of the Black-letter Saints of the English Calendar. By the late Mrs RUNDLE CHARLES. Crown 8vo, cloth boards. 2*s.* 6*d* [*Deals with the Lives of the Black-letter Saints in a Devotional as well as Historical Manner*]

Mazarin.

By the late GUSTAVE MASSON. Crown 8vo, cloth boards. 2*s.* 6*d.*

Mediaeval Church History, A Sketch of.

By the Ven. S. CHEETHAM, D.D. Fcap. 8vo, cloth boards. 1*s.* 6*d.* [*Deals with the history of the Church from the break up of the Roman Empire until the Reformation period.*]

Mitslav; or, The Conversion of Pomerania.

By the late Right Rev. R. MILMAN, D.D. Crown 8vo, with Map, cloth boards. 2*s.* 6*d.*

Monumental History (The) of the Early British Church.

By J. ROMILY ALLEN, F.S.A. (Scot). With numerous illustrations. Fcap. 8vo, cloth 3*s* [*Furnishes historical materials gleaned from the early Christian monuments in these Islands.*]

Narcissus: a Tale of Early Christian Times.

By the Right Rev. W. BOYD CARPENTER, Lord Bishop of Ripon. Crown 8vo, cloth boards. 2*s* 6*d*

North African Church, The.

By the late Rev. JULIUS LLOYD, M.A. Crown 8vo, with Map, cloth boards. 2s. 6d.

Northumbrian Saints, The; or, Chapters from the Early History of the English Church.

By the Right Rev. E. C. S. GIBSON. Post 8vo, cloth boards. 1s. [*Treats of Paulinus, Aidan, Chad, Cædmon, St. Cuthbert, The Venerable Bede, Alcuin, &c.*]

Notes of Lessons on the Church in the New Testament.

By the late Rev. E. L. CUTTS, D.D., Author of " Turning Points of Church History." With Map. Crown 8vo, cloth boards. 2s. 6d.

Notes on the Church in Wales.

By the Ven. W. L. BEVAN, Archdeacon of Brecon. Small post 8vo, cloth. 6d.

Notes on the History of the Early Church.

By the Ven. ARCHDEACON PRYCE. Small post 8vo, cloth boards, 1s. [*A short summary of Early Church History, from the research of a thoughtful writer.*]

Official Year-Book of the Church of England, The.

Furnishing a trustworthy account of the condition of the Church of England, and of all bodies in communion with her throughout the world. Demy 8vo, paper boards, 3s. ; cloth boards, 4s.

Old Churches of Our Land (The): the Why, How and When of Them.

By FRANCIS BALDWIN, Architect. With numerous illustrations. Crown 8vo, cloth boards. 3s. [*This is just such a book as one would like to give to intelligent Sunday Scholars. It indirectly* teaches much Church History.]

Old England.

A Lecture by the late Right Rev. HARVEY GOODWIN, D.D. Post 8vo, paper covers. 3d. [*A graphic account of the sources of England's Power and of her Responsibilities.*]

Parish Priests and their People in the Middle Ages in England.

By the late Rev. E. L. CUTTS, D.D. With numerous illustrations. Demy 8vo, cloth boards. 7s. 6d. [*A work revealing the spiritual condition of England in the Middle Ages. The materials and illustrations are drawn from first-hand sources.*]

Penny History of the Church of England.

By the Rev. AUGUSTUS JESSOPP, D.D. Revised Edition. Small post 8vo, paper covers, 1d.; cloth, 6d.

Richelieu.

By the late GUSTAVE MASSON. Crown 8vo, cloth boards. 2s. 6d.

Side Lights on Church History:

HISTORY OF EARLY CHRISTIAN ART. By the late Rev. E. L. CUTTS, D.D. Demy 8vo, cloth boards. 6s. [*The aim of the book is to throw light from indirect sources on the History and Teaching of the Primitive Church.*]

Liturgy and Ritual of the Ante-Nicene Church, The.

By the Rev. F. E. WARREN, B.D., F.S.A. Demy 8vo, cloth boards. 5s. [*Puts together the chief facts known concerning Early Christian Liturgies, and enables one thus to judge of the doctrines held by the Church at the time.*]

Sketches of Church History from the First Century to the Reformation.

By the late Rev. CANON ROBERTSON. Post 8vo, with Map, cloth boards. 2s. [*A simple and attractive account of the leading events in Church History, from A.D. 33 to the Reformation: for General Readers; suitable also for Use in Sunday and Day Schools.*]

Sketches of Church History in Germany.

By the late Rev. JULIUS LLOYD, M.A. Post 8vo, cloth boards. 1s. 6d. [*A Sketch of German Church History from the Earliest Times to the Present Day: for General Readers.*]

Sketches of Church History in Scotland.

By the late Rev. JULIUS LLOYD, M.A. Post 8vo, with three page woodcuts, cloth boards. 1s. 6d. [*An Account of Church Affairs in Scotland from St. Columba's Mission in Iona until the Present Time.*]

Story of the Church of England, A.

By Mrs. C. D. FRANCIS. Post 8vo, illustrated, cloth boards. 1s. 6d [*A very simple Narrative History of the English Church.*]

Story in Outline of the Church of England, The.

By the late Rev. CANON GARNIER, M.A. Small post 8vo, paper covers. 3d. [*Gives a short and simple Historical Account of the Church of England*]

Theodore and Wilfrith.

By the Right Rev. G. F. BROWNE, D.D., D.C.L. Small post 8vo, with several illustrations, cloth boards. 3s. 6d. [*A continuation of the Series of Monographs on the Early English Church.*]

Tithes and the Poor.

By the Rev. T. MOORE. (No. 2136.) 4s. per 100. [*Deals with the Liberationist Fallacy as to the Claims of the Poor upon the Tithes.*]

Tithes made plain, The Question of.

By the Rev. W. PRESTON, M.A. (No. 2205.) 6s. per 100.

Title-deeds of the Church of England, The.

An Historic Vindication of her Position and Claims. By the late Rev. CANON GARNIER, M.A. Small post 8vo, cloth boards. 3s. 6d. [*The sub-title explains the aims of this book, which is written in a lucid and interesting manner.*]

Turning Points of English Church History.

By the late Rev. E. L. CUTTS, D.D. Post 8vo, cloth boards. 3s. 6d. [*The Leading Events in the Church of England from the Earliest Period of British History to the Present Day, showing the Church Questions that have arisen, and yet remain as our Inheritance: for Churchmen in General.*]

Turning Points of General Church History.

By the late Rev. E. L. CUTTS, D.D. Crown 8vo, cloth boards. 3s. 6d. [*The Leading Events in General Church History from the Time of the Apostles to the Present Day. Useful for a Text-book in Schools, &c., and for General Readers.*]

Two Hundred Years: the History of the S.P.C.K., 1698–1898.

By the Rev. W. OSBORN B. ALLEN, M.A., and the Rev. EDMUND McCLURE, M.A., Secretaries of the Society. Demy 8vo. With a frontispiece and several illustrations. Buckram boards. 10s. 6d. [*The information contained in the Volume is drawn in the main from the Society's Minute Books, and the material thus gleaned furnishes, perhaps, a more complete account of Church life and work during the last two centuries than could be had from any other source.*]

Villa of Claudius, The.

By the late Rev. E. L. CUTTS, D.D. With three page illustrations. Crown 8vo, cloth boards. 1s. 6d. [*An instructive tale of the Roman-British Church.*]

Welsh Church, The Case of the.

By the late Rev. E. L. CUTTS, D.D. Small post 8vo, paper covers. 1d.

Work of the Church of England (The), for the Benefit of England's People.

By the Rev. GUY MILLER. (No. 2195.) 4s. per 100. [*On the Educational Work of the Church.*]

Illustrated Books

BY THE LATE

REV. J. M. NEALE, D.D.

Agnes de Tracy.

A Tale of the Times of St Thomas of Canterbury. 1s. 6d.

Deeds of Faith.

Stories for Children from Church History. Crown 8vo, cloth 1s.

Duchenier; or, The Revolt of La Vendée.

Large crown 8vo, cloth boards. 3s 6d.

Herbert Tresham.

A Tale of the Great Rebellion. Crown 8vo, cloth boards. 1s.

Lent Legends.

Stories for Children from Church History. Crown 8vo, cloth boards. 1s. 6d

Stories from Heathen Mythology and Greek History.

For the use of Children. Crown 8vo, cloth boards. 1s. 6d.

Stories of the Crusades:

I. De Hellingley; II. The Crusade of S. Louis. Large crown 8vo, cloth boards. 3s. 6d.

Tales Illustrative of the Apostles' Creed.

Crown 8vo, cloth boards. 2s.

Tales of Christian Endurance.

Crown 8vo, cloth boards. 1s.

Tales of Christian Heroism.

Crown 8vo, cloth boards. 1s. 6d.

Theodora Phranza; or, The Fall of Constantinople.

Large crown 8vo, cloth boards. 3s. 6d.

The Egyptian Wanderers.

A Story for Children of the Great Tenth Persecution. Large crown 8vo, cloth boards. 2s.

The Farm of Aptonga.

A Story for Children of the Times of S. Cyprian. Large crown 8vo, cloth boards. 2s.

The Followers of the Lord.

Stories for Children from Church History. Crown 8vo, cloth, 1s.

Early Church Classics.

Small post 8vo, cloth boards.

A Homily of Clement of Alexandria. Entitled, "Who is the Rich Man that is Being Saved?" By the Rev. P. MORDAUNT BARNARD. 1*s*.

Bishop Sarapion's Prayer Book. An Egyptian Pontifical (dated probably about A.D. 350–356). Translated from the edition of Dr. G. WOBBERMIN, with Introduction, Notes, and Indices. By the Right Rev. JOHN WORDSWORTH, D.D., Bishop of Salisbury. 1*s*. 6*d*.

Origen the Teacher. Being the Address of Gregory the Wonderworker, to Origen, together with Origen's Letter to Gregory. Translated, with an Introduction and Notes, by the Rev. W. METCALFE, B.D. 1*s*. 6*d*.

St. Augustine's Treatise on the City of God. By the Rev. F. R. M. HITCHCOCK, M.A, B.D. 1*s*. 6*d*.

St. Chrysostom on the Priesthood. By the Rev. T. ALLEN MOXON, M.A. 1*s*. 6*d*.

St. Cyprian on the Lord's Prayer An English Translation, with Introduction, by Rev. T. HERBERT BINDLEY, D.D. 1*s*. 6*d*.

St. Polycarp, Bishop of Smyrna. By the late Rev. BLOMFIELD JACKSON, M.A. 1*s*.

The Apostolical Constitutions and Cognate Documents, with special reference to their Liturgical elements. By the Rev. DE LACY O'LEARY, M.A. 1*s*.

The Doctrine of the Twelve Apostles. Translated into English, with Introduction and Notes, by the late Rev. CHARLES BIGG, D.D. 1*s*.

The Epistle of St. Clement, Bishop of Rome. By the Rev. JOHN A. F. GREGG, M.A. 1*s*.

The Epistle of the Gallican Churches: Lugdunum and Vienna. With an Appendix containing Tertullian's Address to Martyrs and the Passion of St. Perpetua. Translated, with Introduction and Notes, by the Rev. T. HERBERT BINDLEY, B.D. 1*s*.

The Epistles of St. Ignatius, Bishop of Antioch. By the Rev. J. H. SRAWLEY, M.A. In two volumes. 1*s*. each.

The Liturgy of the Eighth Book of "the Apostolic Constitutions," commonly called the Clementine Liturgy. Translated into English, with Introduction and Notes, by the Rev. R. H. CRESSWELL, M.A. 1s. 6d.

The Shepherd of Hermas. By the Rev. C. TAYLOR, D.D., LL.D. Vols. I and II. 2s. each.

The Epistle of Diognetus. By the Rev. L. B. RADFORD, M.A. 1s. 6d.

LARGE FRESCO CARTOONS, ILLUSTRATING ENGLISH CHURCH HISTORY.

SIZE, 45 BY 35 INCHES.

1. Gregory and the English Slaves, A.D. 589.
2. St. Augustine before King Ethelbert, A.D. 597.
3. Manumission of a Slave by an English Bishop.
4. The Martyrdom of St. Alban.
5. Columba at Oronsay, A.D. 563.
6. St. Aidan preaching to the Northumbrians.
7. The Venerable Bede translating St. John's Gospel, A.D. 735.
8. Stonehenge.
9. Iona at the present Day. Founded A.D. 565.
10. Murder of Monks by the Danes, Crowland Abbey, about A.D. 870.
11. The Martyrdom of St. Edmund, A.D. 870.
12. St. Dunstan reproving King Edwy, A.D. 955.
13. Norman Thanksgiving for Victory after the Battle of Hastings, A.D. 1066.
14. The Murder of St. Thomas à Becket, A.D. 1170.
15. The Crusaders starting for the East.
16. Archbishop Langton producing before the Barons the Charter of Henry I, A.D. 1213.
17. Preaching at St. Paul's Cross, A.D. 1547.
18. The Seven Bishops sent to the Tower, A.D. 1688.
19. The Consecration of Matthew Parker as Archbishop of Canterbury, December 17, 1559.
20. The Execution of Archbishop Laud. January 10, 1645.
21. The Savoy Conference. April 15, 1661.
22. The Consecration of Bishop Seabury. Nov. 14, 1784.
23. Bishop Steere building his Cathedral at Zanzibar. Foundation laid, 1873; opened, 1879.
24. The Martyrdom of Bishop Patteson. September 20, 1871.
25. The Lambeth Conference, 1897.
    Assembling of Bishops in Guard Room.

The Fathers for English Readers.

Fcap. 8vo, cloth boards.

Boniface. By the Rev. CANON GREGORY SMITH, M.A.   1s. 6d.

Clement of Alexandria. By the Rev. F. R. MONTGOMERY HITCHCOCK, B.D.   3s.

The Apostolic Fathers. By the Rev. CANON SCOTT HOLLAND.   2s.

The Defenders of the Faith ; or, The Christian Apologists of the Second and Third Centuries. By the Rev. F. WATSON, D.D.   2s.

Gregory the Great. By the late Rev. J. BARMBY, B.D.   2s.

Leo the Great. By the Right Rev. C. GORE.   2s.

St. Ambrose ; His Life, Time, and Teaching. By the Rev. R. THORNTON, D.D.   2s.

St. Augustine. By the late Rev. EDWARD L. CUTTS, D.D.   2s.

St. Athanasius ; his Life and Times. By the Rev. R. WHELER BUSH.   2s. 6d.

St. Basil the Great. By the Rev. RICHARD TRAVERS SMITH.   2s.

St. Bernard, Abbot of Clairvaux, A.D. 1091-1153. By the Rev. S. J. EALES, M.A., D.C.L.   2s. 6d.

St. Hilary of Poitiers and St. Martin of Tours. By the Rev. J. GIBSON CAZENOVE, D.D.   2s.

St. Jerome. By the late Rev. EDWARD L. CUTTS, D.D.   2s.

St. John of Damascus. By the Rev. J. H. LUPTON.   2s.

St. Patrick : his Life and Teaching. By the Rev. E. J. NEWELL, M.A.   2s. 6d.

Synesius of Cyrene, Philosopher and Bishop. By ALICE GARDNER.   2s.

Venerable Bede, The. By the Right Rev. G. F. BROWNE.   2s.

Diocesan Histories.

Fcap. 8vo, cloth boards.

Bath and Wells. By the Rev. W. HUNT. With Map. 2s. 6d.

Canterbury. By the late Rev. R. C. JENKINS. With Map. 3s. 6d.

Carlisle. By RICHARD S. FERGUSON, Chancellor of Carlisle. With Map. 2s. 6d.

Chester. By the Rev. RUPERT H. MORRIS, D.D. With Map. 3s.

Chichester. By Rev. W. R. W. STEPHENS. With Map and plan. 2s. 6d.

Durham. By the Rev J. L. LOW. With Map and plan. 2s. 6d.

Hereford. By the late Rev. CANON PHILLOTT. With Map. 3s.

Lichfield. By the Rev. W. BERESFORD. With Map. 2s. 6d

Lincoln. By the late Rev. CANON E. VENABLES and the late Ven ARCHDEACON PERRY. With Map. 4s.

Llandaff. By the Rev. E. J. NEWELL, M.A. With Map. 3s. 6d.

Norwich. By the Rev. A. JESSOP, D.D. With Map. 2s. 6d.

Oxford. By the Rev. E. MARSHALL. With Map. 2s. 6d.

Peterborough. By the Rev. G. A. POOLE, M.A. With Map. 2s. 6d.

Rochester. By the Rev. A. J. PEARMAN, M.A. With Map. 4s.

Salisbury. By the Rev. W. H. JONES. With Map and plan. 2s. 6d.

Sodor and Man. By A. W. MOORE, M.A. With Map. 3s.

St. Asaph. By the Ven. ARCHDEACON THOMAS. With Map. 2s.

St. David's. By the Rev. CANON BEVAN. With Map. 2s. 6d.

Winchester. By the Rev. W. BENHAM, B.D. With Map. 3s.

Worcester. By the Rev. I. GREGORY SMITH, M.A., and the Rev. PHIPPS ONSLOW, M.A. With Map. 3s. 6d.

York. By Rev. CANON ORNSBY, M.A., F.S.A. With Map. 3s. 6d.

LONDON:

SOCIETY FOR PROMOTING CHRISTIAN KNOWLEDGE,

NORTHUMBERLAND AVENUE, W C.; 43, QUEEN VICTORIA STREET, E C.
BRIGHTON: 129, NORTH STREET.